DEVELOPMENT STRATEGIES IN RURAL COLOMBIA
THE CASE OF CAQUETÁ

Studies on Social Processes and Change

Published with the cooperation of the

INTER-AMERICAN FOUNDATION

UCLA Latin American Studies

Volume 55

MAP 1. Republic of Colombia.

SOURCE. Adapted from the Frontis in Banco de la República, *Guía para el inversionista* (Bogotá, 1965).

DEVELOPMENT STRATEGIES IN RURAL COLOMBIA
The Case of Caquetá

Robin Ruth Marsh

UCLA LATIN AMERICAN CENTER PUBLICATIONS
University of California, Los Angeles

UCLA Latin American Center Publications
University of California, Los Angeles

Library of Congress Catalog Card Number: 82-620032
ISBN: 0-87903-055-0
Printed in the United States of America

A los campesinos del Caquetá,
con mucho afecto y recuerdo

Contents

Illustrations

Tables

Abbreviations and Acronyms

ACPO	Acción Cultural Popular (Action for Popular Culture)
ANUC	Asociación Nacional de Usuarios Campesinos (National Association of the Peasantry)
Caja Agraria	Caja de Crédito Agrario, Industrial, y Minero (Agriculture, Industry and Mining Credit Bank)
Caminos Vecinales	Fondo Nacional de Caminos Vecinales (National Fund for Local Roads)
CARE	Cooperative for American Relief Everywhere
CECORA	Central de Cooperativas de la Reforma Agraria Ltda. (Center for Agrarian Reform Cooperatives)
CIDA	Comité Interamericano de Desarrollo Agrícola (Interamerican Committee on Agricultural Development)
COOPERAGRO	Cooperativa Agropecuaria del Caquetá Ltda. (Agricultural Cooperative of Caquetá)
DANE	Departamento Administrativo Nacional de Estadística (National Administrative Department of Statistics)
DRI	Desarrollo Rural Integral (Integrated Rural Development)
FAO	Food and Agriculture Organization (United Nations)
FARC	Fuerzas Armadas Revolucionarias de Colombia (Revolutionary Armed Forces of Colombia)
IBRD	International Bank for Reconstruction and Development (World Bank)
ICA	Instituto Colombiano Agropecuario (Colombian Agricultural Institute)
ICCE	Instituto Colombiano de Construcciones Escolares (Colombian Institute of School Construction)
IDEMA	Instituto de Mercadeo Agropecuario (Agricultural Marketing Institute)
ILO	International Labour Organization (United Nations)
INCORA	Instituto Colombiano de la Reforma Agraria (Colombian Institute of Agrarian Reform)
INDERENA	Instituto de Desarrollo de los Recursos Naturales Renovables (Institute for the Development of Renewable Natural Resources)

INPES	Instituto Nacional de Programas Especiales de Salud (National Institute of Special Health Programs)
INS	Instituto Nacional de Salud (National Health Institute)
ISP	Instituto de Salud Pública (Public Health Institute)
MRL	Movimiento Revolucionario Liberal (Liberal Revolutionary Movement)
OAS	Organization of American States
PAN	Plan de Alimentación y Nutrición (Food and Nutrition Plan)
SEM	Servicio Nacional de Erradicación de la Malaria (National Service for the Eradication of Malaria)
SENA	Servicio Nacional de Aprendizaje (National Learning Service)
UNIR	Unión Nacional Isquierdista Revolucionaria (National Leftist Revolutionary Union)
USAID	United States Agency for International Development
WHO	World Health Organization (United Nations)

Preface

THIS STUDY IS a product of seven months of field research in the intendencia of Caquetá, Colombia, and several months of subsequent analysis of data and of research into the historical background of the region. The task undertaken is a multidisciplinary evaluation of a series of rural development projects administered by the Colombian Institute of Agrarian Reform (INCORA), and partly financed with World Bank funds.

Caquetá, Colombia, has been an important center of innovative rural development for the past two decades. The region, nevertheless, remains virtually unknown to most Colombians, and receives few foreign visitors, because of its geographic isolation and relatively sparse population. In the course of my field research, I was able to explore and study Caquetá at length, traveling by jeep, bus, boat, plane, horse, mule, and foot. During this exploration, I learned to appreciate the process of colonization, and gradually gained insight into the concerns and hopes of Caquetá *colonos* (settlers) as well as the successes and failures of the region's rural government assistance programs.

This work is an account of my field experiences and an evaluation of what has been accomplished thus far by the people of Caquetá and by their government to fulfill the needs and the aspirations of the rural majority. It is also an attempt to deliver Caquetá from its present obscurity by bringing to light the region's noteworthy efforts to achieve social and economic progress, and by exposing the injustices and neglect that continue to afflict the rural poor and that impede Caquetá from embarking on a steady course of egalitarian development.

It would not have been possible to complete this study were it not for the cooperation and generosity of the INCORA staff, with whom

I worked in Florencia and the countryside for several months. The INCORA veterinarians, social extension agents, credit supervisors, economists, engineers, planners, and drivers all contributed to the field research by passing their knowledge and experience on to me, and by enabling me to gain my own experience. To all of them I am deeply indebted. Moreover, for their difficult but worthwhile endeavors in Caquetá, they deserve great respect and due acknowledgment.

To the Caquetá farmers and their families, whom I visited and interviewed, I want to express special thanks. Their willingness to share with me their daily struggle for survival and change allowed me to grasp the fundamentals of rural life in Caquetá. Through their supply of data was formed the skeleton of this study; their stories and comments gave it flesh and blood.

I gratefully acknowledge the financial and moral support of the Inter-American Foundation and the UCLA Latin American Center, without which my field research and the publication of this manuscript would not have been possible. I am also indebted to Professor David Eiteman and Professor E. Bradford Burns at UCLA and Professor William Thiesenhusen at the Land Tenure Center of the University of Wisconsin for their careful reading of the manuscript, and their insightful comments and suggestions. I thank Elly Simmons for her skillful design and adaptation of the illustrations. Finally, for their love and encouragement throughout this endeavor, I remain ever indebted to the members of my family.

Introduction

The intendencia of Caquetá, Colombia, is unusual in that it occupies an intermediary position between the highly structured and densely populated rural areas of the Colombian highlands to the north, and the isolated, sparsely populated Amazonas region to the south. Caquetá is also unusual in its population mix of farmers, ranchers, merchants, and professionals from all over the country. Most of the Caquetá settlers at one time were victims of rural violence, or experienced land displacement and extreme deprivation in their states of origin. They sought refuge in Caquetá, where land was available and cheap, and life, though arduous in many respects, was overall, more tranquil.

For several decades, and particularly since the mid-1960s, an important aspect of Colombian agrarian policy has been to encourage the landless and unemployed rural population to migrate east and south to Colombia's largely vacant frontier lands. This campaign became especially important after initial efforts at redistributive land reform were circumvented through actions taken by politically influential opponents.

In Caquetá, the government instituted a "direct" colonization program that involved the selection, transportation, and settlement of rural and urban migrants from the highlands to the uncolonized frontier. This program had very poor results, and was subsequently reoriented to provide assistance to self-motivated settlers. Since 1971, the Caquetá Colonization Project, administered by INCORA (Colombian Institute of Agrarian Reform), has been expanded, with World Bank loans, to include a variety of social and technical services, infrastructure projects, and credit for livestock production. Consequently, the development strategy for the region has advanced beyond the simple occupation of uncolonized public land to encompass a complex, long-term plan of integrated rural development.

In this study, the development strategies that have been adopted and implemented in Caquetá have been evaluated in terms of the basic social and economic needs of the rural majority, and in view of the stated objectives of Colombia's Agrarian Reform Law 135 and World Bank planners. The stated objectives of these strategies are evaluated in relation to general development goals, and are then compared to real accomplishments in Caquetá.

The study includes historical material on the area, data and observations collected from interviews, and discussion of the conditions and relationships between and among the study's two principal actors—INCORA/World Bank and the Caquetá farmers. In the study, the impact of government assistance on the productivity, income levels, and the quality of life of the intended beneficiaries, that is, the farmers and their families, is measured quantitatively and qualitatively.

In the course of my field research, I discovered that it was erroneous to assume a simple linear cause-and-effect relationship between the two main actors (INCORA/World Bank and farmers). Instead, I found that to understand the full nature of their relationship, it would be necessary to study the complex network of socioeconomic interrelationships which characterize rural society in Caquetá. This network is schematically illustrated in diagram 1.

The preconditions (refer to diagram 1) describe the life of the farmer before INCORA programs enter the scene. Each family experiences a unique set of preconditions, but generalizations can be drawn for the region as a whole. Various intervening events take place in between the time a farmer receives government assistance and the time benefits are expected to be evident; these events may enhance, inhibit, or neutralize the impact of that assistance. The dependent or desired effect variables, measured in quantitative terms, have various consequences which are best understood in qualitative terms. Where the dependent variables measure increased income levels and social services, the consequences show whether the beneficiaries of government assistance programs also attain greater well-being, personal fulfillment, and self-reliance, leading to a heightened sense of optimism about their future in Caquetá. The arrows between these two sets of variables denote the question of whether changes in income necessarily lead to long-term changes in general well-being. If so, how and when does the transition take place? If not, what are the conditions that prevent better-off farmers from living better-off lives?

The methods I have used to research the area, and to become acquainted with the major and minor actors involved in the process

Diagram 1. Socioeconomic Interrelationships in Rural Caquetá, Colombia: The World Bank/INCORA Land Settlement Project

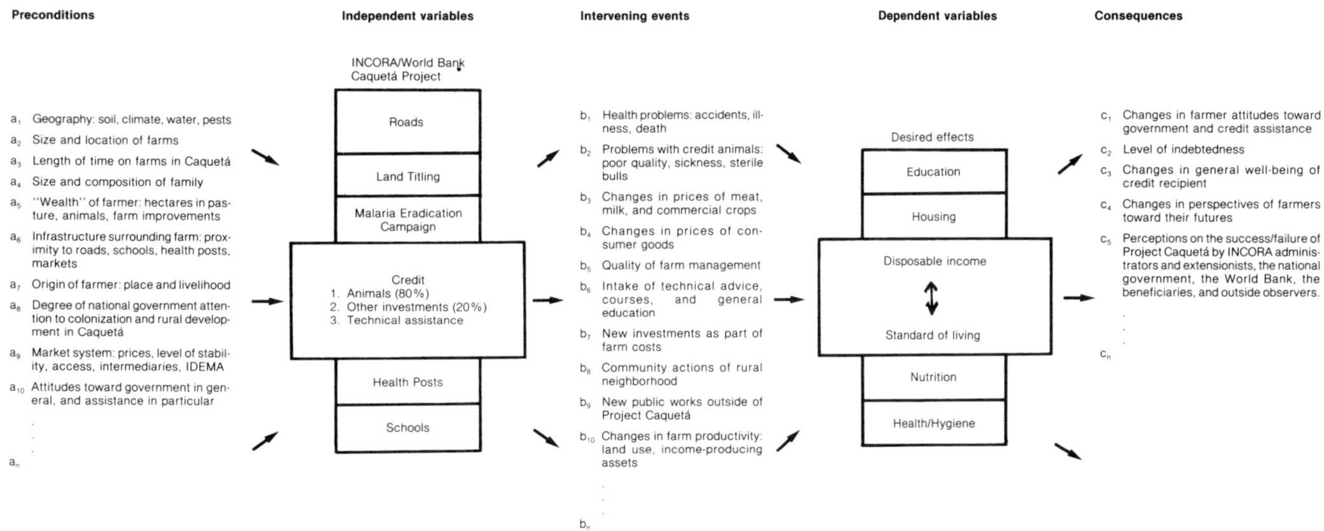

of rural development, were in part chosen from an objective academic standpoint, and in part determined by a set of practical limitations.

Before, during, and after my field research, I reviewed a wide selection of books, articles, and documents pertinent to rural development in general, and the Caquetá experience in particular. I consulted reports and data from such institutions as INCORA, the World Bank, Colombia's National Administrative Department of Statistics (DANE), the National Health Institute (INS), the Agrarian Bank (Caja Agraria), the Cattlemen's Bank (Banco Ganadero), the major agricultural research institution of Colombia (ICA), and the Chamber of Commerce of Florencia, Caquetá. I also sought information and insights from previously written scholarly works on rural Colombia and the intendencia of Caquetá.

Original data were collected from lengthy interviews held over a period of four months with Caquetá farmers, as well as informal talks with INCORA staff members, other government employees, teachers, medical workers, neighbors, and friends. The specific methodology used for selecting the sample of families interviewed is somewhat complex and is discussed in detail in chapter 4. Practical limitations largely determined the methodology used during the sample selection and interview process. As the margin of error is considerable in this area, it has been realistically assessed and incorporated into the tabulation and analysis of collected data.

Altogether eighty-five families were interviewed; fifty were INCORA/World Bank credit recipients, and thirty-five had applied for credit, but their applications were not yet approved. I was able to measure changes in productivity, income, and living standards for credit recipients, and to compare the situation of farmers who had never received INCORA credit with that of those who had. The interviews took place at the homes of the rural families and covered all of the nine geographic zones of credit, an area of approximately 14,000 square kilometers. The interview form was designed by INCORA, with additions made by the author (see appendix 2 for a sample copy), and the interviews were conducted by the author, together with one to three INCORA employees (credit supervisors, veterinarians, and economists). In addition, we visited several schools and health posts built with INCORA/World Bank funds, and traversed nearly all of the roads constructed as part of the INCORA Project over the last decade.

Chapter 1 provides historical background to the colonization of Caquetá through a review of Colombia's agrarian structures, government policies, and popular rural movements from the Conquest to the mid-1970s. The conditions and conflicts that have precipitated

Colombia's political debates on the "agrarian problem" are discussed with reference to the adopted "solutions."

Two frequently proposed alternatives for solving Colombia's lasting tenure crisis have been: (1) the colonization of public, frontier land (the conservative approach), and (2) the parcelization of privately owned land in heavily populated areas (the reformist to radical approach). INCORA's Project Caquetá falls under the category of colonization, rather than parcelization, because it is located where the population is sparse and there is abundant public land, far from the nation's principal cities, markets, and highways. During the 1970s, government programs in Caquetá have encompassed both the colonization "solution" and the more recent integrated rural development strategy.

In chapter 2 the histories, needs, and aspirations of one of the two principal groups of actors—the Caquetá farmers—are explored. I rely heavily on comments made by farmers, direct observation, and technical information on the farming process under tropical agroclimatic conditions. Later I show that the impact of INCORA/World Bank credit varies considerably for different rural families. Though these families have some characteristics in common, it would be unduly simplistic to treat the Caquetá farmers, or even the sample group of INCORA beneficiaries, as a homogeneous group. Chapter 2 provides examples of both shared and divergent conditions within the rural community.

The role of government in the colonization and development of Caquetá is reviewed chronologically in chapter 3. The stated objectives and program goals of INCORA and the World Bank are compared and contrasted with actual accomplishments and the fundamental needs of Caquetá farmers. The INCORA/World Bank Land Settlement Project is described in greatest detail.

Although Project Caquetá is an integrated rural development project with many programs, the credit and road development programs have been given greatest priority, accounting for nearly 80 percent of total invested INCORA/World Bank funds. Owing to the special importance of credit and technical assistance to the Caquetá rural community, I have chosen to evaluate that program in particular, using original data collected from fifty credit recipients and thirty-five nonrecipients.

In chapter 4, I present and analyze these data. The chapter provides a background for the interview process, a description of the survey methodology, and an evaluation of the impact of INCORA/World Bank credit on selected beneficiaries. Emphasis is placed on measurements of change, both quantitative and qualitative. A few examples of the variables measured and compared are: farm assets, gross and net income, and housing, nutrition, and education standards.

In chapter 5, I conclude that the INCORA/World Bank Project succeeds or will succeed in meeting most of its development goals, and that these accomplishments have resulted in substantial economic benefits to middle-income Caquetá farmers, and moderate social benefits to the rural community at large. Nonetheless, I believe that the Project has been marred by serious planning and coordination difficulties, and by problems that stem from limitations inherent to the current national agrarian policy of Colombia. I specify the shortcomings that could be corrected regionally, given a reordering of investment priorities and a larger budget, and the shortcomings that would require major changes in national policy to be overcome, particularly, a greater commitment to the process of making development planning more democratic and to meeting the basic needs of the poorest sector of the *colono* (settler) population.

Finally, I make a series of recommendations for change that would help to solve the problems discussed in the conclusions; I suggest the inevitability of increased frustration and political conflict within Caquetá if these changes are not considered and brought to effect within a reasonable time. I hope these recommendations will prove interesting and useful to the development planners and implementers currently at work in Caquetá, and to all others who are concerned with the planning and implementing of future colonization and integrated rural development projects throughout the developing world.

1

Historical Review of Agrarian Reform in Colombia

IN THE PAST half-century, rapid urbanization has caused dramatic economic changes and social upheaval throughout Latin America. High population growth rates and a concentration of the best land on *latifundia*[1] and large commercial farms have driven the rural poor to the towns and cities in search of work and basic services. The results of forced, rapid rural-to-urban migration are overcrowded cities with high unemployment rates, serious service deficiencies, and enormous wealth, side by side with dire poverty. From country to country the specifics vary, but with few exceptions these conditions have reached critical proportions throughout Latin America. Most of the victims of these shortages and inequities are people of rural origin who have been adversely affected by long-established, undemocratic systems of land tenure. Clearly, the solution to the mounting crisis of the cities and the countryside depends upon the dissolution of present traditional agrarian structures, followed by the institution of a more equitable and productive land tenure system.

LAND DISTRIBUTION IN CONTEMPORARY COLOMBIA

In 1940, 71 percent of Colombia's people lived in the countryside or in villages of less than fifteen hundred people, a figure that diminished to 39.6 percent by 1974. These percentages indicate that Colombia is a part of the Latin American trend of rapid urbanization. In absolute terms, however, the rural population of Colombia has increased over the last 35 years, from approximately 10 million in 1938 to 10.4 million in 1973.[2] Thus, increased human pressure on the land continues despite rural-to-urban migration.

Table 1 shows that nearly 50 percent of Colombian farms in 1970–71 were less than 3 hectares (has.) in size. (1 hectare = 2.47 acres.)

These subfamily plots, called *minifundia*, occupy 2 percent of Colombia's cultivable land, and are concentrated in the western and southern highlands. Owing to mountainous terrain and intensive planting, these small farms frequently experience erosion and nutrient-depleted soils, with consequent diminishing yields. Typically, the survival of *minifundistas* (small farmers) depends upon supplementing work on their own land with work as sharecroppers or day-laborers on nearby large farms.

A major study of Colombia's land tenure system made in 1966 by the Interamerican Committee on Agricultural Development (CIDA) estimates that 175 thousand Colombian rural workers possessed no land at all in 1960.[3] In the past two decades, that figure has increased considerably due to a rapid growth in commercial-crop agriculture, the use of wage labor, and the near-stagnant level of traditional and mixed-crop agriculture, produced by small and medium-sized farms.[4]

According to the CIDA study, family farms, classified as those that fulfill at least half of their labor needs with family hands, range in size from 5 to 50 hectares in the Colombian Andean region. Together, the subfamily (minifundia) and family farms comprised 91.6 percent of total farms in 1970–71 and occupied 22.2 percent of the cultivable land. In contrast, 41 percent of the land, generally the most fertile, was occupied by farms of 500 hectares or more, representing 0.5 percent of the total number of farms (see table 1). These 1970–71 figures adequately represent the present tenure system as well, for no significant reforms have been instituted in the past decade.

What can be seen in these figures is an acutely unequal distribution of land, which contributes significantly to the great economic hardship and insecurity suffered by the majority of Colombia's rural families. This situation goes back centuries, throughout which peasant rebels and political reformers have been thwarted in their attempts to bring about significant structural change; nevertheless, their efforts have played a vibrant role in Colombia's history. If we are to understand contemporary agrarian politics, this history requires study.

Creation of Colombia's Minifundia/Latifundia, Seventeenth-Nineteenth Centuries

The latifundia evolved from the land distribution and tenure systems dominant during Colombia's colonial era. Spanish conquerors, along with relatives and friends, were originally granted huge landed estates by the crown in reward for "valiant" service.[5] In

TABLE 1

Land Distribution in Colombia, 1960–1971

Size of farms (in hectares)	Farms				Hectares (thousand)			
	1960		1970–71		1960		1970–71	
	Number	Percent	Number	Percent	Number	Percent	Number	Percent
Less than 3	606,423	50.2	559,052	47.5	678	2.5	625	2.0
3 - 9.9	319,327	26.4	300,832	25.6	1,726	6.3	1,609	5.2
10 - 49.9	201,020	16.6	217,873	18.5	4,211	15.4	4,653	15.0
50 - 99.9	39,990	3.3	47,763	4.1	2,680	9.8	3,198	10.3
100 - 499.9	36,010	3.0	42,897	3.6	6,990	25.6	8,253	26.6
500 - 999.9	4,141	.3	4,927	.4	2,731	10.0	3,299	10.6
1,000 or more	2,761	.2	3,467	.3	8,322	30.4	9,426	30.3
Total	1,209,672	100.0	1,176,811	100.0	27,338	100.0	31,063	100.0

Source: DANE, *Agricultural Census*, 1960, 1970–71, Colombia.

addition to the land grants (*capitulaciones* or *mercedes*), the Spanish were permitted to extract labor and taxes from the native population (encomiendas or repartimientos), thus forcing the abandonment of indigenous farmsteads and nucleated villages.

In the sixteenth, seventeenth and eighteenth centuries, several crown proclamations and laws were enacted to encourage the encomenderos to cultivate idle land, and to permit new settlers to clear and use unclaimed land. In 1790, the viceroy of Santa Fe (now Bogotá) stipulated that all landowners must cultivate, put to pasture, rent or sell their land, or it would revert to the crown's possession.

The phrase, "Se obedece pero no se cumple" (one obeys but does not comply) came to symbolize New World reaction to these obligations, and to all crown land laws and proclamations concerning social obligations. Wealthy colonizers were able to secure and increase their landholdings by buying their "irregular" possessions at low prices from the nearly penniless crown. These new land grants (*composiciones*), as well as the theft or cheap purchase of small bordering holdings, permitted a few people to acquire huge extensions of the most fertile land. Poorer Spanish newcomers were left with no other alternative than to gradually establish themselves on small plots of land in the eastern and southwestern highlands. The Indians continued to be transported from place to place as their labor was required, or pushed onto reservations (*resguardos*) in order to free their lands for sale and occupation.

In the early nineteenth century, Colombia's large landholders, who were anxious to release themselves from the crown's reforms and restrictions, joined with discontented merchants and miners to battle for the independence of Gran Colombia beside their leader, Simon Bolívar. For the first few decades after Colombia achieved its independence in 1819, the Conservative elites used their dominant political power to preserve, expand, and legalize their private landholdings. In the second half of the nineteenth century, the traditional elites were challenged by an emerging manufacturing and commercial class. This elite group advocated and accomplished the emancipation of the slaves and the disintegration of the Indian resguardos, which freed rural labor for work on commercial plantations and helped create an internal market for goods. As the best land was already incorporated into latifundia, former slaves, Indians, and poor *mestizos*, who sought land of their own, were obliged to settle on the steep mountainsides or venture into virgin territory to colonize state-owned lands (*baldíos*).

In the mid- and late-nineteenth century, thousands of courageous farmers colonized the western Colombian highlands, corresponding to the present states of Antioquia, Caldas, and Quindío. In the beginning, as slash-and-burn agriculturalists, they were afflicted by malaria, malnutrition, unstable earnings, and miserable living conditions. Later in the nineteenth and early twentieth centuries, the colonists converted their farms to coffee cultivation, and as producers for export, their general economic position improved. The problem of unstable earnings continued, nevertheless, as a result of their dependence on fluctuating world market coffee prices.

These pioneer settlers, or colonos, were officially lauded for their hard work and contribution to the development of marginal lands. As soon as they had developed the forests and jungle into economically viable farms, however, neighboring latifundistas began to process eviction procedures, claiming previous ownership of the colonos' newly-settled plots. Although the large landholders were usually unable to provide legal proof of title, and had never worked the land they claimed, political influence with local politicians won them generous settlements in the courts. Consequently, the colonos were forced to pay for their land and self-made improvements or risk total dispossession.

Peasant Rebellion and Liberal Reformism, 1920s–1940s[6]

By the early 1900s, the Colombian agrarian structure was characterized by huge extensively exploited cattle ranches and coffee haciendas spread out over the fertile coastal lowlands and the interior foothills and valleys, and by a growing rural population which was concentrated on small coffee and traditional-crop highland holdings. Subsistence tenant farming and daywork were done on the haciendas and plantations (see diagram 2).

The 1929 stock market crash, and the depression that followed, resulted in further inequities in the countryside. Thousands of laborers from rural areas, who had migrated to the cities to work in construction and manufacturing during the twenties, were put out of work. Many of the unemployed returned to the countryside to become squatters on the latifundias, alongside the tenant farmers and colonos settled on the fringe. With additional labor, the output of agricultural staples increased; however, diminishing demand and falling prices pushed rural incomes downward. The rural situation had reached a critical juncture. The scarcity of land, insecure ownership, declining incomes, and oppressive labor relationships on the

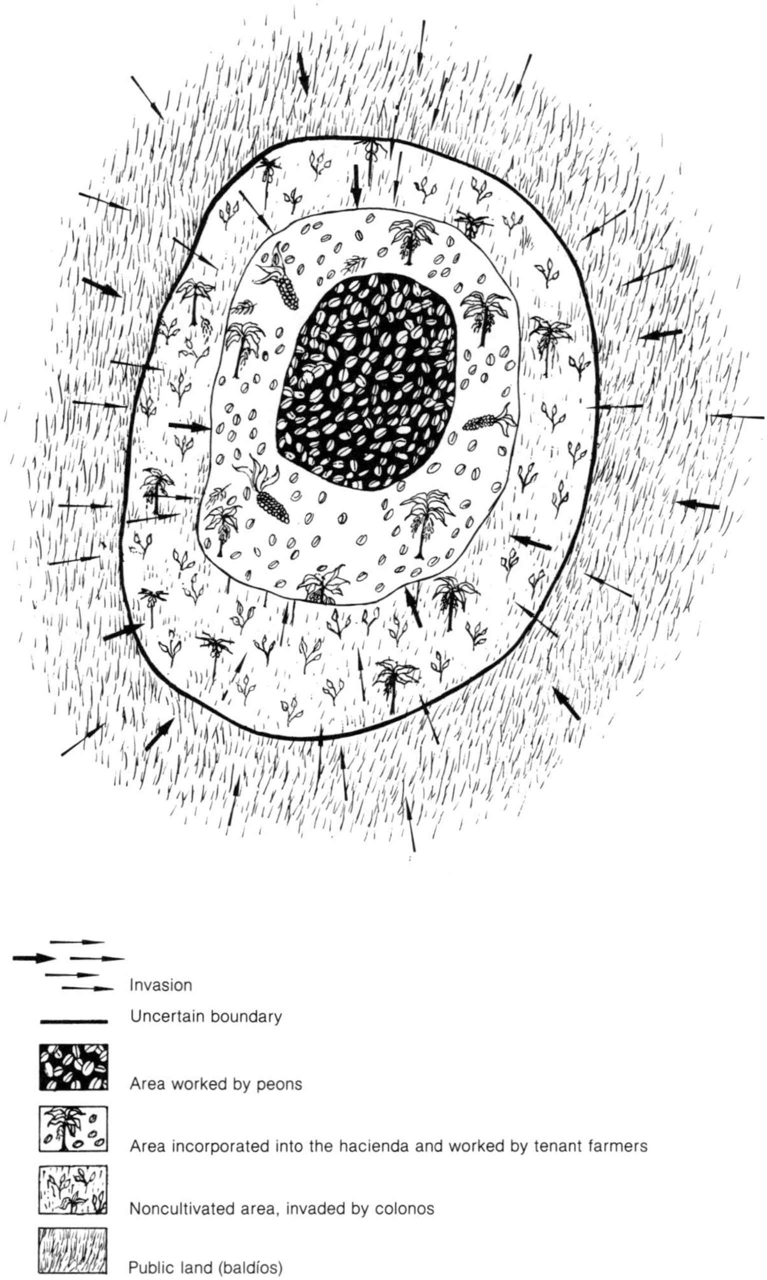

DIAGRAM 2. Schematic Plan of a Colombian Coffee Hacienda, 1930

large estates, made survival for the rural masses more difficult than ever. Having nothing to lose, they began to organize and rebel.

Peasant Leagues (Ligas Campesinas), often organized with the assistance of the Communist Party, were formed to put forth the demands of their rural constituencies. Over 100 peasant organizations were officially registered between 1917 and 1945; others worked unofficially.[7] The Leagues led dozens of land invasions, usually in areas from which tenant farmers and colonos had been evicted. Their ideology hinged upon the belief that the land should belong to those who work it. In addition to demanding land, they fought for an end to unpaid labor service, the right for tenant farmers to plant cash crops on their subsistence plots, and higher wages. Large landowners reacted to these pressures by continuing to evict colonos, sharecroppers, and tenant farmers, and by hiring less politically conscious wage laborers to take their places. In the process they acquired, free, all farm improvements made by the previous tenants.

As the conflict intensified, it developed into class warfare: the rural elites, their armed gangs, and government friends on the one side, out to defend the status quo; and the colonos, peons, and tenant farmers on the other side, demanding land and an end to semifeudal labor relations.

At the height of the Peasant League land invasions, Alfonso López Pumarejo became president (1934–1938), and led the country into an era of liberal reformism under the slogan, "Revolución en Marcha." López tried to promote economic development and political stability at the same time. His method was to incorporate leftist rural and urban demands into the reformist program, rather than exacerbate class conflict by identifying too closely with the traditional landed elite. In a message to Congress he stated: "Some landowners . . . asked the State to use the weapons of public order for ridding titles and the land itself of all dangerous ideas. . . . The eviction procedure was to be followed by the machine gun. . . . My government advised that such was not its attitude . . . toward the colono who invaded a piece of land which he believed in good faith to belong to the public domain."[8]

In 1936, López signed Law of Land Tenure 200. The law was intended to: (1) correct a long history of confused land titling criteria, which had provoked violent confrontations for many decades, and (2) stimulate latifundistas to make "economic" use of their land. Article 6 stipulated that all privately owned lands that remained more than 50 percent uncultivated after a period of ten consecutive years were to revert to the public domain, excluding landholdings of 300 hectares or less. Titles would be administered to colonos who had peacefully occupied and exploited a plot of land for five years. Evictions were permitted only when the original land title could be offered as proof of ownership, and after the evicted tenants had been compensated for farm improvements in cash.

Land judges were appointed to resolve eviction disputes and enforce the tenets of the new law. Since the state had no consistent way of distinguishing public from private land, disputes were usually settled through monetary arrangements rather than expropriation. The state bought up large extensions of uncultivated lands claimed by latifundistas, and distributed them in small plots to colonos (often already settled on the land) for a moderate sum to be reimbursed in monthly payments over five to ten years. Otherwise the colonos bought their plots directly from the supposed owners, sometimes exchanging land for labor service. Many of today's minifundia were created through these arrangements.

During the 1930s, the Conservative party responded to Liberal party reforms with an alternative plan to solve the land problem, that is, colonization. Rather than infringe upon the rights of private property owners by imposing government-sponsored redistribution programs, which encouraged illegal land invasions, Conservatives supported mass emigration to Colombia's sparsely populated hinterland—the Amazon basin and eastern plains (llanos). López disputed the idea that colonization could appease peasant demands, and favored, instead, land reform within the settled interior. His reform efforts were vigorously attacked, especially since the Liberal party was increasingly associated with the Communist party and UNIR (Jorge Gaitán's popular left-wing party). As before, threatened and angry landholders reacted to demands for land and Law 200 by dislodging sharecropper and tenant farmers before their claims could be heard, and by converting the labor system to one of full-time and seasonal salaried work, with no land options.

In the 1940s, under President Santos and during López's second term in office, Liberal party politics moved toward the right, offering a tentative peace to the landed elite. Law 100, legislated in 1944, was aimed at reassuring landowners of their right to hold property by providing generous compensation terms in case of expropriation, and by extending proof of "economic" land use another five years, to 1951. Still, Gaitán continued to support peasant demands and encourage class struggle for land reform in the 1940s.

During Conservative Ospina Perez's term in office (1946–1950), and particularly under Laureano Gómez (1950–1952), who was vehemently against agrarian reform, all remnants of the "Revolución en Marcha" were extinguished. In the late 1940s, capitalist agriculture began to replace the semifeudal labor and land structures of rural Colombia. Government attention was placed on increasing agricultural productivity, particularly for export. The landed elites were indulged with cheap credit, tax incentives, and large government investments in commercial enterprises. Meanwhile, state attacks against peasant rebellion continued as Laureano Gómez attempted to wipe out Gaitanismo and the Peasant Leagues once and for all.

"La Violencia," The National Front, and Agrarian Reform Law 135

The Conservatives may have hoped that by assassinating Jorge Gaitán on April 9, 1949, they would be able to quell the rebel movement of his rural followers. Instead, the assassination marked the beginning of nearly two decades of struggle and violence. This dark, poorly understood era of Colombian history called "La Violencia" took between 200 thousand and 400 thousand lives and left 800 thousand homeless and landless.[9]

From 1948 to the mid-1950s, under Laureano Gómez and the military dictatorship of Rojas Pinilla, peasants fought attacks by state police and army troops with revolutionary fervor. Rural guerrillas, still identified with the Liberal reformist wing, formed defense groups in the eastern llanos and central highlands, while Conservatives paid gangs of indigent workers and peasants to terrorize and assassinate within the Liberal strongholds, thus pitting peasant against peasant. At the same time, army troops arbitrarily evicted people from their land, enriching themselves and their government with the booty. What began as class warfare turned into bloody combat between the manipulated constituencies of the Liberal and Conservative parties, each leadership intent on using the violence for political gain and land acquisition.

When the Liberal outposts had been eliminated and hope for true reform through the political system extinguished, the victims of this manipulative warfare turned against each other and the system with vengeance. Self-motivated banditry replaced ideological revolt. The sons of landless peasants, and the victims of rape and pillage, joined in the plunder to take what they could from whomever they could. Extortion, burning, kidnapping, and assassination plagued the countryside with wanton fury. A new consciousness began to unfold in the peasant mind, for "La Violencia" had evoked

> a change in attitude toward the structures, the leaders and the very mentality of the people . . . the peasant population withdrew from the State because it was destroyed by

> the State . . . the violence engendered distrust in the Government. . . . For the peasant masses, the demagogue and cacique as political leaders no longer held weight . . . the peasant became conscious that he is the vital nerve of the nation, with the right to put forward his problems, and fervently demand his rights.[10]

In 1958, the Conservative and Liberal parties made a truce in order to quell a situation which had taken on a dangerous character, one that threatened the economic security of the elites as well as the poor. Under the National Front, the Liberals and Conservatives would automatically alternate control of the presidency for sixteen years, and share equal power in Congress and on the boards of all government institutions. This imposed peace created an atmosphere of popular apathy toward traditional politics, especially as the two parties began to temper their differences in the spirit of diplomatic, but unpopular, compromise.

With the National Front, and coordinated efforts to depoliticize rural violence and hunt down the bandits, a semblance of political stability was obtained. Nevertheless, "La Violencia" had caused the country to suffer great social upheaval at high economic cost, and feelings of insecurity (spurred by sporadic murders and kidnappings) continued to haunt the countryside. If Colombia was to see the defiance and desperate conditions of its masses neutralized (real wages had slipped 15 percent between 1948 and 1958[11]), and at the same time continue early efforts to modernize agriculture, balance its international accounts, and create a propitious atmosphere for investment, then the government would have to regain control of the countryside.

The first president of the National Front, Liberal Alberto Lleras Camargo, signed Colombia's most ambitious agrarian reform act to date, Law 135, on December 13, 1961. Written in the spirit of the Alliance for Progress, it reflected the thinking of moderate, practical reformers. The Reform was intended to restore peace in the countryside by instituting a land redistribution program in the areas hardest hit by "La Violencia" and, at the same time, increase total agricultural production through intensive exploitation and mechanization.

The law was debated for a full year in the Senate and the House of Representatives before sufficient adjustments had been made to satisfy a majority of both parties. The leftist MRL party (Movimiento Revolucionario Liberal), led by López Pumarejo's son, López Michelsen, and the Laureanista Conservatives consistently opposed the Reform. The primary beneficiaries-to-be, Colombia's rural masses, never participated in its design nor in the debate that followed. The Reform, thus, was an effort engineered from above by moderate Liberals and Conservatives, with no mass constituency.

Agrarian Reform Law 135 is a complex, lengthy document that encompasses all of Colombia's previous attempts at agrarian reform as well as additional, more radical mandates for change. If the law and its implementing agency, INCORA (Instituto Colombiano de la Reforma Agraria), had been given adequate financing, had enjoyed long-term government and popular support, and had been consistently staffed with committed individuals, its intended goals might have been accomplished. However, what might have happened and what has happened are two different stories. One can see from table 1 that during the reform decade of the 1960s, when support for Law 135 was at its peak, land distribution in Colombia changed very little. Indeed, some observers note that land concentration today is greater than it was prior to agrarian reform, primarily owing to the rapid growth of commercial, export-oriented agriculture since 1950.[12]

In the making and attempted implementation of Law 135, the most controversial aspects were the articles and subsequent decrees on expropriation and compensation. INCORA was allotted a fairly generous budget (100 million pesos annually, about 10 million U.S. dollars in 1961) to carry out the Agrarian Reform Law objectives. The allocation would have been insufficient to provide for an adequate number of parcelization and colonization projects and finance needed rural services, if, at the same time, expropriated landowners were to receive the compensation terms they desired. After long debate, a compromise was reached which stipulated several different payment terms depending upon the size and exploitation of the farms.

Farms with less than 100 hectares of exploited land were exempt from expropriation, leaving approximately 43 thousand farms as possible areas for redistribution efforts. Adequately exploited commercial farms would be subject to expropriation only if noncultivated land or land worked by tenant farmers and sharecroppers were not available, and only with the voluntary consent of the titled landowner. If and when the state chose to incorporate rationally exploited farms into a parcelization project, they were to be paid 20 percent in cash and the rest in eight-year nonnegotiable bonds at 4 percent interest. Idle land would be totally paid for in low-interest, long-term government bonds.

More controversial than the payment terms was the question of how to determine land values. Landowners pushed for the present commercial value while Reform advocates argued for cadastral (tax) values. By government decree, the latter system was instituted, though it was vehemently opposed by landowners who, for decades, had been underestimating the value of their land in order to avoid paying higher taxes. To stall for time and put pressure on the government, opponents argued that the whole valuation and compensation process was unconstitutional. Although they lost their argument in court, the decree was eventually amended to allow for self-valuation for both compensation and taxation purposes. This dealt a crippling blow to INCORA by weakening its powers vis-à-vis agrarian reform opponents. According to the 1966 CIDA study, the amount the government would have to pay in increased compensation under the new valuation system would exceed additional revenue collected in taxes by more than twenty times.[13] Thus, despite sincere initial attempts by INCORA to implement both the redistributive and rational exploitation objectives of Law 135, political opposition, combined with financial and legal restraints, made progress difficult and slow.

By the mid-sixties, government enthusiasm for agrarian reform was already waning. INCORA propaganda and funds were directed toward colonization, land reclamation, and technical assistance projects, while parcelization began to be criticized as being adverse to increased food production, the nation's foremost need. This criticism was spurious—a rationalization—for agricultural productivity (per unit land) had increased by more than 3 percent a year since 1962. Small farmers continued, as in the past, to contribute a larger share to total agricultural production than their corresponding shares of cultivated land.[14] INCORA workers who remained true to the law's original intent and refused to accept the rationalization process filtered down from above, were either eased out of their responsibilities or quit in frustration.

Aside from internal considerations, influential international bodies (USAID, OAS) began to encourage rural policies that stressed technical over structural change. John Kennedy and his dual counter-insurgency/social change doctrine were replaced with Lyndon Johnson's more direct capitalist approach. "There have been indications that the Johnson Administration intends to emphasize the technical features of land reform under the Alliance for Progress, rather than the expropriation features written into the Charter of Punta del Este. Assistance will be forthcoming, but the emphasis will be on colonization rather than parcelization, in an attempt to increase private investment in the agricultural sector by bettering the investment climate."[15]

The Colonization Argument

Land reform in Colombia has come nearly full circle since its beginnings in the 1930s. Demands for reform, first manifested in organized protests led by the Peasant Leagues, degenerated into political confrontation between the manipulated constituencies of the two traditional parties during "La Violencia," and eventually were quieted with the forced peace of the National Front. Whereas outright repression had failed, moderates of the new coalition hoped that a limited land reform program (lauded and partially financed by the Alliance for Progress) might finally stabilize rural unrest and dismantal uneconomical semifeudal labor and land structures. Efforts to implement land reform met with fervent political opposition from the landed elite and right-wing Conservatives. Reform advocates lacked the commitment and a mass constituency to overcome these obstacles. Consequently, a new approach to the rural "problem" unfolded, justified by the government's altered concept of what constituted reform. By the late 1960s the main criteria for investment in the agrarian sector had changed from social obligation to political feasibility and commercial profitability.

Colonization of Colombia's frontier lands fulfills the above criteria. Settlement and development of public lands do not pose an immediate threat to private property and potentially could boost total national production by incorporating isolated areas into the market economy. Although costs per settler are very high, they can be deferred to some degree through long-term international loans. Colonization is not agrarian reform, for it does not alter established structures. Nevertheless, proponents claim that landlessness and underemployment in the interior could eventually be resolved through the settlement of Colombia's scarcely populated eastern half.

Renewed government enthusiasm for colonization projects has been complicated by the soured relationship between the state and the peasantry. A long history of broken promises of reform, expulsion by latifundistas, and violent repression, have made Colombian peasants wary of colonization ventures and government assistance.

Historically, colonization in Colombia has been a process of migration from the interior's most fertile land, occupied by latifundia, to isolated areas where colonos have converted virgin forest and jungle into subsistence plots and small coffee farms. Once the frontier was cleared and put to agricultural use, colonos were frequently evicted or bought out by large landowners and commercial enterprises. Liberal reforms to protect colonos and tenant farmers were consistently thwarted by influential political opponents. The colonos' existence, therefore, has been a precarious one, troubled with land insecurity, unstable earnings, arduous work, and sporadic violence. This history of suffering largely explains why Colombians today are reluctant to migrate to the eastern llanos, Caquetá, Putumayo, and Amazonas. For most, frontier settlement is viewed as a last resort. "This form of adjustment (colonization), even when it is called spontaneous, is not necessarily voluntary, given the necessity that induces it . . . due in part to the lack of capital resources and remunerative employment opportunities available to small producers."[16]

Government efforts to direct a portion of the highland's displaced, rural population toward the frontier and away from private property and overcrowded cities have met with little success. In 1948, the Institute of Colonization, Parcelization, and Forest Defense was established with a one-time endowment of 10 million pesos. Beyond the usual opening fanfare, little activity was accomplished, owing to insufficient funds and personnel. The Institute of Colonization and Immigration was created during the administration of Rojas Pinilla. Despite more activity, this Institute fared little better than its predecessor. "Under inexperienced management, with hardly any prior study, the Institute plunged into several colonization ventures, built airstrips, bought machinery to set up in sawmills, brought volunteer settlers to work poor soils in inhospitable climates and . . . met with total disaster."[17] Colombia's Agrarian Bank (Caja Agraria) took charge of colonization efforts in 1956. After six years of planning, field experience, and heavy investment, the Caja had settled only one thousand families on frontier land. In 1962, colonization responsibilities were ceded to the newly-formed Institute for Agrarian Reform (INCORA).

The following table sums up INCORA's accomplishments during its first, most inspired, eight years of work. The figures in table 2 show that the greatest achievement of Colombian agrarian reform has been the opening of the agricultural frontier, and not the redistribution of underused land in heavily populated areas. Between 1962 and 1970, title to public land was granted to an average of thirteen thousand families per year, some of whom also benefited from scattered infrastructure projects, rural services, and government loans.

INCORA's first few parcelization projects on redistributed private land are estimated to have cost approximately Col. $60,000 per rural family, or U.S. $5,400 using the 1963 exchange rate. The high cost of these initial land reform efforts (projects Tolima and Nariño) is explained by the variety of integrated services financed, in addition to basic land purchase, distribution, and titling. These

TABLE 2

INCORA Land Incorporation, Titling, Redistribution, and Credit Activities Compared with Total National Resources, 1962–1970

	National total	INCORA activity	Percent INCORA activity over national total
Total cultivated land compared to land incorporated by INCORA (hectares)	30,993,000	3,295,332	10.6
Total number of farms compared to number of farms titled by INCORA	1,176,811	107,773[a]	9.2
Total cultivated land compared to land INCORA redistributed by purchase or expropriation (hectares)	30,993,000	77,428	0.25
Total number of farms compared to number of farms receiving INCORA credit	1,176,811	29,849	2.5

[a]Of which, 5,347 (0.45 percent of total farms, 5 percent of INCORA titled farms) were a result of redistribution; the remainder a result of titling of public land (*baldío*).

Source: Updated from Alonso Tobon, *La tierra y la Reforma agraria en Colombia,* 2d ed. (Bogotá: Ediciones Cancer, 1972), p. 155.

included the provision of housing, electricity, running water, sewage, schools, health clinics, churches, roads, farm implements, seeds, fertilizers, several small animals per family, credit for coffee growers, technical assistance, and the organization of production and marketing cooperatives.

The cost of settling a Colombian rural family in an area of colonization in the early sixties was estimated by the Export-Import Bank at Col. $80,000 to $100,000, or U.S. $8,000.[18] The colono family, however, would receive only minimal services: land titling, penetration roads, six months of seeds and fertilizers, and supervised credit. Therefore, at one-third higher cost to INCORA, the agency could attempt to settle rural families on the eastern frontier while providing only a fraction of the assistance and possibilities of long-term success offered by other redistributive land reform projects. The decision to finance colonization rather than parcelization incurred a high economic opportunity cost that makes sense only when analyzing it from the political perspective of Colombia's ruling elites.

Even with state assistance, the new colono's life is in many ways as precarious as that of his late nineteenth-century predecessors. Difficult agroclimatic conditions, the lack of a basic infrastructure, disease, and opportunistic middlemen are constant impediments to economic mobility. In addition, of the 3.3 million hectares newly titled by INCORA, more than 60 percent are occupied by large ranchers who have gradually expanded their holdings by buying the surrounding farms of the poorer colonos cheaply. One of the largest frontier latifundia is owned by the Lara family in the intendencia of Caquetá. Over a period of forty years the Laras accumulated over 40,000 hectares of land and in 1966 owned forty thousand head of cattle.[19]

Colombia's rural population has passed the ten million mark and continues to grow by more than fourteen thousand families per year (net of rural-urban migration). Approximately 70 percent of rural families do not possess the means—land, capital, and wages—to live above subsistence levels. The argument by agrarian reform opponents that a substantial portion of this interior rural population could be transferred to frontier public land with minimal trouble has proven fallacious. Owing to their high costs and difficult agroclimatic and technical problems, colonization schemes are able to accommodate relatively few families on economically efficient farmsteads. Spontaneous migration occurs only as a last resort. Therefore, while frontier settlement has attracted a small number of Colombia's rural poor, it is at best a Band-Aid solution. The National Front chose to colonize and abandon its program of redistribution. To preserve calm within its own ranks and promote large-scale export-oriented agriculture, the Front essentially abandoned the peasantry.

Current Strategies of Popular Rebellion and Government Policy in Rural Colombia

Since the late 1960s, Colombia has experienced periodic peasant rebellion in response to the failures of agrarian reform. In 1968, the National Association of the Peasantry (ANUC) was formed under the auspices of Liberal president Carlos Lleras Restrepo to gather rural support for INCORA programs, and to give the Liberal party greater credibility among the popular classes. Shortly after its creation, the ANUC leaders went beyond their intended role, and became militant organizers and supporters of rural revolutionary demands.

ANUC's first mandate for change, published in 1971 under the heading Tierra sin Patrones (Land without Bosses), summarized the demands that the Colombian peasantry have consistently voiced in response to the inequities built into the land tenure system:

1. An end to the land monopoly and the final elimination of latifundia.
2. Prohibition and liquidation of the archaic systems of tenant farming, sharecropping, and peonage.
3. Rapid and free distribution of land to those who work it or wish to work it.
4. Substitution of large cooperative peasant-managed farms based on voluntary association and adequate technological change for the present systems of land tenure and labor exploitation.
5. Protection for those with small and medium-sized farms, with assistance for them to achieve more economical and technically advanced methods of development, and for their gradual transition to cooperative farming under peasant control.
6. Protection for the farmers with small and medium-sized properties, who were victims of the incumbent regime, by eliminating attempts by merchants, middle-men, and usurers to expel peasants from their rightful land through indebtedness.[20]

Under this basic program and a coordinated decentralized peasant leadership, ANUC launched over two thousand land invasions nationwide in the early 1970s. More land was given to peasants and organized into cooperative farms in three years of ANUC activity than had been distributed during the fourteen-year existence of INCORA (1961–1975).[21]

The militant activities of ANUC polarized the Liberal and Conservative parties. The latter blamed the former's reformist politics for the current state of rural lawlessness. In a conference held at Chicoral, Tolima, in 1972, the leaders of the National Front gathered to plan a new agrarian policy designed to reassure the property rights of latifundistas. The proceedings of this conference, ratified in 1973 and reiterated in Law 6 of 1975, essentially mark the end of Colombian agrarian reform. Landowners were given guarantees against expropriation, and in the remote case that it might occur, assured the bulk of compensation in cash. In exchange, latifundistas were again pressured to put their idle hectares to economic use, through a property tax of 8 percent on the value of the land whether it was income-producing or not. They were to receive subsidized credit to assist in the transformation to commercial farming.

Government funding of ANUC was cut off and soldiers were sent out to restore invaded areas to their original owners. What was once a strong and growing peasant organization became two debilitated factions, one associated with the government and the rights of wealthier peasants, and the other still supportive of the original demands, but now leaning toward the path of electoral politics rather than armed confrontation.[22]

In addition to ANUC, several small guerrilla groups have been working in the countryside with varying degrees of success since the late 1960s. The Colombian priest and sociologist, Camilo Torres, who joined the guerrillas and was killed in combat in 1966, remains a hero and inspiration to idealistic revolutionary youth all over Latin America.

The guerrillas see their immediate role to be defenders of the rural poor against attacks by bandits and hired armed gangs, while their long-term goals are the elimination of the present labor and land structures and the establishment of a democratically managed workers' state. Although the guerrillas number only a few thousand, they can count on general popular support when they are hunted down by the military, which makes their presence more threatening to the authorities than their numbers alone might indicate. In the areas of colonization, where ample hideout territory exists and uprooted colonos are struggling to make ends meet, the guerrillas are particularly strong. In Caquetá, the FARC (Revolutionary Armed Forces of Colombia) has carried out assaults on nearly all of the frontier towns, and in 1978 was considered a dangerous enough force by the national government and the local elite to have the area militarized with anti-guerrilla troops.

The Colombian government's most recent efforts to establish legitimacy in the countryside, and at the same time to raise agricultural productivity, have been centered around the agency called DRI (Integrated Rural Development), created in 1975. The stated objective of this institution, to be implemented through a five-year extendible program, is to "benefit the poorest 50 percent of the rural population by delivering to small rural enterprises a series of integrated services."[23] The services are administered by the Agrarian Bank, in coordination with twelve other governmental institutions, and are financed 50 percent with internal funds and 50 percent with World Bank and Inter-American Development Bank loans. DRI serves selected farmers directly with credit and technical assistance, and assists a larger group indirectly, with marketing associations, reforestation, road development, aqueducts, sanitation units, construction of schools and health posts, and provision of personnel and supplies.

According to the DRI plan, assistance is to be directed toward farmers with less than Col. $500,000 worth of assets (approximately U.S. $16,000), and less than 20 hectares of land. Nevertheless, because DRI is aimed at raising farm productivity through technological innovation, the minifundia (less than three hectares), which are often too small and eroded to be economically transformed through technology, are essentially excluded from the credit and technical assistance programs. Consequently, DRI's direct services do not reach nearly 50 percent of Colombia's landholders, nor do they benefit the landless rural wage workers.

Most of the six areas where DRI activities are concentrated (Nariño and Cauca, Cundinamarca and Tolima, Antioquia, Córdoba and Sucre, Boyacá, and Santander) were heavily affected by "La Violencia," and still experience some banditry and right-wing repression as well as guerrilla assaults. Students skeptical of Colombian agrarian reform see the current Integrated Rural Development Program as just another attempt by government to quell peasant rebellion, without seriously tackling the problems that provoke the unrest. "The current strategy for rural development in use in Colombia, rests principally on the control of "rural violence," together with the adoption of agrarian projects that have no real social benefit."[12]

The programs of Project Caquetá encompass both the colonization and the integrated rural development strategies described above. By evaluating these few programs and their impact on a select number of beneficiaries, I am able to draw certain conclusions that may shed light on the overall effectiveness of these strategies, currently employed in projects nationwide.

While colonization and integrated rural development are not adequate replacements for agrarian reform, for in neither is there an attempt to dismantle the established land tenure system, their programs are aimed at benefiting poor farmers by raising productivity levels and income and by improving their general well-being. These, by themselves, are laudable goals. We will see whether, in the case of Caquetá, the strategies adopted do have "real social benefit." But first, let us take a close look at the histories, economic means, and needs of the rural people toward whom these benefits and services are directed.

Notes

1. Large rural estates, typically underused and owned by absentee landlords (*latifundistas*). The land tenure system dominated by latifundia is generally marked by a grossly inequitable distribution of land wealth.

2. Salamón Kalmanovitz, *Desarrollo de la agricultura en Colombia* (Bogotá: Editorial la Carreta, 1978), pp. 34–39.

3. Comité Interamericano de Desarrollo Agrícola (CIDA), *Tenencia de la tierra y desarrollo socioeconómico del sector agrícola: Colombia* (Washington, D.C.: Unión Panamericana, Secretaría General de la Organización de los Estados Americanos, 1966), p. 300.

4. Kalmanovitz, *Desarrollo de la agricultura*, table 2-B, pp. 68-69. Between 1950 and 1976 the annual average growth rate of commercial crops was 7.6 percent, more than five times greater than the growth of mixed crops. In 1976, 64 percent of the value of total agricultural production was generated from a modern, capitalist system of production.

5. Several authors were consulted for the research and writing of this section. Of special importance were the following: Ernest a. Duff, *Agrarian Reform in Colombia* (New York: F.A. Praeger Publishers, 1968); Hermes Tovar, *El movimiento campesino en Colombia durante los siglos XIX and XX*, 2d ed. (Bogotá: Ediciones Libres, 1975); and Albert O. Hirschman, *Journeys toward Progress* (New York: Twentieth Century Fund, Inc., 1963).

6. In addition to the two references cited in notes 7 and 8, the following authors were consulted for ideas on the 1920s-1940s period: Duff, *Agrarian Reform*; Alonso Tobon, *La tierra y la reforma agraria en Colombia*, 2d ed. (Bogotá: Ediciones Cancer, 1972); Tovar, *El movimiento campesino*; and CIDA, *Tenencia de la tierra y desarrollo*.

7. Gonzalo G. Sánchez, *Las ligas campesinas en Colombia* (Bogotá: Ediciones Alcaraván, 1977), pp. 70-77.

8. Alfonso López Pumarejo, Annual Message to Congress, 1935, quoted in Hirschman, *Journeys toward Progress*, p. 106.

9. Wolfgang Brucher, *La colonización de la selva pluvial en el piedemonte amazónico de Colombia* (edited by the Instituto Geográfico "Agustín Codazzi," 1974), pp. 43-44. Figures on human and economic losses due to "La Violencia" vary from source to source, averaging approximately 200,000 deaths, or 1.5 percent of the total population in 1958.

10. CIDA, *Tenencia de la tierra y desarrollo*, p. 253.

11. Kalmanovitz, *Desarrollo de la agricultura*, p. 32.

12. Observers include Salamón Kalmanovitz, Alonso Tobon, and CIDA.

13. CIDA, *Tenencia de la tierra y desarrollo*, p. 284.

14. Duff, *Agrarian Reform*, p. 119. Increase in agricultural production, per unit of land, averaged 4.6 percent between 1962 and 1964, and slightly less than 3.0 percent for the period 1956-1960. Farms less than 5 hectares in size comprised 6.1 percent of total cultivated area, and contributed 20 percent to total agricultural production in 1963.

15. Ibid., p. 168. Statement by Ernest A. Duff.

16. CIDA, *Tenencia de la tierra y desarrollo*, p. 253. Translated from Spanish by Robin Marsh.

17. Hirschman, *Journeys toward Progress*, p. 139.

18. Duff, *Agrarian Reform*, p. 100. Cost estimates for both colonization and parcelization projects are taken from this source.

19. Kalmanovitz, *Desarrollo de la agricultura*, pp. 279-280. In the mid-1960s, the head of the Lara family was kidnapped and killed by rebellious workers employed on his estate. Since then the latifundia (Larandia) has been divided amongst the rest of the family, and part has been sold. Today, in Caquetá, the Laras own approximately 28,000 hectares with as many cattle. They also own several other large farms and businesses throughout Colombia.

20. Ibid., p. 285. Quoted from the Peasant Mandate passed in the municipality of Fuquene in August 1971, and adapted and translated from Spanish by Robin Marsh.

21. Ibid., p. 286.

22. In their Fourth Congress, held in the town of Tomala, Sucre, in 1977, ANUC leaders proposed a more moderate land reform program and geared up for the 1978 elections, prepared to participate as part of the Popular Unity Front, an alternative to the Liberal and Conservative Parties.

23. Quoted from a pamphlet called "Qué es el DRI?" published in 1976 by the Caja Agraria, in coordination with the Ministry of Agriculture.

24. Emil Haney, "El dilema del minifundia en Colombia," reprint no 85-S (Madison, Wisconsin: University of Wisconsin Land Tenure Center, 1973), p. 155.

2

Socioeconomic Conditions of Rural Caquetá

THE INTENDENCIA OF Caquetá is called the "Gateway to the Amazon" because of its intermediary location between the Colombian Eastern Andean Range and the lowland rainforest of the Amazonas (see *frontis.*). Approximately 15 percent of the region has been cleared and settled by colonists (14,000 square kilometers) and the rest is "unclaimed" public land (baldíos), partially occupied by indigenous tribal societies. While situated only a twelve-hour bus ride, or fifty minutes by plane, from the nation's capital, Caquetá is still perceived by most Colombians as a forbidding place to live, though perhaps an adventurous place to visit. This image is changing as the area slowly progresses toward modernity.

Caquetá is a melting pot of farmers, ranchers, merchants, and professionals from all over Colombia. It exudes an atmosphere of both calm provinciality and bustling commerce. According to studies by the local Public Health Institute, the current population of Caquetá is 239,000, giving the intendencia a density of 2.4 persons per square kilometer. Sixty-four percent of the Caquetá population is classified as rural, living on farms or in villages of less than twenty-five hundred people. Of the urban population, 75 percent live within the municipality of the capital city, Florencia, and the remaining 25 percent are distributed among seven other municipalities and three smaller divisions called *corregimientos*.[1]

Since the 1930's, the intendencia of Caquetá has experienced a steady influx of spontaneous colonists; in general, these have been refugees from economic and political injustice suffered in their areas of origin. Other settlers have been "directed" toward Caquetá via government-sponsored colonization projects. Most of the immigrants arrived believing that the open space, informality, and potential for economic mobility characteristic of a newly developing land might provide a more promising future than the highly structured economic and social divisions of the "civilized" *interior*, the densely populated highlands of western Colombia. The degree to which expectations for economic mobility are fulfilled during the colonization process will be discussed. First, let us turn to a brief history of Caquetá settlement.

Settlement History of Caquetá

Immigrant settlement of Caquetá began in earnest in the late nineteenth century as a result of a short-lived rubber boom. Rubber-collection companies contracted their labor from migrants, some of whom remained to clear and cultivate the land after the boom fizzled out around 1920.

It was during this early stage of colonization that the native population experienced its first and most brutal contact with the white man. Indians were forced to provide free labor services for the rubber companies. Those who resisted domination were severely punished—some fled and the less fortunate were killed. The infamous Casa Araña Peruvian rubber company, which spread its domain throughout southeastern Putumayo and Caquetá, was responsible for decimating nearly all the native peoples whose lands it invaded. Moreover, the company intimidated recently arrived mestizo colonists into leaving their subsistence plots, increasing the land available for rubber exploitation. Largely owing to the crimes of Casa Araña, "by 1908, at least 20,000 natives had been kidnapped, enslaved and assassinated."[2]

Further to the north, Indians were violently evicted from their land and homes by land-seeking mestizos, which forced them to migrate to the yet unpenetrated hinterland. Even today one hears of Indians being murdered by colonists who claim to believe that natives are not protected under the law.

Catholic missionaries from the interior of Colombia, and from Spain and Italy, established several refugee settlements for the Indians in the early 1900s. They attempted to curb the brutality of Casa Araña by publicizing its excesses in Bogotá. In exchange for protection, the missionaries paternalistically converted and educated the natives, and taught them the ways of sedentary agriculture. Missions, which later grew into the principal frontier towns of

Caquetá, were established all along the lowland edge of the eastern Andes and are today connected by a single, partially paved highway. Florencia was christened on December 25, 1902, as was Belén to the south in 1917, and Guacamayas to the north in 1921.

Colonization of Caquetá was further advanced by a territorial conflict between Colombia and Peru. In the early 1930s, Peruvian troops invaded southern Colombia through the port of Leticia, intent upon pushing their national border northward. From Bogotá, a massive counterattack was organized to halt the aggressors and claim firm authority over Colombia's nearly abandoned Amazonas territory. A road was built to facilitate the movement of troops from the interior to the lowlands, and military posts were set up along the way. The counterattack proved successful and helped to open the threatened region to a gradual process of exploration and development. Stores were established to provide soldiers with supplies, and some troops remained to become farmers and ranchers after the conflict. The newly constructed road opened the way for a small but steady stream of land-seeking migrants. By 1938, the non-Indian population of Caquetá had reached twenty-one thousand.

During the next thirteen years the population of Caquetá more than doubled, reaching 46,558 in 1951. By 1964 it had doubled again, 75 to 80 percent from immigration and the rest owing to local population growth.[3] About 70 percent of the immigrants came from Huila and Tolima, both areas that experienced extreme land concentration during the 1930s and 1940s as a result of expanding cattle haciendas and commercial farming. Many small highland farmers could no longer feed their families from the diminishing yields of the tiny plots left to them, and therefore sold their farms to become salaried workers on large farms and construction projects, or work-seekers in the cities. Each year a few thousand families opted for the frontier alternative, attracted by the prospect of acquiring land, cattle, and tranquillity.

Frontier settlement experienced an upsurge during the era of "La Violencia," when hundreds of thousands of rural folk were forced to hastily flee their homes. As refugees, they spread out over all corners of the nation. The vast majority migrated to the cities and some sought sustenance in more tranquil areas of the rural interior, although this option was closed to most because of the unavailability and high cost of land. A small number of the refugees chose to make their new homes in the sparsely populated, relatively calm tropical lowlands. Among them, approximately four thousand a year migrated to Caquetá. During the peak years of violence, many arrived from the state of Tolima, where 300 thousand persons were expelled between 1948 and 1958.[4]

The first government-sponsored effort to assist in the agricultural colonization of Caquetá grew out of the social chaos created by "La Violencia." Something had to be done about the thousands of indigent, idle, and bitter men and women converging upon cities that were totally unprepared to receive them. Conservative agrarian reform opponents and moderate Liberals agreed that as many as possible should be transported to Colombia's marginal lands, vis-à-vis "directed" colonization. "Directed" refers to the intervention of the state in selecting the families which are to migrate; in choosing and distributing the parcels of land; and in providing credit, roads, technical assistance, and supervision as means to economic survival. The colono in a sense becomes a ward of the state until he/she is able to survive independently.

Toward this end, the state authorized the Caja Agraria (Agrarian Bank) to select families, deprived of the means for subsistence as a result of "La Violencia," for settlement on 698,000 hectares of land in the Intendencia of Caquetá. Between 1959 and 1961, the Caja established three centers of colonization in Caquetá—Maguaré, La Mono, and Valparaiso (map 2). Together they were divided into 749 parcels averaging 50 hectares each and housed 1,043 families.[5] Inexperience and the urgency of the social crisis at hand largely explain why the selection process, the planning, and implementation of this project were hastily and shoddily executed. As a consequence, these new "directed" settlers—many of whom were not farmers, but urban and rural day-laborers—found the struggle for survival under unfamiliar tropical agroclimatic conditions to be hopelessly difficult.

Although credit for subsistence and supplies was made available until the first harvest, both the project supervisors and the new farmers lacked the experience, the endurance, and the commitment to tackle the harsh environment and convert it to economical use. Ill-prepared for the deprivations of frontier life and disappointed with unfulfilled government promises, a good many of the selected colonists abandoned their parcels to return to more familiar environments in the rural and urban interior. What they had been assured of in Bogotá—a new start, a decent life, and government assistance to make them possible—did not in fact materialize. By mid-1961, more than half of the "directed" colonists had left the area, while those who remained continued to produce poorly, averaging 2 hectares of subsistence crops per year.

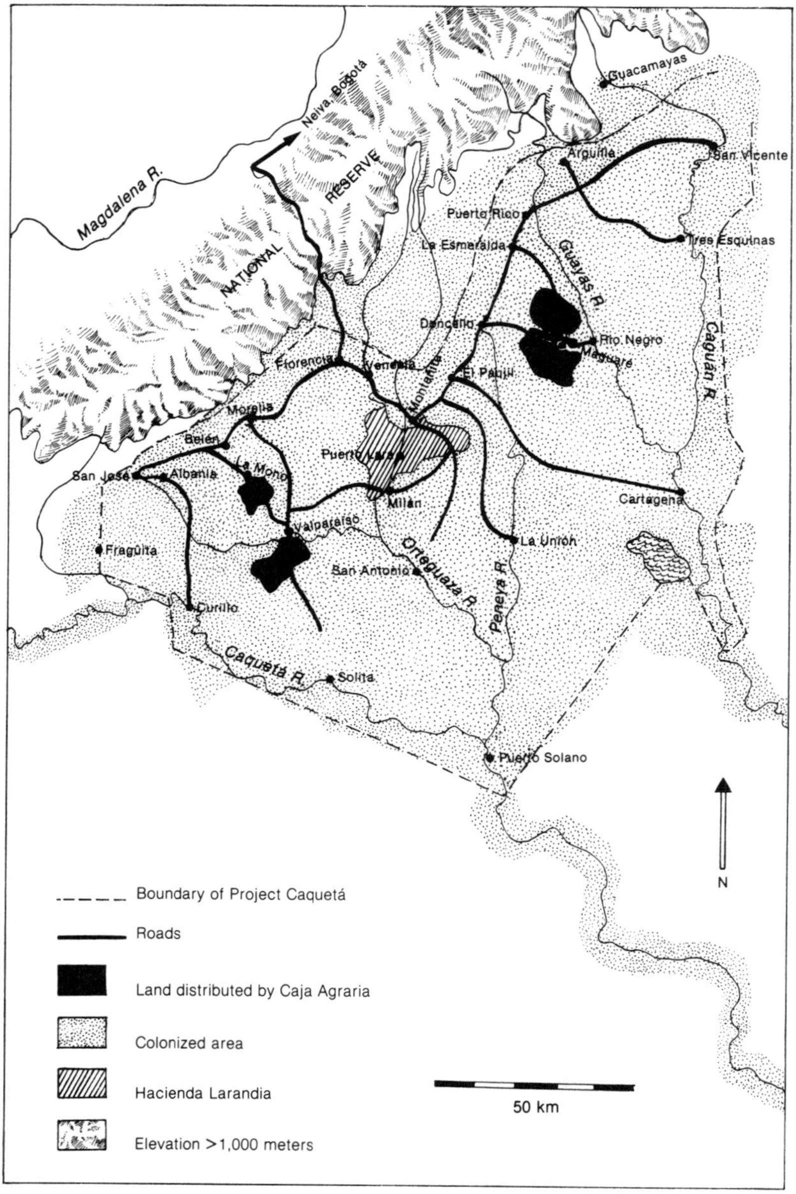

MAP 2. Colonization of Caquetá.

SOURCE. Adapted from a map in Wolfgang Brucher, *La colonización de la selva pluvial en el piedemonte amazónico de Colombia* (Bogotá: Instituto Geográfico "Agustín Codazzi," 1974), p. 172.

The shortcomings of the Caja Agraria experiment served to strengthen the subsequent INCORA rural development project in Caquetá. "Directed" colonization was discredited and replaced with government programs designed to assist spontaneous or "voluntary" frontier settlers. The experiences of the Caja Agraria, as well as previous colonization schemes, had shown the weakness of a strategy aimed at physically rerouting families from overcrowded cities, areas of concentrated minifundia, and rural violence to the unfamiliar tropical lowlands. It was decided that permanent rural development programs, administered by INCORA, should be established in the marginal areas to assist spontaneous, self-motivated migrants. In this way, indirectly, the government might encourage new settlers to remain in Caquetá, and moreover, stimulate further migration of their friends and families. The new colonization strategy, therefore, sought to incorporate self-motivated recruits into the government program, rather than to recruit reluctant families by nurturing false hopes, a policy which had failed both politically and economically.

In summary, migration to Caquetá has been propelled principally by negative conditions within the densely populated interior. Of the spontaneous settlers, almost all were employed in the rural sector prior to migration, the majority as small landowners. Approximately half of the "directed" colonists brought by the Caja Agraria were wage workers, 20 percent urban and 30 percent rural.[6] The wage workers went to the frontier in search of work, and possibly a farm of their own. The minifundistas went for more and cheaper land. Unable to survive and progress in their homelands, they believed their luck might change in Caquetá.

Overall between 10 and 20 percent of the migrants were directly affected by "La Violencia," and fled to Caquetá as a matter of immediate survival. A much higher percentage of the "directed" colonists migrated because of "La Violencia" than did the spontaneous settlers, although the latter group, whether directly or indirectly affected, also arrived in large numbers during the peak violent years. Table 3 shows the dates of arrival and length of stay in Caquetá for the eighty-five farmers interviewed for this study, none of whom were part of the Caja Agraria project ("directed" colonists). Those arriving before 1963 (61.9 percent of the total) were probably "touched" by the rural conflict, if not through actual loss, then through a declining standard of living and concern over the general climate of insecurity.

Of the families interviewed, 16 percent were born in Caquetá and 84 percent migrated from seven different states. More than half of

TABLE 3

Arrival Dates to Caquetá of 85 Surveyed Families

Dates of arrival	Years in Caquetá	Percent of families
1974–1978	less than 5	12.7
1969–1973	5–9	12.7
1964–1968	10–14	12.7
1959–1963	15–19	32.4
1954–1958	20–24	8.5
1953 or before	25 or more	21.0

the immigrants were originally from Huila (39 percent) and Tolima (21 percent); 18 percent came from Caldas and Quindío; and the rest migrated from Valle, Cundinamarca, Santander, and Norte de Santander. Map 3 succinctly illustrates the areas of origin of settlers in Caquetá, Putumayo, and the eastern llanos. The dots refer to areas of concentrated minifundia (Huila, southern Tolima, Caldas, eastern Valle), and the diagonal lines refer to heavy zones of violence (Tolima, Caldas, Quindío). Aside from economic and political reasons, the geographic location of Huila and Tolima explains why a high proportion of Caquetá settlers migrated from those states.

While the push toward Caquetá has been analyzed in terms of negative forces present in the more developed areas of Colombia, it is also true that migration has been stimulated by a variety of economic opportunities within Caquetá, particularly since the mid-sixties. A large section of Caquetá has already been exploited and incorporated into the national economy. The colonized area is penetrated with a network of roads connecting several growing, commercially active towns. The lands closest to navigable rivers, roads, and towns are principally occupied by medium- and large-sized cattle ranches that produce for export to the interior. Daily flights connect Florencia to Bogotá and air travel is available between several peripheral towns within Caquetá.

As the area becomes less isolated and "forbidding," it becomes more attractive to a new class of migrants. Middle-class farmers, merchants, and some well-to-do landowners and businessmen are arriving in greater numbers to take advantage of good land deals and opportunities to tap a growing market. As migrants from all classes and occupational backgrounds stream in, structures and institutions within Caquetá begin to resemble those of "modern-day" Colombia.

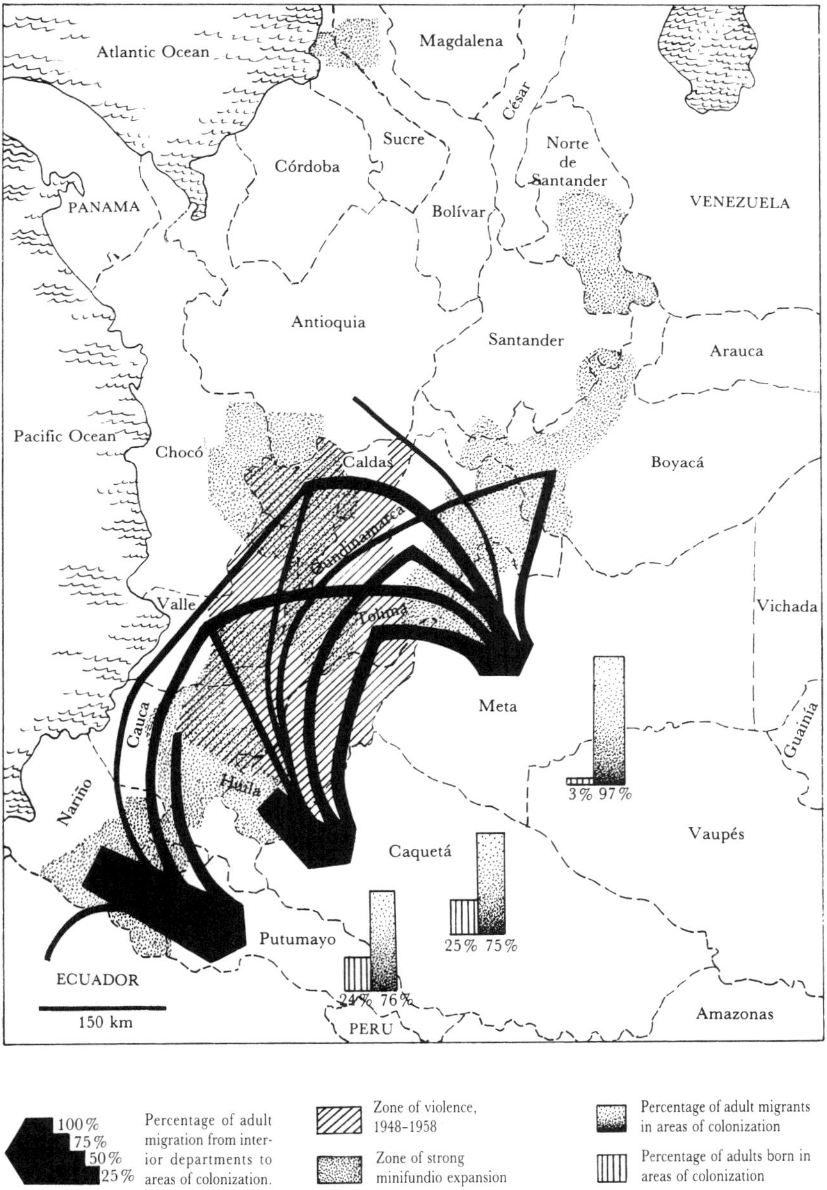

MAP 3. Origin of Caquetá (Putumayo, Meta) Migrants. SOURCE. Adapted from a map in Wolfgang Brucher, *La colonización de la selva pluvial en el piedemonte amazónico de Colombia* (Bogotá: Instituto Geográfico "Agustín Codazzi," 1974), p. 76.

Signs of progress visible today would not have been possible were it not for the grueling colonization process endured by the early settlers. Nevertheless, after decades of sacrifice, only a small portion of these colonists has been able to secure a decent living, and poor newcomers face a long life of struggle.

Making a Living

Caquetá settlers are not a homogeneous group. Migrating from different regions of the country for a variety of reasons, each family arrives with a unique package of experiences, skills, and aspirations. The occupational and educational backgrounds of the migrants, the size and composition of their families, and their initial material worth all affect their chances for achieving economic mobility within the frontier society of Caquetá.

This section focuses upon those settlers who have migrated due to economic and political hardships suffered in the interior, and who share low educational levels and poverty. Though each settler family has a distinct story to tell, its experiences farming in Caquetá are sufficiently similar to treat the group as a whole when discussing the fundamentals of making a living on the frontier.

The goal of the Caquetá settler family is to establish a successful family farm on public or purchased land. Toward this end, the migrants must follow a series of steps which require, as a minimum, a great deal of physical endurance and some agricultural and ranching know-how. Lacking one or the other, the colonist will usually fail.

Often the men arrive first, to explore the area and stake out a parcel of land. Initially the man may need to work on an established farm in order to save a small sum to invest in his own farm and to pay for subsistence expenses before the first harvest. As soon as possible, the women and children join in the agricultural tasks, and some sort of shelter is built. In a World Bank report, the colonization process is described as follows:

> Arriving with little more than a machete, an ax, and perhaps a mule, colonists laid claim to public lands by staking out their property, clearing pieces at the corner boundaries, and gradually clearing larger pieces for cultivation and/or pasture. Because soils are poor, colonists were forced either to continue with slash and burn rotational cultivation producing only for subsistence or develop a larger livestock enterprise. Without financial credit, however, most colonists could not obtain cattle; many colonists

spent years in the process of building up even a small herd. Others simply sold their land to wealthier migrants and moved on, returning to towns or seeking to use their capital to develop a farm further into the jungle.[7]

Agriculture

The constellation of climatic, topographical, and soil conditions characteristic of the tropical lowlands largely determines which cultivation methods to undertake and which crops to grow. Caquetá has a rolling topography; the eastern mountain range dividing Caquetá from Huila gradually levels off into hills, plains, river valleys, and finally the vast tropical jungle. Caquetá has a nine-month rainy "winter" season and a three-month dry "summer" season. Rainfall begins in March and continues to mid-December, with the heaviest storms falling from April to July. During these months the principal waterways are easily navigable, but foot trails and roads become nearly impassable due to the build-up of mud, stones, and natural debris. In mid-December, as the dry season begins, Caquetá's landscape changes dramatically. The lush foliage and green pasture turn brown; rivers reach dangerously low levels; creeks dry up, and a humid heat settles over the entire area.

The jungle is cleared and burned during the dry months in preparation for the sowing season in late February and March. Machetes are used to clear secondary growth, and all but the very largest trees are felled with hand axes. Then the area is burned until leveled, leaving scattered logs to rot over the next few years. One man can clear from 3 to 5 hectares of jungle per season.

Corn, rice, and yuca, the three dominant annual crops of Caquetá, are planted in the newly cleared area and harvested some four months later, in June and July. A second, smaller harvest, called the *mitaca*, is sometimes sown in September and collected in January. Corn and rice are used for home consumption and surpluses are sold in towns to local residents or for export to the interior. Yuca is rarely sold, as it constitutes a family staple eaten in huge quantities on the farm, and the producer's price is so low that it does not compensate to sell small surpluses.

Caquetá farmers frequently maintain a few hectares in the perennial crops plantain (banana-like fruit) and sugar cane, partly to feed themselves and their animals and partly to sell. Owing to government promotion, a few farmers cultivate African palm and rubber trees, though a history of unsuccessful attempts has shown that palm and rubber production is not appropriate for modest family-sized farms. The initial capital investment required is too high, especially since there is a four-to-six-year waiting period before the oil-producing palm nuts can be harvested and the rubber trees tapped. A small number of farmers cultivate cacao (chocolate beans), another crop currently promoted by the local government in Florencia. Some of the colonists who migrated from coffee-producing highland areas continue to grow coffee in Caquetá, but with little success. Some tropical fruits (banana, papaya, pineapple), are also produced in Caquetá, principally for local consumption.

Repeated use of the described "slash-and-burn" method of agriculture results in a damaging alteration of an otherwise naturally balanced ecological system. The soils of Caquetá hillsides are, for the most part, unfertile and poorly suited to continuous annual planting of crops. They contain low levels of phosphorus, calcium, and potassium, are typically very acidic, and drain poorly. The natural jungle cover acts as a barrier which protects the topsoil from being washed away by heavy rains, and which also continually replenishes the earth with falling debris.

When deforestation occurs, this natural protection is withdrawn, resulting in further mineral depletion and the erosion of hillsides and river banks throughout the nine-month rainy season. During the dry months, the sun's rays, no longer diluted by tree cover, shine so strongly that they often damage the summer vegetation, including the corn and rice crops. Moreover, summer clearing fires frequently spread out of control, burning pasture, crops, animals, and even homes. In January and February, the smoke is so thick and pervasive that air travel becomes dangerous, at times impossible, and general air quality becomes very poor.

Caquetá's most desirable lands, the vega, are located along the shores of the major waterways. Since these have better soils and a flatter topography, they are more suitable for agriculture than the hillsides. Still, as colonists deforest the river banks, these relatively fertile valleys become vulnerable to flooding. Minor floods occur annually and every few years a devastating flood ruins the farms of entire rural communities, such as occurred in 1971 with the inundation of the Caquetá river near the towns of Puerto Solano and La Solita.

Another damaging consequence of riverbank deforestation has been the widening and shallowing of the waterways. Soil, sand, and debris are washed down from the hillsides, and without trees to protect the shoreline, eventually erode the banks and collect on the river floor. Consequently, the waterways have been filled with shifting sandbars, making navigation in large boats impossible nearly all year, and travel in small boats difficult during all but the rainiest months.

The naturally difficult climate and poor soils of Caquetá, combined with the ecological havoc created by the colonization process, make Caquetá a very difficult place to establish a successful agricultural farm. Typically, after one or two harvests, the land will no longer produce, and the farmer must let it go fallow for at least three or four years, or seed the area with grass for pasture. Vega land can be exploited for up to five consecutive years, if the topsoil has not been diluted by flooding.

Aside from "natural" hardships, which frequently result in poor quality and low quantity harvests, market conditions further aggravate the agricultural situation. Farmers who live close to the major roads and towns, particularly those near to Florencia, are able to avoid the uncertainties and high costs of long distance transportation, and market their goods directly to the consumer at the going market price. On the other hand, isolated and poorer settlers, who sometimes live days away from the nearest market place, are pressed to sell their surplus goods to intermediaries at less than the market price. These intermediaries (middlemen), either working for themselves or hired by small town entrepreneurs, buy the harvest surpluses for cash on the farm or in local villages, and later transport the goods for sale in Caquetá's principal markets or to other middlemen buying for Bogotá and Cali. Only the relatively prosperous farmers among this group of isolated settlers can afford to pay the high transportation, storage, hotel, and food costs involved in personally carrying their goods to the final market place.[8]

IDEMA, the government agricultural marketing agency, pays higher prices per kilo than middlemen, but farmers complain that the range of their services is insufficient, and most important, they are unreliable. Farmers who bring their surpluses to IDEMA warehouses in town are guaranteed a fixed price, but payment is not received until two to three months after delivery. As farmers need to pay off short-term debts shortly after the harvest, and often feed their families for several months from harvest earnings, they usually prefer to forego IDEMA's higher price (about 25 percent higher) for immediate cash. It is also said that IDEMA officials tend to fill up their quotas with large orders from the wealthier producers, and many believe they receive some personal compensation in return. In any case, because Caquetá farmers must make themselves available to IDEMA, rather than vice versa, and because payment for goods is delayed up to three months, IDEMA has acquired a bad reputation with the rural community. If IDEMA is to better its image, services will have to be expanded and improved significantly, and corrupt practices, to the extent that they favor wealthy farmers over poor farmers, will have to be eliminated.

During the course of several interviews, farmers remarked that the high costs, hard work, and other aggravations involved in growing and marketing corn and rice outweighed the financial benefits. Aside from production for home consumption, it simply was not worth it. A few farmers had lost the greater part of their crop during the unusually long 1978 summer; others were discouraged by the highly competitive, quickly saturated market, which drives prices steadily downward. During the summer of December 1978–April 1979, Caquetá experienced a devastating worm plague which destroyed the corn crop and resulted in widespread hunger and disease. According to a report received in June 1979, nutritional levels were so deficient in certain areas that health workers in Caquetá feared people's lowered resistance would lead to typhoid and malaria epidemics, and perhaps even an outbreak of tuberculosis.

One farmer was so upset about the bad harvest of 1979 that he resolved never to plant corn again: "I'm not going to grow [corn/rice] again; it's such a damn bother and you don't get anything for it." That year he had planted 10 hectares of corn and rice, but harvested only 1 ton of surplus (net after home consumption). Normal production should yield about 850 kilos per hectare[9], given Caquetá's climate and soil conditions; however, much lower yields seem to be the rule rather than the exception.

Another farmer lives in the zone of Cartagena, one and a half hours from a navigable river and two and a half hours from town. We estimated his costs and income received from 1 hectare of corn, in order to predict his personal "profit and loss statement" for that year's corn harvest. The costs per hectare of corn, not including family labor, were as follows:

Col.$	
$2,000	Hired labor to clear 1 hectare of jungle (ten work days at $200/day)
50	Seed
475	Hired labor to plant and harvest
200	Hired labor to shell the corn
650	Transportation
$3,375	(approximately U.S $85)

The farmer produced seven cargas per hectare that year, 1,750 pounds (carga = 250 pounds); two were for home consumption and five were sold at Col.$550 per carga for a total income of Col.$2,750. Thus, even though this farmer had produced normal Caquetá yields, his costs per hectare were greater than his monetary income by Col.$625. If the two cargas consumed on the farm were calculated at their commercial value, the farmer would have registered a profit of Col.$475/hectare, or U.S.$12. This farmer received an exceptionally low price for his corn (average rate - Col.$650/carga) because he harvested late and had to sell to an oversupplied market. Even given the average price, costs would have exceeded income on the surplus sold. After this calculation the farmer concluded, "You see, it's not worthwhile. One invests more than one gets."

As a result of these ecological and marketing difficulties, Caquetá agriculture has delivered very few farmers from poverty. In order to change this situation, yields would have to increase substantially, and prompt and adequate compensation for surpluses be forthcoming. Institutional efforts to bring about these changes are noticeably absent in Caquetá.

The use of artificial fertilization would increase yields, but it is very expensive and subsidized prices for small farmers are not available. The use of cow manure or natural compost for fertilizer would also be likely to increase yields substantially, and minimize the need to burn the forest and rotate so frequently. Compost production is a simple but time-consuming process, more suitable for communal farming or some sharing effort than for use on individual, labor-scarce farms. Campaigns to encourage farmers in these pursuits have never seriously been tried.

Caquetá farming is also hindered by the use of traditional, archaic tools. Clearing and weeding are all done by hand with machetes and axes. Planting is done with a pointed stick. These methods are extremely time consuming and physically trying. Besides, using these primitive tools, the land is never properly cleared, which adversely effects production. In general, farmers lack the capital, knowledge, and enthusiasm to invest in more sophisticated tools. Not enough research has been conducted or disseminated to demonstrate to sceptical farmers that new methods would be worth their while. It is not easy to convince farmers to forego traditional practices under any circumstances, but if persuasive efforts on the part of qualified experts and financial institutions are lacking, the prospects for change become dim indeed.

Part of the difficulty of agricultural life in Caquetá stems from the dependence upon very few sources of sure income. For months at a time, many families live from hand to mouth, often on credit.

Of the eighty-five families interviewed, one farmer stood out from the others, not only because of higher earnings, but because of his successful efforts at farm diversification. He struck me as a "model" colonist. Señor X moved to Caquetá from Huila over twenty years ago with only a few pesos. He colonized several farms on public land and with accumulated earnings bought his present farm, located ten minutes from a road and two hours from a town. His 100-hectare farm (median landholding size for all interviewed farmers = 94 hectares) is distributed, in hectares, as follows: natural pasture, 48; artificial pasture, 15; plantain, 10; yuca, 1; corn, 10; secondary growth, 6; jungle, 10.

Señor X owns no cattle of his own but raises thirty-four cattle from the Fondo Ganadero (receiving 65 percent of profits after sale), and thirty-four cattle *al partir* (on a sharing basis, fifty-fifty). In addition, he owns eight pigs, three horses, and a dozen chickens. His average expenses are Col.$12,000 per month and for the last six months before the interview his monthly income averaged $Col.40,000. The biggest income-producing items were plantain (a perennial crop bringing in approximately Col.$140,000 annually), and corn, that year sold to IDEMA at Col.$850/carga. Additional money was brought in weekly from the sale of milk and eggs, and on occasion, pigs. The Fondo Ganadero and al partir contracts brought in substantial, but infrequent, sums of money.

Señor X and his wife know how to read and write but only completed one year of schooling. They have three children; their eldest is studying mathematics at a prestigious university in Bogotá with a partial scholarship; the second had studied commerce for three years at the high school level but temporarily left to get married; the youngest has completed two years of high school and wishes to continue, but is at home now helping on the farm.

Their house is modest but comfortable. It is made of clay and wood, has four rooms, a wood fire stove, and an outdoor latrine. They enjoy the farm and the tranquillity, but are worried about being left alone when their youngest child leaves. Señor X is in his late fifties and cannot work as hard, nor tolerate the climate as well as he once could. They would like to find reliable help, preferably family or live-in workers. He mentioned going back to Huila to live in town, but she balks at the idea: "What would we do there?" It is likely they will stay a good while longer.

Señor X has several factors going for him: a farm close to the road and not too far from town; sufficient capital to pay workers year-round; a relatively level, pest-free farm with sufficient water; several steady income-producing activities, and many years of agricultural experience. He and his wife, despite little schooling, manifest a great interest in new ideas and technological innovations. Their children have attained unusually high educational levels, which is a tribute to their parents' concern about the future. In sum, the family has achieved considerable economic and social mobility over the course of more than twenty years of hard work in rural Caquetá.

During another interview in a moderately isolated area, I mentioned the example of Señor X to point out the advantages of farm diversification. The two farmers present agreed with the concept but felt it was very difficult, in practice, to overcome the obstacles of scarce resources and natural impediments. The conversation went like this:

> Señor Y: Sure that's true. If one were to have an establishment with stable weekly income—30 *racimos* of plantain, two or three cargas of yuca, milk, things like that, it would be fine.
>
> Señor Z: But we don't have stable income. There are times when we haven't enough to buy food for the family. We make by with nothing.
>
> Señor Y: We say we're going to sell 30 or 50 racimos of plantain, 10 cargas of yuca—but there isn't enough; we're going to sell two or three pigs, but there aren't any.
>
> Señor Z: So do you know what we do? That creek over there helps us a lot. We go there with our shotguns and perhaps catch a *bocachico* (type of fish) or two, to pull us through the week. This is no lie, *Doctora*, because that is how we live.

Cattle Raising

Caquetá's rural settlers believe that their chances for attaining economic mobility hinge on whether or not they succeed in developing a good-sized, healthy herd of cattle. Nearly every landholder hopes and strives to become a rancher, rather than simply a subsistence and/or cash crop farmer. As we have seen, the latter pursuit is viewed as a dead end due to a variety of natural and institutional obstacles.

In the Colombian interior, and on the coasts, the means to acquire a stock of animals and manage a ranch have been limited to a small elite of large landholders. In Caquetá, however, poorer farmers have been able to obtain relatively large plots of public land, and some have acquired cattle through access to public credit and through private arrangements with wealthier neighbors.

Aside from the prestige factor, the aspiration to become a rancher arises from the following reasons:

1. Caquetá's soils, although unsuitable for intensive cropping, are appropriate for long-term pasture use.
2. The demand for meat in Colombia is growing, as are exports of cattle (both legal and extralegal) to the border countries Ecuador

and Venezuela. Seventy percent of Caquetá cattle is exported to the interior of Colombia, principally to the cities Cali and Bogotá, and 30 percent is consumed internally.

3. The price of cattle has risen sharply in Colombia, particularly since 1972, and the meat market is not as vulnerable to short-term demand fluctuation as the basic food market, especially when international exports are included.[10]
4. Ranching is less trying, physically, than slash-and-burn agriculture. Once the forest is cleared and put to pasture, it should be weeded two to four times a year, but needn't be cleared again for decades.
5. More local institutions provide credit and technical assistance for cattle raising than agriculture. Also cattle loans are larger, longer term, and generally at lower interest rates than the loans available for agricultural investment.

According to the Caquetá Cattle Census, taken in March 1975, the total cattle population equaled 625,524 animals, distributed among 23,159 farms, giving an average of 27 animals per farm. The census included nine geographical divisions, with Florencia registering the highest head-per-farm average at 61.45 and Belén the lowest at 8.58. The middle zone average is 22.83 head per farm. The most recent census, 1978, shows a total cattle population of 731,086 animals, but shows no distribution breakdown.[11]

The statistics available are insufficient to determine the full distribution curve, but sample studies indicate that the majority of farmers who raise cattle have considerably less than the average of 23 animals, and that at least a third of the landholders do not own any cattle.[12] Of the 35 non-INCORA recipients interviewed for this study, the median rancher raised 9 head, though the average for the group was 28 head, indicating a marked unevenness in cattle distribution among the farmers interviewed. From a survey of 121 Caquetá farms, conducted by an American anthropologist in 1975, 51 farmers had no cattle on their farms at all and 62 did not own any cattle, whereas 9 farmers owned more than 100 head each.[13]

Another indication of skewed cattle distribution is the land tenure situation shown in table 4. In 1971, 33.7 percent of Caquetá farms had less than 30 hectares of land, representing 4.3 percent of the total area surveyed. Most of these farmers do not have enough land in pasture to qualify for institutional credit, and probably are not in a viable position to buy cattle independently, though they may raise a few head on a sharing basis with larger landholders.

Poor migrants, as described earlier, are initially engaged in subsistence and cash crop cultivation. When the cultivated land is no

TABLE 4

Land Distribution in Caquetá, 1971

Size of farms in hectares	Number of farms	Percent	Cumulative percent	Number of hectares	Percent	Cumulative percent
0–29	2,977	33.7	33.7	34,509	4.3	4.3
30–49	1,790	20.2	53.9	66,102	8.2	12.5
50–99	2,271	25.7	79.9	134,391	16.7	29.2
100–199	1,189	13.5	93.1	150,905	18.7	47.9
200–499	505	5.7	98.8	129,070	16.0	63.9
500 or more	106	1.2	100.0	291,835	36.1	100.0
Total	8,838	100.0		806,812	100.0	

Source: World Bank, *Project Performance Audit Report: Colombia, Caquetá Land Colonization Project (Loan 739-CO)*, 1978. Originally from the Instituto Geográfico Agustín Codazzi, Bogotá, 1971.

longer productive, it is either allowed to go fallow or is seeded with grass. Then farmers look for an opportunity to acquire cattle in order to make good use of their pasture. At this stage, the farmer is not sufficiently financially solvent to undertake a high-interest loan or buy cattle outright; therefore, he commonly enters into an al partir arrangement with a wealthier rancher or an independent businessman. Under this system, the poorer rancher raises the owner's cattle on his land until it is ready for sale and then the two parties divide the net return fifty-fifty, i.e., the return from the sale minus the original value of the animals when first contracted out.

Al partir is widely used in Caquetá because it meets certain needs of both the owner and the "caretaker." The owner, on the one hand, lends out his cattle for one of the following reasons: (1) his own farm does not have enough cleared pasture for his growing herd; (2) he does not want to be bothered with the daily maintenance of more than a set number of animals; (3) he does not own land but simply deals in the cattle purchase and sale business; (4) al partir is cost efficient. The "caretaker," on the other hand, accepts the animals because he does not want unused pasture to go to waste; and because he needs the income.

As an example of an al partir contract,[14] in October 1975, Señor X lent six cows with calf to Señor Y for a total value of Col.$35,000, the average local market price at that time. A three-year contract was signed before witnesses and a notary public, which stated that Señor X would be paid for the full value of the cattle loaned plus 50 percent of the profits when sold; that Señor Y was responsible for the loss of any of the twelve animals; and that Señor Y could receive payment (50 percent of profits) in cash or in cattle. In September 1978, the original herd had developed into twenty-one head of cattle, worth Col.$150,000. The profit, Col.$115,000, was divided between the two parties giving Col.$57,500 to each, or $19,166 per year for the three-year contract. From the gross profit, Señor Y had to deduct the costs of animal and pasture maintenance to determine his net earnings, but Señor X walked away clear. Subtracting costs, Señor Y made no more than Col.$5,000/year (U.S.$125) on the contract.[15] While this sum is small in comparison to what Señor X earned (U.S.$479), the income did help to make ends meet and allowed the "caretaker" to buy a heifer of his own.[16]

This system is open to abuse if the animal owner decides to take advantage of his superior position at the time the contract is liquidated. Either he may remove the cattle to another farm and make a spot valuation at lower than the commercial price, thus reducing the earnings of the "caretaker," or when the "caretaker" is paid in kind, the owner may upvalue the cattle in order to give up less for a higher price. If the animals are steers, ready for slaughter when the contract is terminated, the opportunity to "cheat" is minimized, since the two parties go to the slaughterhouse together and must accept the commercial value quoted.

The Fondo Ganadero (FG), a mixed institution with private and public equity, offers another al partir arrangement for Caquetá ranchers. Under the FG system, profits after sale are shared 65 percent–35 percent for the rancher and the Fondo, respectively. Then the rancher must revert 5 percent of his profit to the Fondo, a requirement for being a member of the association.

The Fondo purchases livestock from large Caquetá ranches and distributes it mainly among medium-sized ranches as shown in table 5.

Dividing the strata of number of cattle received into small (30 head or less), medium (31–75), and large (76 or more) size of herd, the figures show that 29.13 percent of total beneficiaries received small herds, accounting for 12.24 percent of total cattle distributed; 50.41 percent received medium-sized herds, accounting for 42.10 percent of total cattle, and 20.46 percent received large herds, accounting for 45.70 percent of total cattle. In all, the Fondo has distributed 40,734 head of cattle among 728 farms, which represents approximately 5.6 percent of the total cattle population of Caquetá and 2.4 percent of total rural households.

Another source of institutional credit in Caquetá is the Caja Agraria. The Caja has the largest loan portfolio in the area. In 1978, 42 percent of its ordinary (demand deposit) funds went toward

TABLE 5

Distribution of Cattle Loaned by Fondo Ganadero del Caquetá, S.A., September 1978

Number of cattle loaned	Beneficiaries		Cattle	
	Number	Percent of total	Number	Percent of total
0–15	17	2.34	138	.34
16–30	195	26.79	4,849	11.90
31–45	198	27.20	7,282	17.87
46–60	102	14.01	5,328	13.08
61–75	67	9.20	4,544	11.16
76–90	38	5.22	3,139	7.71
91–105	29	3.98	2,824	6.93
106–120	29	3.98	3,308	8.12
121–150	23	3.16	3,091	7.59
+ 150	30	4.12	6,231	15.30
Total	728	100.00	40,734	100.00

Source: Fondo Ganadero del Caquetá, S.A.

agricultural loans and 45 percent were invested in livestock. Small landholders (total worth = Col. $750,000 or less) received 95.2 percent of the loans and 80.3 percent of total funds.[17] The majority of these loans are small and short term, at 18 percent interest, and are used to pay for preharvest agricultural costs. Agricultural loans must be paid back as soon as the crops are collected and sold. Frequently farmers ask for extensions, based on harvest failure and insufficient sales. Extensions are granted for a few months at 21 percent interest, and beyond a specified time, the interest rate is doubled from the original 18 percent to 36 percent annually. In 1977, 6,148 farmers with small-sized farms received Col.$144.2 million of Caja credit, averaging Col.$23,454/loan; 384 with medium-sized farms received Col.$35.9 million, averaging Col.$93,490/loan, and 15 with large farms received Col.$6.6 million, averaging $440,000/loan.[18]

Although the bulk of the Caja loans are too small to use for livestock development, a number of Caquetá settlers have used Caja funds to acquire one or two animals, especially cows to produce milk for home consumption. The rest of Caja funds directed toward livestock go to well-established large ranchers in the area. The Banco Ganadero, a large Colombian bank with 80 percent private ownership, also services large cattle enterprises in Caquetá.

Since 1964, INCORA has administrated several livestock development credit programs in Caquetá. These programs will be discussed in detail in the following chapter. Briefly, over the course of fourteen years and five different programs, 9,310 loans, totaling Col.$435.5 million, have been distributed among holders of small and medium-sized Caquetá farms.[19] Since 1971, INCORA beneficiaries have received more than 80 percent of the value of their loans in cattle, and the remainder in cash for farm investments. The funds have come from diverse sources: USAID, the Inter-American Development Bank, the World Bank, Colombia's Banco Ganadero, the national budget, and from INCORA's own financial resources.

Of all the public credit institutions, INCORA has had the best coverage rate. In 1978, according to SEM (Service for the Eradication of Malaria) figures, there were 29,136 rural households in Caquetá, of which approximately 17,482, or 60 percent of the total, meet farm size qualifications for an INCORA cattle loan (farms from 30 to 200 hectares). In October 1978, 3,456 families (20 percent of total eligible rural property owners) were in the process of paying back INCORA loans, and another 5,854 loans had been fully paid. Thus, INCORA programs provide more cattle for more Caquetá ranchers than either the Fondo Ganadero or the Caja Agraria. Nevertheless, nearly half of the eligible population has not had access to INCORA credit. It must resort to private al partir arrangements, perhaps buy a few head independently, or remain cattleless. Farmers with less than 30 hectares of land (approximately 33 percent of all farms) are not eligible for INCORA credit, and even if credit were available, usually do not have enough pasture to develop an economically viable herd.

For the eighty-five families interviewed for this study, the total number of cattle raised, excluding INCORA credit, was distributed as follows: 20 percent, farmer owned; 25 percent, Fondo Ganadero; 54 percent, al partir, and 1 percent, Caja Agraria. Fifty of these eighty-five families are INCORA credit beneficiaries. Among them cattle was distributed, including INCORA credit, as follows: 9 percent, farmer owned; 66 percent, INCORA, and 25 percent, "other."

As this information indicates, the opportunities for acquiring a viably sized herd of cattle in Caquetá are quite limited and do not meet the needs of the rural population at large. The supplies of funds and cattle for incipient ranchers are scarce compared with the demand, partly because of an unequal distribution of land and capital resources and partly because of the emphasis, by large ranchers, on cattle for export rather than on internal reproduction and development.

Aside from the problem of obtaining cattle, Caquetá ranchers are often troubled with poor quality pasture and livestock. The tropical climate and mineral-deficient soils subject cattle in Caquetá to a variety of diseases and pests that can only be controlled with regular investments in disinfectants, vaccinations, mineralized salt, quarterly pasture weeding, and insecticides. Good farm management also requires that the owner construct and maintain such installations as wire fences, a corral, various salt trays, and a loading chute.

Cebú and Crillo, the principal cattle races of Caquetá, are mainly used for meat, rather than milk production. A healthy animal should consume 10 percent of its weight daily until ready for sale at 450–500 kilograms. Given Caquetá's poor soils and generally disorderly pasture cover, the capacity rate averages only one adult animal per hectare of grass, and this on a rotational basis. If the owner overstocks the cattle and has limited pasture, or does not divide his farm into several pasture plots among which cattle can be rotated at different stages of growth, the herd will not develop normally. Poor-quality and underweight animals will naturally bring in smaller earnings.

Often incipient ranchers do not possess sufficient income-producing assets to make consistent investments in their newly acquired livestock. Moreover, they may lack the experience or the know-how to invest what funds they have in appropriate technological and structural improvements. Some cattle raisers receive technical advice from INCORA and ICA (Colombian Agricultural Institute), but the overall coverage rate is still inadequate, and suggestions are generally not considered if the resources necessary to implement them are unavailable. When a farmer experiences a series of discouraging setbacks (cattle that die, low reproduction levels, pasture pests, or high personal and agricultural expenses that cannot be managed alongside additional livestock costs) he will be likely to sell off the herd and to return, eventually, to subsistence/cash crop farming.

In sum, the major obstacles to cattle raising in Caquetá, for the incipient rancher, are: (1) abuses of the al partir system; (2) an institutional credit shortage; (3) poor climatic, soil, and pasture conditions; (4) insufficient incomes to invest in good livestock and farm management; and (5) lack of technological know-how.

While most of Caquetá's poor settlers who would like to become successful ranchers are prevented from doing so by one or more of these obstacles, some manage to surmount the obstacles and effectively transform their principal economic activity from agriculture to ranching. This latter group has attained a certain amount of economic mobility in Caquetá; no longer solely dependent upon unstable agricultural earnings, it possesses sizeable capital assets. Nevertheless, the transition from higher economic potential and more farm assets to higher disposable incomes and better living standards is complex—and not assured. This transition process is discussed in this chapter's section on Basic Needs, and in a later chapter where the experiences of specific INCORA beneficiaries are discussed.

Other Means of Making a Living

The principal income-earning activities of Caquetá rural landholders—agriculture and cattle raising—have been discussed in some detail in the previous two sections. Within the agricultural category, corn, rice, plantain, and sugar cane were mentioned as the principal cash-earning crops. In cattle raising, income is earned from the sale of cattle and surplus milk and cheese. Additional income is earned from the sale of chickens and pigs, although generally on an irregular basis.

Besides these on-farm activities, most "lower" level farmers, who are principally agriculturalists and own little or no cattle, must hire themselves out to other farms as another source of income.

"Middle" level farmers (who own a few cattle, may raise up to seventy-five head al partir, or are in the process of paying off long-term INCORA loans) occasionally engage in wage labor as well. Of the rural families interviewed for this study, 24 percent derived income from outside labor (18 percent of the INCORA borrowers, 31 percent of the nonborrowers).

Both agricultural and ranching activities are cyclical, with especially busy months as well as slack periods. While earnings are irregular, most personal and some farm expenses tend to be fairly consistent throughout the year. Consequently, "lower" and "middle" level farmers engage in wage labor during the slack periods to bring in money when no other income is forthcoming. They may work on prosperous ranches that hire many outside laborers year-round, or on smaller farms that hire a few workers during the peak clearing, harvest, and weeding periods.

One farmer, an INCORA borrower, who raises forty-three head of cattle and owns a 100-hectare farm, explained his situation as follows: "When we have no money to pay for the *remesa* (food bill), the store-owner gives us credit for the week. In eight days we return and have only enough to pay our debt, but not enough to buy more food. It's bad to buy on credit again—you build up a bad reputation and it never stops. So we get day-work on a farm and pay for our *panalita* (unrefined sugar) that way."

A few farmers derive income from extracting and selling wood from their farms (6 percent of those interviewed). However, this practice diminishes over the years, and eventually the stock of wood left after burning is just sufficient for home and farm use—cooking-wood, house construction and repair, corrals, the local school, etc. Caquetá once possessed large quantities of valuable wood, principally cedar, but this resource is now practically exhausted. The potential economic utility of ordinary wood, cleared and burned by colonists, is overlooked, either because of its poor quality or because of the hard labor and high costs involved in its extraction and transportation. The colonists would rather not be bothered. As one farmer put it: "Those logs aren't worth a thing. You know what they're good for? They're good for making you sweat like mad!"

Finally, the following are occasional income supplements for a few farmers: (1) financial help from children employed outside the farm; (2) tailoring and sewing; (3) buying and selling cattle at a profit; (4) small warehouse businesses; (5) small beer, soda pop, and cigarette stands on farms located near the roads, and (6) sales from hunting and fishing. Of the farmers interviewed, 5 percent said they derived some income from one or more of these activities.

Basic Needs

In the previous section I explored the principal economic activities of rural Caquetá settlers. It was argued that the majority of farmers are seriously limited by environmental and institutional constraints in their efforts to establish economically viable farms that provide for adequate, secure incomes. Even so, it was demonstrated that some colonos have managed to acquire sufficient resources and skills to overcome these obstacles and achieve significant economic mobility. These are the farmers who have crossed the threshold from a "lower" level existence of subsistence and cash-crop farming supplemented by frequent wage labor, to a "middle" level existence geared toward cattle raising, some farming, and occasional wage labor. Their progress has been evaluated in terms of farm development and diversification, the accumulation of valuable assets—land, animals, installations—and rising gross incomes.

In this section, progress is discussed and evaluated in terms of the general welfare of Caquetá's rural population. The living standards of the people, not the farms, are in question here. To what degree does society provide for the basic needs of its citizens? To what degree does economic "progress" bring about improved living standards?

The terms "welfare," "living standards," and "basic needs" require some explanation. I define improved "welfare" and "living standards" in terms of the gradual fulfillment of "basic needs." These needs, according to an International Labour Organization report include: ". . . certain minimum requirements of a family for private consumption: adequate food, shelter and clothing are obviously included. . . .

"Second, they include essential services provided by and for the community at large, such as safe drinking water, sanitation, public transport and health and education facilities."[20] Hence, basic human needs are divided between those that can be privately attained and those that should be fulfilled through community action.

On the pages that follow, the welfare of Caquetá settlers is discussed, with the focus on the most fundamental of human needs—nutrition, housing and hygiene, health, and education. For each need, the following elements are included: (1) current standards; (2) private and public attempts to improve standards; and (3) the relationship between economic progress and needs fulfillment.

Nutrition

"Under- and mal-nutrition are by far the most serious health problems in Caquetá."[21] This statement from a World Bank Appraisal Report indicates that the typical Caquetá diet is both deficient in calories and poorly balanced. Undernourishment is usually the result of scarce resources and low incomes, while malnutrition is as much a result of ignorance and tradition as it is a function of economic status.

More prosperous farmers tend to eat more and better than poorer farmers.[22] They can supplement starchy home-grown foods (yuca, plantain, rice, corn) with purchases of meat, beans, and vegetables in town. Living closer to roads and markets, they are able to shop more often and maintain constant supplies at home despite the lack of refrigeration.

Nonetheless, even families with "middle" level incomes often subsist on poorly balanced diets that weaken the organism and occasion perpetual health problems. Though the total worth of these families has increased, cash flow is still slow and unstable, and recent memories of having nothing at all affect their current decisions to avoid unnecessary risk and change. Farmers who have only recently achieved some economic progress are fearful of "throwing away" money into nonproductive expenses. Rather than invest increased incomes on more nutritious, expensive food for themselves and their families, the farmers choose to invest in cattle, land, and other farm improvements. Again, this kind of thinking stems from an insecure economic position. Any number of disasters—a flood, a plague, sharp changes in market conditions—could wipe out hard-won gains. So the farmers hedge disaster by fortifying their assets and sacrificing their personal needs.

Many farmers who appear to be well-off because they "own" a good-sized herd of cattle, are actually deeply in debt and dare not spend a penny beyond what is absolutely necessary. As one INCORA beneficiary put it:

> What happens, Doctora, you need to know this and we need to tell you—there are people who say we're well-off because we have cattle; I have forty-three head. But if I sell my cattle (for food, housing, etc.), how am I going to make good on the loan? I have to keep things quiet. When I have a grave necessity like I just had [malaria], I'm convinced to sell. But the day may arrive when, sincerely, we don't have with what to buy our food.

In addition to insufficient resources and feelings of insecurity, many Caquetá families eat poorly because they do not understand the basics and importance of good nutrition. For generations, in their places of origin and on the frontier, they have survived on a few homegrown staples. In Caquetá the typical diet is based on yuca and plantain, which are plentiful and cheap; *panela*, which supplies quick energy, and some milk and eggs. Fruits are rarely consumed, even when they are readily available. Papaya is often left to rot on the trees or is fed to the pigs, and pineapple and oranges are mostly valued because surpluses can be sold at a decent price. Vegetables must be imported and tend to be expensive and poor quality. However, irrespective of their price, vegetables simply do not play a part in what is considered to be a "good" Caquetá meal. Meat is still a luxury, even among cattle raisers. Only on a rare occasion would a "lower" or "middle" level farmer slaughter a cow for home consumption; this would be considered a waste of an income producing asset.

While Caquetá farmers understand that their cows need to be nourished with healthy grass and mineralized salt in order to grow strong and healthy, often they do not understand that the same principle applies to their own constitutions and those of their families. Health problems that arise directly or indirectly from undernourishment and malnutrition, such as nutritional anemia, gastroenteritis, and amebic dysentary, are "cured" with pills and injections, but the diet continues to be deficient and poorly balanced. What need to be changed are certain traditional values and customs, and this could be effected, in part, with decentralized education facilities that teach preventive health and good nutrition. Once the farmers clearly understand their nutritional needs, they may seek to fulfill them with more vigor. Still, it must be remembered that ignorance is only part of the problem; the greater part will be resolved only when rural people can depend upon adequate and secure incomes.

At this point, I think it important to add a specific case study to the general discussion of nutritional standards. Data collected on monthly food expenses for thirty-nine Caquetá rural families, which fall generally within the "middle" income range, show a median food expenditure per month of Col.$3,054 (U.S.$76). This equals approximately one-third of total monthly expenses. Total food intake includes market purchases plus "free" food grown for home consumption.

Table 6 lists the specific purchases of a representative family within the sample. The family consists of two adults and seven children between the ages of two and eleven. Because the children are so young, per capita intake is calculated on the basis of a seven-member family, counting the three youngest members as one person.

In addition to the foods listed on table 6, assuming that a farmer is self-sufficient in yuca and plantain, his family of seven will consume approximately 2,520 pounds of each product annually, 52

TABLE 6

Monthly Food Expenses of Surveyed Family X, October 1978

Item	Col.$ spent	Market price (Col.$) per pound or unit noted	Quantity purchased/ month (pounds or unit noted)	Quantity purchased/ week (pounds or unit noted)	Per capita intake/ week (pounds or unit noted)
Meat	$ 700	25.0	28.0	7.0	1.0
Chocolate	231	33.0	7.0	1.8	.3
Lard	324	24.0	13.5	3.4	.5
Coffee	182	28.0	6.5	1.6	.2
Panela	341	6.2	55.0	14.0	2.0
Salt[a]	415	5.0	83.0	21.0	3.0
Eggs	12	4 each	3 eggs	.75 egg	.1 egg
Beans	200	20.0	10.0	2.5	.4
Dried peas	167	18.0	9.3	2.3	.3
Carrots	46	10.0	4.6	1.2	.2
Potatoes	178	4.0	44.5	11.0	1.6
Refined sugar	60	10.0	6.0	1.5	.2
Onions	60	18.0	3.3	.8	.1
Spices	56	2/package	28 packages	7 packages	1.0 package
Dried soup	80	10/package	8 packages	2 packages	.3 package
Pasta	32	18.0	1.8	.5	.1
Total	$ 3,084		189.5 lbs.[b]	47.6 lbs.[b]	6.9 lbs.[b]

[a]Salt is used principally to feed the livestock, and therefore is not included in any of the totals except Col.$ spent.

[b]These totals do not include eggs, spices, dried soup, or salt.

pounds per week, or 7 pounds of yuca and 7 pounds of plantain per family member per week.[23] Adding the 6.9 pounds of purchased food to the 14 pounds of home-grown food, the total sum of food intake per capita, per week equals 20.9 pounds.

These figures are approximate. They combine specific data collected for one representative family and general information on typical consumption of home-grown foods. Rice, corn, and milk are not included, because this particular farmer did not grow cash crops and was not milking at the time of the study. Furthermore, the sample family consumes more meat than what is typical of a family in their income bracket.

In a study on Caquetá nutritional levels made in 1973, the average per capita calorie intake of the rural population was estimated at 1,390 calories per day.[24] This figure was derived from a similar list of food items, in similar proportions, to the list in table 6, plus yuca and plantain. For a family of seven, this study approximated per capita consumption of purchased foods at 7.94 pounds per week, versus the total of 6.9 pounds per week for Family X.

Recommendations from studies on adequate calorie consumption vary considerably. According to FAO/WHO standards, an "average" level of calorie adequacy for an adult is 3,000 calories per day. In a quantitative study on basic human needs, authors John and Magda McHale lower acceptable calorie intake to 2,370 calories per day to allow for the age-mix composition of a total regional population.[25] In the 1973 study on Caquetá, minimum calorie requirements are set at 2,800 for men and 1,800 for women. However, to account for the specific climatic and work conditions of Caquetá rural families, which are particularly demanding, this latter study suggests that average calorie intake per person should be 3,100 calories per day (compared with actual intake of 1,390 calories/day in 1973).[26]

Given all of the standards presented here, and taking into consideration a substantial margin of error, one can safely say that adequate nutritional standards are not being met in much of rural Caquetá. Calorie intake is insufficient and the supply of minerals, vitamins, and protein in the dominant foods (yuca, plantain, panela) is low. As mentioned previously, the most serious impact of poor nutrition is poor health, and poor health undermines the work potential of the colonos and provokes premature signs of old age. Thus a "vicious cycle" ensues: low productivity, low yields → low, unstable incomes → inadequate, poorly balanced food intake → poor health, lowered work capacity → low productivity.

In Caquetá there are no institutions with far-reaching programs on nutrition. Some of the local health clinics and hospitals sponsor informal discussions on nutrition and counsel specific patients with nutrition-related illnesses; however, they admit to a low, inadequate coverage rate. INCORA employs two social extension workers who travel throughout the countryside giving talks and lessons on nutrition as well as proper hygiene, sewing, furniture making, and community organization. In addition, many farmers listen to the educational radio programs of the Catholic organization *Acción Cultural Popular* which are especially directed toward rural communities. The programs include lessons on reading and writing, technical information for farmers and cattle raisers, and the basics of good nutrition, hygiene, and health care.

From surveys of past and present studies on Caquetá development, as well as current interviews with farmers and health workers, it appears that nutritional levels in Caquetá are gradually improving. This is principally due to higher incomes and less isolation. Still, for reasons already mentioned, "lower" level colonos continue to suffer from undernourishment and "middle" level colonos often are poorly nourished even when their absolute calorie intake approaches adequate levels. The possibilities for improving nutritional standards at home are hampered by insufficient resources, insecure cash flows, traditional values, and lack of education. Public nutritional programs lack the personnel, financing, and coordination to disseminate needed information to the population at large.

Housing and Hygiene

Housing and hygienic conditions in rural Caquetá vary according to the length of time lived on one farm, the location of the farm, income levels, personal priorities, and the accessibility of pertinent information. When colonos first arrive and stake out a piece of land, they build a rudimentary shelter with supplies easily available on the land—palm leaves for the roof, a dirt floor, and slabs of wood or palm for walls. Many years may go by before house improvements are made, because, as in the case of nutrition, farm development takes precedence over personal needs and comforts.

The two most salient problems of Caquetá housing are overcrowding and poor sanitation. Fifty percent of the eighty-five families interviewed live in houses of one (20 percent) or two (30 percent) rooms. Another 31 percent live in three-room houses. Sixty-five percent of the families have less than three beds. Average family size is 8.5: six children, two adults, and other live-in relatives or workers. Thus there are several children crowded into each small room, sleeping together in one bed, on the floor, or on overhead wooden planks. Germs spread quickly since the sick and the healthy live in close, constant contact.

The house structures and layout are not conducive to good hygiene. Kitchen fumes travel freely into the eating and sleeping space, as do the pigs, chickens, dogs, and cats. Even when attempts are made to prevent the animals from "invading" human space, the main living space is open-air so that as soon as the animals are chased away, they come back again. Bacteria-carrying animals and ground parasites are particularly dangerous for the barefoot children and crawling infants; also, basic house construction is often not strong enough to withstand the heavy winter rains, causing constant drafts and leaks and consequent respiratory infections.

Practically no rural homes have running water or piped sewage systems. Water is carried in pots from nearby creeks and springs to use for washing, drinking, and cooking. The water is rarely boiled, although it is often unsafe to drink owing to its high bacteria content caused by inadequate waste disposal. After continual exposure, the people become somewhat immune to its harmful effects, but water-borne diseases are still endemic to the area.

As Caquetá farmers become well established and begin to reap some profit from their farm labor, they start to make structural improvements on their homes. A new room is built; the walls are replaced and strengthened; a wooden floor is put in; a new roof is built with metal "zinc"; more kitchen and eating space is incorporated, etc. Consequently, hygienic conditions improve and the house becomes a more congenial place in which to live. Large investments, however, such as an electrical generator, a piped sewage system, or cement walls, are undertaken almost exclusively by "upper" level farmers with substantial and secure incomes.

Institutional efforts to improve housing and provide safe drinking water and sanitation facilities are concentrated in the villages and towns. INCORA and the National Health Institute (INS) have distributed ceramic latrines to some rural homes and have installed sanitary units, wells, and pumps in many of Caquetá's rural primary schools. However, no program has been organized to systematically disseminate information and supplies to individual rural homes. As with nutrition, Caquetá farmers learn about hygienic needs after related health problems develop and require visits to local clinics. Otherwise, the only sources of information and advice are the Acción Popular radio programs and very occasional visits from social extension agents.

Health

The most prevalent health problems in Caquetá are directly or indirectly caused by poor environmental conditions, that is, undernutrition and malnutrition, overcrowded housing, lack of sanitation, and unsafe water sources. Under these living conditions the human body functions at a subnormal level and its natural abilities to resist infection and recuperate from illness are severely weakened. Given immediate medical attention, environment-related illnesses can be "cured," but unless preventive measures are taken—that is, improved living standards—the same health problems recur indefinitely.

Infants and young children are particularly vulnerable to environment-related diseases, resulting in disproportionately high infant and child mortality rates. According to Caquetá's local public health agency, the infant mortality rate in 1976 was 10.54 percent. That means that for every 1,000 live births, 105 of the newborn did not survive the first year of life. Of the eighty-five families interviewed for this study, 46 percent of the couples had lost one or more children. Of a total of 582 live births, 69 of the children (11.8 percent) had died, the majority as infants.

The three primary causes of death among the general Caquetá population are: (1) bronchopneumonia; (2) gastroenteritis and colitis; and (3) avitaminosis and other nutritional deficiencies. Pneumonias are often induced by inadequate shelter and clothing in inhospitable climates. Gastroenteritis, or "stomach-swelling," is caused by the consumption of water and food contaminated with harmful bacteria and parasites. Avitaminosis, or nutritional anemia, results from insufficient and poorly balanced food diets.

Among Caquetá's rural population, the most frequently mentioned health problem is malaria. Although it is no longer a significant killer because of curative drugs and widespread fumigation (malaria causes 0.5 deaths per 1,000 inhabitants today), the incidence of malaria is still high, reaching epidemic proportions in 1977 with 7,602 reported cases.[2]

SEM (Service for the Eradication of Malaria) has launched an extensive door-to-door fumigation campaign in Caquetá, in coordination with INCORA and the World Bank. In the mid-seventies SEM was thwarted in its fumigation efforts because of its use of DDT, which is lethal to farm animals, and therefore unacceptable to rural people. Since joining the INCORA/World Bank Project in 1976, SEM has replaced DDT with the nonlethal substance Baygon, and acceptance rates have increased significantly. Between January 1977 and September 1978, 81.1 percent of Caquetá households were fumigated, protecting 165,476 inhabitants out of a total of 219,023.[28] The fumigation campaign must reach a 90 percent level in order to avoid a rapid recurrence of infestations.

Today, the main problem for SEM in eradicating malaria is not its coverage rate nor the availability of finances and supplies, but rather the exposed structures typical of Caquetá rural housing.

Homes without walls or with cracked and leaky roofs cannot be properly protected by fumigation. The malaria-carrying mosquitoes that infest and reproduce in and around these poorer homes will inevitably spread to better-protected homes as soon as the fumigation poisons lose their potency, some three to seven months after SEM's last visit. Here again an impoverished physical environment becomes the major obstacle to fighting a debilitating and costly health problem.

To date, the intendencia of Caquetá offers the following medical services: three major hospitals (Florencia, Doncello, and San Vicente), two minor hospitals (Belén, Puerto Solano), one large health clinic (Florencia), and eleven health centers and thirty-four small health clinics spread throughout the region. Two of the centers and eight of the small clinics were built as part of the integrated services of INCORA's Project Caquetá. Most of the health centers employ a full-time doctor and are supplied with the infrastructure and equipment to undertake minor operations; health clinics are only periodically visited by doctors and their principal functions are to distribute first aid, drugs, and vaccinations. The hospital and clinic in Florencia are the only medical facilities equipped to handle laboratory testing and major surgery.

According to information collected from visits to several small health clinics and centers, and interviews with numerous technicians and patients, the following appear to be the more serious inadequacies of Caquetá's health services: (1) an insufficient and unstable supply of qualified medical personnel—dentists, public health workers, and lower-level technicians, but particularly doctors and nurses; (2) lack of instruments and laboratory and x-ray equipment in the peripheral centers and clinics, causing dangerous and costly delays while tests are conducted in Florencia, and subutilization of local space and manpower, and (3) public health programs—family planning, child care, vaccinations, nutrition, hygiene—which do not reach the rural population at large due to insufficient mobile outreach. In sum, curative medicine is hindered by an inadequate supply of qualified personnel and equipment in the peripheral health centers and clinics, and preventive health programs fall short of meeting local needs because of the deficiency in decentralized communication with rural communities.

Any strategy designed to promote good health in Caquetá should include these three elements: (1) the improvement of living conditions vis-á-vis higher and more stable incomes; (2) easier access to reliable information on nutrition, proper hygiene, and childcare, and (3) the consistent availability of low-cost supplies and services which are necessary for both preventive and curative health care, i.e., disinfectants, vitamin and protein supplements, laboratory equipment, mobile medical units, decentralized drug distribution, etc.

Caquetá health professionals and administrators with whom I have spoken recognize the need for decentralized, preventive health care. They believe that in order to implement the above three-part health strategy in Caquetá, planners must focus on institutional coordination and consistent, widespread outreach to the rural communities.[29] The more "progressive" public health workers suggest that rural communities should be encouraged to organize and communally express their health needs and demands, and that the rural population should be allowed to participate in health planning and administration. Working from the bottom up, at a neighborhood level, health technicians would have a greater impact on the population that is most needy.

In order to tackle all of the "poverty ills" simultanously, and thus offer an effective preventive health program, a better coordination of resources, information, and expertise is needed among all the local government agencies concerned with development and basic needs, i.e., ICCE (Colombian Institute for the Construction of Schools), ICA (Colombian Agricultural Institute), INCORA, the Ministries of Health and Education, CECORA (Center for Agrarian Reform Cooperatives), IDEMA (Agricultural Service Marketing Institute), the Caja Agraria, SENA (National Learning Service) and SEM. By coordinating efforts, the objectives of all of the entities would be advanced. INCORA has coordinated resources with a number of other agencies to carry out the programs of Project Caquetá. The impact of these efforts will be discussed in the next chapter.

Education

We have discussed how basic needs fulfillment depends upon the combined efforts of the individuals in need and of public institutions established to assist in human and economic development. Effective communication within and between these two groups is greatly enhanced when the participants are literate. Knowing how to read and write and express oneself confidently is important for tackling the obstacles that impede economic and social mobility. "Literacy is closely related to meeting many basic needs. For example, information on health and family planning is hampered when literacy does not exist; improvements in nutrition and agricultural development are much harder to disseminate; self-help in shelter and services provision slows with the inability to read simple instructions; and job training for skill improvement is made much more difficult."[30]

Table 7 sums up the literacy levels of the 578 individuals, over seven years of age, belonging to the eighty-five households visited for this study. Slightly more than a third of the sample adult population is illiterate; slightly less than a third has had no formal education. Some adults who received minimal education never picked up reading and writing skills while at school; others have forgotten, and others have maintained literacy through daily use and by following the Acción Cultural Popular literacy programs. Of the children over seven years of age, less than 20 percent have had no schooling, but a larger percentage is still effectively illiterate. This is principally due to erratic school attendance and the large number of children in the first and second grades. Supplemental information indicates that although over 80 percent of school age children (ages seven - sixteen) have attended school at some point, only 59 percent were attending school regularly at the time of the interview. Differences between the two sexes are insignificant except in the case of child literacy—more girls are literate than boys. This is probably because more boys than girls are withdrawn from school to assist in farm work.

The sample is not truly representative of the entire rural Caquetá population because the territory covered did not include the most inaccessible populated areas, where educational facilities are very scarce and the colonos tend to be poorer and less educated. Therefore, it is assumed that overall rural illiteracy is somewhat higher than indicated in the sample. Nonetheless, as a general trend, the children of colonos are receiving more education than their parents did and can be expected to achieve higher literacy rates. This can be attributed to the proeducation attitudes of most Caquetá parents both the literate and the illiterate; to the economic gains accomplished in Caquetá, and to the increased construction of rural primary schools.

TABLE 7

Education and Literacy of 85 Surveyed Families, 1978

Individuals surveyed (578)	No schooling[a] percent of total	Illiteracy[b] percent of total
Male adults	31.0	35.5
Female adults	32.0	34.5
Male children	18.3	34.0
Female children	17.7	26.0

[a]For population seven years of age and older.

[b]Do not read or write, or do so "poorly."

There are three kinds of problems which need to be worked on in order to improve educational standards in Caquetá: (1) the problem of too few schools and teachers; (2) the problem of low school attendance, and (3) the problem of low quality education.

Most Caquetá rural schools are community built. In Caquetá it is common for rural neighborhoods to form a community organization, called Junta de Acción Comunal, for the purpose of meeting local needs communally—the construction and maintenance of schools, roads, bridges, and occasionally small cooperatives or drugstores. Registered Juntas receive some annual funding (approximately U.S.$75) from the municipal government to assist in their tasks. Typically the Junta's primary task is the construction and maintenance of a community school; the members contribute gratis their land, labor, and wood. These schools are usually rudimentary structures lacking piped water, sanitation units, and electricity.

Aside from community-built schools, INCORA and the Ministry of Education, in coordination with ICCE, have built rural schools throughout the more developed rural areas and are beginning to build in the more isolated zones. The INCORA/World Bank Project has financed the construction of sixty-eight one- and two-room primary schools so far, and plans include the construction of twenty-two more in the next two years.

Many more schools are needed to accommodate the growing population, particularly the new colonos who are settling in the hinterland. An even more immediate problem, however, is the deficiency of stable, qualified teaching personnel. Rural teachers are very poorly paid, which results in high turnover rates, frequent strikes, and a generally inadequate supply. As a consequence, many schools are underused or totally abandoned for months and years. Part of the problem arises from the inability of the communities to pay their share of the teachers' salaries. The Ministry of Education pays 40 percent (Col.$1,200 per month), and the Junta is expected to pay the remainder (Col.$1,800 per month plus room and board). Apparently it is common for members of the Junta to promise to pay their monthly share of the costs, but when the salary is due—their pockets are bare. Expressing a common sentiment, one farmer explained: "No. I can't. It's true that I promised, but I don't have the money now—not even for the market." Naturally if the teacher is not paid regularly, he/she will eventually leave to look for work elsewhere.

Another major problem is low school attendance. During a visit to a meeting of one Junta de Acción Comunal, this problem was brought up by the teacher, who was very upset that only nine of the original fifty enrolled students had attended school regularly until the end of the year. The parents had withdrawn their children for three reasons, all of which are common throughout rural Caquetá: (1) the school was too far away—up to one and one-half hours for some; (2) children were needed at home to help in house and farm work, particularly during harvest season, and (3) some parents were dissatisfied with the teacher, especially with his attitudes. They complained that the teacher had not adapted to the life of poor rural folk: "The professors aren't here to teach children of the rich; they must conform with teaching the poor, and eating and living in our homes the same as we do." Obviously, communication between the community and the teacher was poor, but it is unclear to what degree the parents were defending the withdrawal of their children by unjustly attacking the teacher.

Asked about the quality of education their children were receiving, 55 percent of the families in our interview sample expressed satisfaction, and 45 percent expressed dissatisfaction. The three most frequent explanations for dissatisfaction were: (1) poor and/or unreliable teachers; (2) the school was too far away for regular attendance; and (3) the school structure was very poor, furniture was scant, and teaching materials were totally inadequate. All of these deficiencies are closely related. Without teaching materials and a decent school structure, it is difficult for teachers to teach well and for students to learn well. Also, if students must walk a long distance to school, through winter storms and summer heat, and perhaps without proper nourishment, then they will be less alert in the classroom, making the teacher's job even more difficult. All of these difficulties combined have led to considerable tension and unhappiness among parents and teachers alike. As one dissatisfied farmer put it: "Look, I just don't have faith in the quality of the little rural school because if it's not one problem, it's another."

In sum, although the basic need for literacy and primary education is being gradually attended to through the efforts of government agencies and local communities, full need attainment is still a long way off. In order to expand effectively and improve upon existing educational services, local and regional Caquetá planners will need to consider all of the following elements: (1) government subsidies for higher wages and better working conditions for rural teachers, perhaps a "hardship" allowance; (2) building more schools in less developed areas or providing local Juntas with sanitary and construction materials to make community-built structures adequate; (3) decentralized distribution of community-approved teaching materials; (4) encouragement of better parent-student-teacher communication, and (5) the provision of nutritious meals at school for those students who must travel far to school and arrive hungry.

Summary

In this chapter I have explored the economic, political, and social dimensions of the colonization process in Caquetá. We have seen that colonization of public lands is a politically feasible, though economically costly, alternative for the rural poor of the Colombian interior. On the one hand, the colonos are pushed away from the interior by its highly inequitable system of land tenure, high underemployment, and history of devastating rural violence; on the other hand, they are drawn toward Caquetá by its abundance of cheap land.

It has been shown that economic mobility on the Caquetá frontier depends upon many interwoven variables, i.e., location and size of farm, access to cattle credit, farm management skills, market fluctuations, etc. While the majority of Caquetá colonos depends upon wage work and subsistence crops for its livelihood, a substantial number have developed viable income producing activities on their farms, principally cattle raising and cash cropping, and are earning correspondingly higher gross incomes.

It is generally assumed that the accumulation of farm assets (land, animals, installations) will inevitably lead to greater productivity, and consequently, more income and a higher standard of living. In the section on Basic Needs this assumption was disputed because of the occurrence of "intervening events" (see diagram 1), which often impede the transition from economic "success" to greater well-being. Unstable environment and market conditions, indebtedness, escalating farm costs, and traditional attitudes frequently influence Caquetá colonos to reinvest higher gross incomes in asset accumulation rather than personal needs and comforts. In addition, Caquetá government and community health, housing, and education programs are sorely inadequate to meet rural needs.

Signs of economic and social progress are evident in rural Caquetá, particularly among the earlier settlers and credit recipients. The benefits of progress, however, are unequally distributed, repeating to a less marked degree the class divisions of the Colombian interior.

Next I discuss Colombian government efforts to promote colonization and integrated rural development in Caquetá, particularly the INCORA/World Bank Caquetá Rural Settlement Project. The stated objectives and accomplishments of the Project to date are reviewed, using World Bank and INCORA data and reports as well as observations made in the field. While the programs discussed are specific to Caquetá, the problems encountered there are also frequently found in colonization and rural development projects throughout the developing world.

Notes

1. Demographic statistics were collected from the Public Health Institute of Caquetá and are based on DANE (Departamento Nacional de Estadística) and SEM (Servicio para la Erradicación de Malaria) censuses.

2. Wolfgang Brucher, *La colonización de la selva pluvial en el piedemonte de Colombia* (Edited by the Instituto Geográfico "Agustín Codazzi", 1974), p. 33. Brucher's original source: Uribe Uribe R., *Por la América del Sur*, vols. 1 and 2 (Bogotá: Text of 1908).

3 Ibid., table 3—*El Aumento de Población en el Putumayo y el Caquetá de 1938, 1951, and 1964*, p. 42. Data based on DANE censuses of 1938, 1951, and 1964.

4. Ibid., p. 44, and Comité Interamericano de Desarrollo Agrícola (CIDA), *Tenencia de la tierra y desarrollo socioeconómico del sector agrícola: Colombia* (Washington, D.C.: Unión Panamericana, Secretaría General de la Organización de los Estados Americanos, 1966), p. 340.

5. Brucher, *La colonización de la selva pluvial*, p. 46 and p. 189.

6. Ronald L. Tinnermeir, "New Land Settlement in the Eastern Lowlands of Colombia", no. 13 (Madison, Wisconsin: University of Wisconsin Land Tenure Center, December 1964), pp. 7-8. An abbreviated version of the author's Ph.D. dissertation of the same title.

7. World Bank, *Project Performance Audit Report: Colombia, Caquetá Land Colonization Project (Loan 739-CO)*, June 1978, pp. 1-2, para. 4.

8. Ralph Leon Roberts, "Migration and Colonization in Colombian Amazonia: Agrarian Reform or Neo-Latifundismo" (Ph.D. dissertation, University of New York, Syracuse, 1975). See sections on Transport, pp. 171-176, and Marketing, pp. 176-186. Information on marketing and middlemen was also obtained from interviews with farmers and conversations with INCORA credit supervisors.

9. According to the FAO Production Yearbook of 1976, average Colombia corn yield was 1,365 kilos per hectare, for the U.S., 5,517 kilos per hectare, and for Caquetá, approximately 850 kilos per hectare.

10. For a discussion of cyclical cattle production and price trends in Colombia, see: Salamón Kalmanovitz, *Desarrollo de la agricultura en Colombia* (Bogotá: Editorial la Carreta, 1978), pp. 167-183. Kalmanovitz points out that cattle price inflation in Colombia results from insufficient supply vis-à-vis national and international demand, and is only minimally associated with rising input costs.

11. Cattle statistics collected from the Florencia Chamber of Commerce, Caquetá Cattle Census of March 1975, and from a report entitled *Regional Seminar on Cattle Production*, November 1978. Seminar coordinating agencies were: INCORA, ICA, and an international dairy industry with operations in Caquetá.

12. See: (1) R. L. Roberts, "Migration and Colonization in Colombian Amazonia," pp. 220–222; (2) R. L. Tinnermeir, "New Land Settlement," pp. 37–39; and (3) World Bank, *Caquetá Land Colonization Project Completion Report*, June 1978, p. A–8, para. 6.02; data based on INCORA household survey of October 1976.

13. Ibid., Roberts, table 5, p. 220.

14. This example refers to an al partir arrangement between an INCORA agronomist (Señor X) who owns cattle but no land, and a local farmer (Señor Y) with underused pasture. The facts were related to me by the agronomist.

15. The costs of cattle raising (salt, drugs, labor, fencing) were calculated from the lists of farm expenditures of Caquetá farmers with similar sized herds to Señor Y. Data were collected from the household survey of 85 families conducted for this study.

16. To determine Señor X' annual rate of return (rr) on his three-year investment:

$$
\begin{aligned}
(\$35{,}000)(1 + x)^3 &= (\$35{,}000) + (\$57{,}500) \\
(1 + x)^3 &= \$92{,}500 \div \$35{,}000 = 2.6429 \\
1 + x &= \sqrt[3]{2.643} \\
1 + x &= 1.38 \\
x &= .38 \\
rr &= 38 \text{ percent per annum}
\end{aligned}
$$

If Señor X were to invest his money in the bank, instead of an al partir arrangement, he would have earned a maximum of 2 percent per month in interest, or 24 percent annually. Thus, in general, it is more profitable to invest in cattle raising.

17. Statistics were collected from the Florencia branch of the Caja Agraria on two separate occasions: (1) from an interview with a bank economist and a review of the Caja annual reports; and (2) from a public relations talk given by the Caja president and sponsored by the recently appointed Intendente of Caquetá.

18. Ibid., Caja Agraria annual reports.

19. Data from the Credit Department of INCORA, Florencia; summary of credit statistics from 1959 to October 1978.

20. International Labour Organization, *The Basic Needs Approach to Development* (Geneva: ILO Publications, 1977), p. 9. Quoted in the ILO report, "Employment, Growth and Basic Needs".

21. World Bank, *Caquetá Rural Settlement Project Appraisal Report No. 501–1–CO*, annex 7 on Education and Health Programs, May 1975, p. 4.

22. Calculations of incomes and expenditures for 85 households surveyed indicated that "middle" income families spend approximately 20 percent more on food than "lower" income families. Average family size is almost equal for both groups.

23. PiDelta Ltda. Consultants, *Plan de desarrollo del Proyecto de Colonización del Caquetá: etapa 1*, vol. 3, anexo 10 (Bogotá: PiDelta Ltda., 1973). Their findings are based on a survey of 55 rural Caquetá households conducted in 1972.

24. Ibid., vol. 3, anexo 10.

25. John McHale and Magda Cornell, *Basic Human Needs: A Framework for Action*, (New Jersey: Rutgers State University, Transaction Books, 1978), p. 67.

26. PiDelta Ltda. Consultants, *Plan de desarrollo del Proyecto*, vol. 3 anexo 10.

27. Data on the incidence of malaria in Caquetá were collected from the Florencia SEM office. Their data are collected from field workers and from local health clinic records.

28. Ibid. SEM visited 39,547 households between January 1977 and September 1978; however, only 32,085 were actually fumigated, representing an acceptance rate of 81.1 percent. In 1976, before DDT was replaced with Baygon, the acceptance rate was 62 percent.

29. At a public meeting in October 1978, Caquetá public health workers employed by the Ministry of Health discussed their plans to promote community participation in health problem solving. They were to start with a micro-model project in the town of Puerto Rico. In addition, the speakers stressed the need to coordinate their activities with other government agencies in the area.

30. McHale, *Basic Human Needs*, p. 89.

3

Government Efforts to Promote Colonization and Integrated Rural Development in Caquetá

In 1961, the Colombian Agrarian Reform Institute was created to promote the objectives of Colombian Social Agrarian Reform Law 135, and to design and administer the nation's agrarian reform projects and programs. Chapter 1 of Law 135 outlines the law's objectives as follows:

1. Modify the social agrarian structure through measures aimed at eliminating and preventing unfair concentration of rural property or uneconomical division of the same. Reconstruct adequate farm units in small farm areas and give the land to those who have none, preferably to those who cultivate their own land and contribute their own labor resources.
2. Promote the economical exploitation of unused or underexploited land in accordance with the programs providing for orderly distribution and rational utilization of the same.
3. Increase overall agricultural and livestock production simultaneously with the development of other economic sectors; increase farm productivity through the use of modern techniques and see to it that the lands are used in the manner most suited to their location and characteristics.
4. Create conditions that offer better guarantees to small land tenants and land parcellers and secure the means whereby these and the salaried agricultural workers may easily acquire land ownership.

5. Raise the standard of living of the rural sector as a consequence of the previous measures and through coordination and development of services related to technical assistance, agricultural credit, housing, marketing organization, health and social welfare, warehousing, and conservation of products and the promotion of cooperatives.
6. Insure conservation, defense, improvement, and suitable utilization of natural resources.[1]

All of these objectives apply equally to parcelization and colonization projects. The colono of the frontier, as well as the small highland farmer, by law should be provided with an "adequate farm unit," "easily acquired land ownership," "better guarantees," assistance to "increase farm productivity through the use of modern techniques," and a variety of integrated services that would "raise [their] standard of living."

Project Caquetá No. 1, 1963–1971

In 1962, INCORA took charge of the colonization projects initiated by the Caja Agraria, among them the programs of "directed" colonization in Caquetá. The first phase of INCORA's involvement in Caquetá, Project Caquetá No. 1, 1963–1971, continued the programs initiated by the Caja Agraria and assisted in the settlement of new groups of "spontaneous" colonos.[2] The project zone covered approximately one million hectares (map 4), and was designed to benefit, directly or indirectly, the entire rural population within that area (90,000 by 1971) with construction of penetration roads and the provision of land titling services, supervised credit, technical assistance, social development programs, and financial support for the Caquetá marketing cooperative, COOPERAGRO.

The accomplishments and investments of Project Caquetá No. 1 are summarized in table 8.

Land Titling

Between 1963 and May 1971, INCORA's legal section granted 10,274 temporary and permanent land titles to Caquetá colonos, approximately 1,400 per year. A legal property title enables the owner to defend him/herself against possible "invaders," permits the sale of property at will, and fulfills one of the requirements for receiving institutional credit. In order to be eligible for a permanent property title, the applicant must have cleared and developed at least two-thirds of the total farm area, which cannot exceed 450 hectares

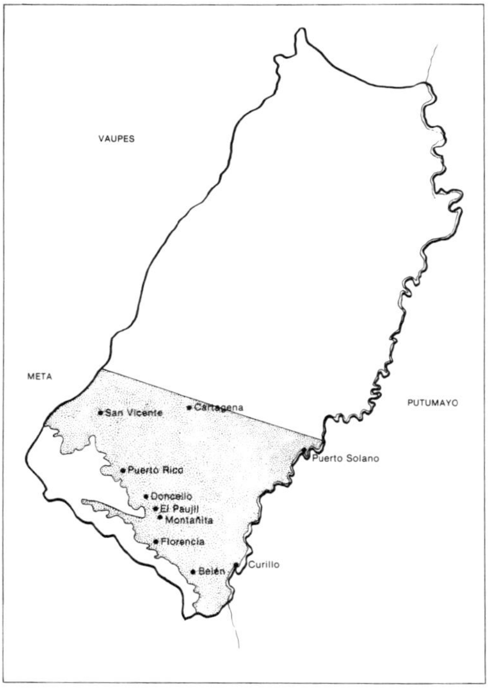

MAP 4. Project Caquetá: Area of Influence. SOURCE. Adapted from INCORA diagram, Graphic Arts and Cartology Department, Florencia INCORA Office.

nor extend for more than 500 meters along a major road or navigable river (applies only to baldío land). Because of the particular conditions of occupied public land, often underexploited for long periods for lack of labor and capital, the colono may apply for an intermediate title, Contrato de Asignación, which guarantees land ownership for a period of five years and permits the colono to receive INCORA credit. If, at the end of the five years, the farmer has developed at least one-half of his farm (in crops or pasture), then he may apply for a permanent land title. Baldío (public) land is granted gratis for up to 50 hectares. The colono is charged Col.$25 for each additional hectare, and must pay for administration and registration costs, usually about Col.$500.

The land titling process, from the initial application to final registration, usually takes several months and sometimes years. Delays are attributable to insufficient personnel and the complex network of bureaucratic and legalistic procedures. From beginning to end, the procedural stages are as follows[3]:

TABLE 8

Caquetá Colonization Project No. 1, 1963–1971

Project activities	Number of loans	Col.$ (thousands)
Supervised credit	3,818	$103,382
Rotating fund	1,618	43,340
Land credit		6,287
Subtotal	5,436[a]	$153,009
Cattle inventory	86,000	
Agricultural development		$ 16,700
Roads	110 km	31,100
Administrative centers	4	5,292
Number of titles granted	10,274	
Total hectares granted	545,282	
Administration[b]		59,436
Total		Col.$265,537[c]

[a]Number of beneficiaries is smaller because many families received two loans.

[b]Includes the costs of social development programs and titling services.

[c]Approximately U.S.$15.6 million at the official 1967 exchange rate.

Source: INCORA Planning Office, Florencia, Caquetá.

1. The colono solicits a land title from INCORA.
2. Announcements of the application are posted in municipal government offices and are publicized over the radio for a period of ten days, during which time any opponent can lodge his/her complaint.
3. If there is no opposition or if the opponent has no valid claim, INCORA topographers visit the applicant's farm to measure the boundaries and draw up a topographical plan.
4. The topographer fills out a Dictamen stating that the applicant fulfills the requirements for titlement.
5. The Dictamen is posted in INCORA offices for three days, and if no opposition is voiced, then:
6. An Announcement of Titlement is posted for ten days in government offices, again to allow for opposition.
7. The Legal Department of INCORA in Florencia decides whether the title should be granted, rejected, or postponed until an opposing claim is resolved.
8. If the title is granted, it is sent to the INCORA office nearest to the applicant, where it can be picked up upon paying Col.$25 for each hectare over 50 and approximately Col.$250 in administrative costs.

9. The colono brings the title to the Registration Office in Florencia and pays Col.$250 in fees and stamps. The registered Property Title is issued to the colono.

Although it is important to resolve any potential conflict with competing claims before a legal title is issued, the present system of posting announcements could be simplified and shortened. As it stands, accumulated backlogs prevent INCORA from attending all of the applicants, and in some cases, initiated title procedures are never completed because the colono becomes discouraged and impatient with the delays.

INCORA estimates that a minimum of 80 hectares is needed for the establishment of an economically viable family livestock ranch in Caquetá. Therefore, according to the "adequate farm unit" objective of Agrarian Reform Law 135, every rural family in Caquetá should be entitled to 80 hectares of public land. According to World Bank estimates, in 1971, 54 percent of Caquetá farms were smaller than 50 hectares and 26% of farms were 50 to 100 hectares, with an average size of 59 hectares (see table 4). These farms combined (80 percent of total) occupied only 30 percent of the total farm area.

Even though, legally, every colono has an equal right to occupy up to 450 hectares of public land, in fact the colonization process favors certain settlers over others. The earliest settlers are favored because of the large expanse of uncolonized land available to them, including the most desirable land along navigable rivers, roads, and near to frontier towns. Colonos with greater financial resources, who arrive subsequently, buy the plots developed by the former tenants; a few of the wealthiest manage to consolidate large holdings of purchased land, which do not fall under the same legal limits as baldío land. The poorer and newer colonos, meanwhile, are left with small hillside plots or larger but more isolated holdings in the uncolonized hinterland. These newer colonos sometimes avoid the titling process because they are unable to pay the price of owning more than 50 hectares, or because they fear that part of the land they hope to clear and develop in the future will be taken away if it comes to the attention of the "authorities" when in an unused state.

It would seem reasonable to raise the 50 hectare limit for free public land to 80 hectares in order to allow poorer colonos an equal opportunity to acquire an "adequate farm unit." Also, "to eliminate and prevent unfair concentration of property," one of the objectives of Law 135, INCORA could regulate the "spontaneous" colonization process, which has led to an unequal distribution of land, by applying the 450-hectare farm limit to all holdings—baldíos and purchased land. A politically difficult, but legally justified action would be to divide the already established latifundia in Caquetá among needy newcomers.

Although conscious of the land tenure problem, INCORA has not yet attempted to prevent further unequal land concentration in Caquetá through its land titling services. INCORA's failure to act on this problem contributes to one author's conclusion that "frontier settlement [in Caquetá] is in practice duplicating the Andean system of land tenure, rather than assuring a more equitable distribution of land wealth."[4]

Credit and Technical Assistance

During Project Caquetá 1, 1963–1971, 3,800 rural families received 5,436 INCORA loans. The credit program was allocated over half of total Project funds, 70 percent for Supervised Credit, 30 percent for the Rotating Fund.

The Supervised Credit program was part of a nationwide effort, financed by USAID as part of the Alliance for Progress, to increase the productivity levels of owners of small and medium-sized farms in Colombia. In order to be eligible for supervised credit, the colonos had to fulfill the following requirements: (1) have legal title or a temporary Contrato de Asignación to their land; (2) have a farm no smaller than 30 hectares and no greater than 250 hectares; (3) have at least 5 hectares of cleared and exploited land, and (4) accept the planning decisions and the supervision of INCORA.

INCORA supervisors were sent to visit the farms of eligible credit applicants to plan the distribution of a future loan among cattle, crops, fencing, housing, and corral, and to design a specific farm development program for each colono. If the application and investment plan were subsequently approved by INCORA's Credit Committee in Florencia, the recipient would have a personal bank account opened for him with the loan deposited. Cattle were distributed in kind.

As part of INCORA's policy to promote cattle raising in Caquetá, 55 percent of Supervised Credit funds were invested in livestock purchase. In addition, credit from the Revolving Fund, partially financed by the Cattle Bank (Banco Ganadero), was used exclusively for the purchase and distribution of breeding cattle. Many families received credit from both programs; however, the total value permissible per beneficiary was Col.$80,000. The average value per loan for both programs was Col.$27,000 (approximately U.S.$1,600 at the 1967 exchange rate). Interest rates for Supervised Credit began at 5 percent, and rose to 12 percent for short-term loans (2–3 years) and 10 percent for long-term loans (7–10 years) by the end of the program. The Revolving Fund loaned at 8 percent interest.[5]

Project Caquetá 1 was successful in providing credit to hundreds of families who would have been denied credit by other institutions. However, a greater positive correlation between credit and farm productivity and income was hindered by a variety of planning errors. In part these errors resulted from the technical inexperience of the INCORA field personnel, and in part from the unrealistic demands of their supervisors in Florencia and Bogotá. Moreover, the credit recipients, most of whom were recently settled, poor, disoriented, and inexperienced in tropical agriculture and cattle raising, had considerable difficulty in fulfilling their credit obligations.

In order to accommodate as many applicants as possible, INCORA credit supervisors were given quotas to fill—so many visits/plans per month. Pressured to move quickly, the supervisors often selected farmers at random and drew up development plans without adequate consideration of the farmer's resources and needs. Also, to promote INCORA's experimental rubber and African palm program, supervisors were instructed to allocate credit on the condition that the applicant agree to cultivate these crops on his farm. INCORA later discovered that this program was inappropriate for poor farmers due to the long waiting period before the first harvest (4–6 years). Eventually loans for rubber and palm cultivation had to be cancelled as "irrecoverable."

According to INCORA supervisors today, the paternalistic attitudes of credit supervisors during Project Caquetá 1, largely induced by the pressures to "force" development and investment plans on farmers who were frequently ill-prepared to implement them, led to poor INCORA-colono relations and a substantial number of credit default cases. Rather than invest the credit money as they were told, some recipients, usually the poorest, drained their accounts on food, alcohol and other personal expenses. Also, beneficiaries of the credit-in-kind program, most of them novice ranchers, were not provided with adequate complementary technical assistance and supervision. Each supervisor, on average, was responsible for eighty farms and colonos were only occasionally visited, if at all, by the ten veterinarians and agronomists. As a result, instead of developing self-sustaining herds, the least experienced ranchers sold their livestock too early or too quickly, leaving them without the means to pay back their INCORA loans. The poorest beneficiaries, particularly those located on the small hillside farms, were simply unable, even when well-intentioned, to manage personal expenses, increased farm costs, and monthly interest payments all at the same time. In their cases INCORA's assistance became more of a burden than a help.

Road Development

Of total Project funds, 12 percent were used to design and construct 110 kilometers of penetration roads. Since one of the most problematic conditions of rural Caquetá is its isolation from market centers and urban-based social services, the construction of roads that connect farms and villages to the principal towns is very beneficial. Specifically, these roads: (1) stimulate further colonization of the affected area; (2) reduce the time, cost, and discomfort of travel; (3) facilitate direct marketing, versus sales through intermediaries; (4) enable more frequent use of urban-based schools, health facilities, and government offices, and (5) increase the land value of the surrounding farms.

Construction costs in Caquetá are generally very high. This problem and other engineering and financial problems are discussed later in the sections on Phases 1 and 2 of the INCORA/World Bank Project.

Social Development

The Project's Social Development section was created to assist in the resolution of common social deficiencies in the Caquetá countryside: social isolation, poor hygiene and housing, malnutrition, and low educational levels. "Logically it is necessary to rectify these deficiencies, if one wants to obtain true development for each one of the settler families."[6] Thus, this department, by providing social services complementary to economic assistance, would help colonos and the Caquetá region generally to achieve a higher level of "integrated" development as opposed to economic growth alone.

Unfortunately, only slightly more than Col.$3 million (around U.S.$200,000), or 1.2 percent of total Project funds, were funneled into this effort.[7] The money was mainly used to promote the programs of other agencies (SENA, National Learning Service, and COOPERAGRO, Agricultural Cooperative of Caquetá), and to encourage the creation of Juntas de Acción Comunal by supporting their activities (school-building, cooperative marketing, handicraft associations, literacy, and nutritional campaigns).

Project Caquetá 1 planners recognized the need for an "integrated" approach to development in Caquetá, specifically the importance of combining social services and community development with increased production and income. Nevertheless, the resources allocated to the Social Development section were not adequate to build, nor even begin to build, an effective outreach service program; neither were the funds and personnel adequate to equip the rural community with the resources to meet their own needs effectively.

The land titling, credit, and road development programs were all useful and beneficial endeavors. Still, the failure of Project Caquetá 1 to grapple with the basic social needs of the rural poor through adequate services and extension work, even at the cost of reducing the scale of other investments, was an important flaw of Project planning.

World Bank/INCORA Caquetá Land Settlement Project: Phase 1, 1972–1976, and Phase 2, 1976–1980

The rural development programs of Project Caquetá 1 began to suffer from a severe lack of funds when USAID assistance ended in the mid-sixties. At that time, the population of Caquetá was growing by 8 percent annually, 5 percent from immigration. The Colombian government was anxious to support this trend with development assistance to new colonos, the idea being that a successful colonization strategy would open new opportunities for the rural and urban poor of the interior. In 1968, the government approached the World Bank for a loan to continue and expand support for Caquetá colonists. The proposed project (Caquetá Land Settlement 1) was appraised by Bank staff in January 1970, and the loan agreement for U.S.$8.1 million (Loan 739-CO) was signed in May 1971. The original closing date, October 31, 1974, was later extended two years to September 30, 1976; the loan was fully disbursed by November 4, 1976. Caquetá Land Settlement Project 1 was refinanced with a second World Bank loan for U.S.$19.5 million (Loan 1118-CO) in June 1975. Caquetá Settlement Project 2 is expected to be completed by 1980 or 1981. Negotiations for a third loan, to finance a third phase of the Project, are now in progress.

Project Objectives

The Caquetá Land Settlement Project 1 was one of the first integrated rural development projects financed by the World Bank worldwide, and the first of its kind in Colombia. Out of a total of U.S.$1,147.2 million in World Bank loans to Colombia through March 1975, only 7.2 percent had been invested in agriculture, principally to finance large-scale farming and ranching.[8] The Caquetá Project loans correspond with over-all changes in World Bank policy, which since the early seventies has focused more attention on agriculture generally, and on raising productivity and income levels of poor and small farmers specifically. "It was in September 1973, that Bank President Robert S. McNamara called for a target of five percent growth in productivity on small farms by 1985. For the Bank, he set a goal of bringing improved technology and other inputs to over 100 million small farmers over the same time span."[9]

The changes in World Bank orientation culminate years of international debate on development objectives and strategies, prompted by the serious shortcomings of the traditional growth strategies that were implemented at high cost during the fifties and sixties throughout the Third World. These strategies were designed to raise per capita GNP (Gross National Product) levels of poor countries to a certain dollar amount (U.S.$500–$1,000) and annual growth rates to a certain percentage (5 percent to 7 percent), with the idea that growth, no matter how it was achieved, would inevitably lead to the development of these countries and their people, i.e., development as it is known in Western Europe and the United States.[10]

Many countries did attain higher GNP levels and annual growth rates in the sixties because of the massive and costly importation of foreign capital and technologies, and because of increased industrialization and farm mechanization. The development follow-up only benefited a small minority, however, while the vast majority continued to suffer, sometimes more acutely, from impoverishment and its accompanying ills. As a result, development theorists and planners began to realize that growth must be accompanied, simultaneously, with redistribution, more employment opportunities, and basic social services. Social changes as well as economic change were needed, and their achievement would require a high degree of commitment by national governments and multinational development institutions and banks, the largest being the World Bank.

In the reworked development strategies (redistribution with growth, basic needs, decentralized development), underdevelopment would not merely be tackled from the top down, which assumes the benefits of growth will trickle down to the poor, but also from the bottom up, by addressing the needs of the poor directly, particularly the rural poor who make up the majority. Consequently, the World Bank was pressured by academics and government advisors, especially from Third World country members, to increase financial and technical assistance to the agricultural sector, particularly among poor and small farmers.

Beyond this, emphasis would be given to integrated rural development as opposed to simply higher agricultural growth rates. The "integrated" approach developed principally from the failure of the "Green Revolution" experimental technologies to achieve higher living standards for the rural poor, despite cases of miraculous yield increases. Planners learned that if benefits are to be widely distributed and self-sustaining, higher productivity must be combined with more jobs, transportation, storage and marketing facilities, educational and health services, land tenure reform, and community organization. Furthermore, where the application of Green Revolution techniques was generally limited to large tracts of fertile agricultural land, the integrated rural development strategy could be applied to small and medium scale agriculture and ranching, under a variety of agroclimatic conditions (including colonization areas).

These development ideas are beginning to be implemented, with external and internal financing, in many Third World countries. Their success, in practice, depends upon a variety of conditions but perhaps most important of all, the condition of commitment. "Recent evidence points to the fact that, over the past few years, developing countries have, in fact, increased their commitments to such a policy (involving small farmers in development). The lesson—that a country's commitment to project objectives is an essential precondition to success, and that without commitment, most efforts are futile—is one that is not confined to the rural development sector."[11] Expressed differently, "The amount of the input and the form in which it is supplied—its "technical" aspects—are secondary in importance to the quality of commitment and power of the supplying institution."[12]

The Caquetá Land Settlement Project presented an opportunity for the World Bank and the government of Colombia to aid poor farmers through a project that combined the colonization and integrated rural development strategies and, given a reasonably successful outcome, would serve as a model for future Bank efforts in other areas of colonization throughout Latin America.

With the assistance of INCORA, two Bank missions prepared the Project appraisal report (taking into consideration the errors and shortcomings of Project Caquetá 1), which summarizes over-all

Project objectives as follows: (1) stabilize and equalize the land tenure system of Caquetá by legalizing the holdings of colonos and by assisting the poorer farmers to establish viable farm enterprises (via cattle credit), inducing them to remain on their land; (2) increase the total worth, productivity, and income of Caquetá small farmers and of the region generally by importing breeding cattle from other regions of Colombia for development in Caquetá; (3) raise nutritional, health, and educational standards of the colonos; (4) connect the hinterland to the central towns through the construction of access roads and bridges, and (5) encourage more efficient planning, administration, implementation, and coordination within INCORA and among other related government agencies.[13]

These objectives correspond well with the stated objectives of the Colombian government vis-à-vis Caquetá and the nation generally. As mentioned previously, government support for the Caquetá Project after the mid-sixties stemmed from its withdrawal of support for land reform in the interior and its increased emphasis on colonization and land reclamation projects. Moreover, if the Project were successful in increasing cattle production for regional and national consumption, then in the long run it would indirectly increase foreign exchange earnings by permitting other cattle areas (Cali, Atlantic Coast) to export their surpluses abroad. Of course, if Colombia were to realize a net gain, the additional export earnings would have to exceed the cost of Project loan repayments to the World Bank and imported equipment; the full value of these transactions will not be known for at least another decade.

Project Organization and Administration

While the World Bank played a large role in initial planning and periodic revisions, and sent biyearly supervisory missions to Caquetá through Phase 1 and now in Phase 2, day-to-day Project activities have been and continue to be the responsibility of INCORA's staff in Florencia and the countryside. The Project manager is responsible for coordinating field operations in Caquetá, and maintaining contact with the national INCORA office in Bogotá. He reports to the Colonization Division which is part of the larger Engineering Department, and all divisions and departments are headed by INCORA's general manager and board of directors. The general manager is appointed by the president of the Republic.

The Project activities are organized into five functional sections: Administrative, Legal, Farm Settlement, Engineering, and Planning (an umbrella division), as shown, along with affiliated committees and groups, in diagram 3. There are 187 INCORA employees in Caquetá at present (January 1979), twenty of whom are university-educated professionals. The staff is distributed as follows: Legal, 41; Engineering, 9; Farm Settlement, 100; Administration and Planning, 36; and one medical doctor (for a full breakdown see Appendix 1).

To carry out the programs of Phases 1 and 2, INCORA enlisted the collaboration of several other institutions in the area. During Phase 1, agreements were signed with the Banco Ganadero, ICCE (for the construction of rural schools), and CECORA (Central Cooperativa de la Reforma Agraria, in coordination with Caquetá's COOPERAGRO). INCORA also assisted, financially, in the establishment of an experimental research farm, staffed and managed by the agricultural research institute, ICA. At present, under Phase 2, INCORA maintains agreements with CECORA, ICCE, and ICA and has signed additional contracts or made informal agreements with INDERENA (for forestry and erosion control), Caminos Vecinales (for road maintenance), SEM (for malaria control), the Ministries of Health and Education (to staff, operate, and maintain health and education facilities), SENA (technical training), the Caja Agraria, and the Fondo Ganadero. These institutional agreements and the percentage of INCORA financing for each contract are shown in diagram 4. The specifics of these agreements (*convenios*) are discussed further on.

Phase 1, 1971–1976

On May 28, 1971, the Minister of Finance and Credit of the Republic of Colombia and the International Bank for Reconstruction and Development (World Bank) signed the Caquetá Land Settlement Project 1 loan agreement for U.S.$8.1 million at 7.25 percent interest per annum on the principal withdrawn and .75 percent interest on the principal withheld. The effective interest rate, given an average annual devaluation of the Colombian peso by 10.6 percent, has been estimated at 19.12 percent.[14] The Colombian government was given 20 years, including a four-year grace period, to repay the loan, beginning November 1, 1975, and ending November 1, 1990. Total Project cash expenditures—U.S.$20.3 million—were distributed over five years to farm development (42 percent), road development (26 percent), health and education (3 percent), administration (13 percent), and seasonal input (17

Diagram 3. Project Caquetá: Organizational Chart

Source. Adapted from INCORA diagram, Graphic Arts and Cartology Department, Florencia INCORA Office.

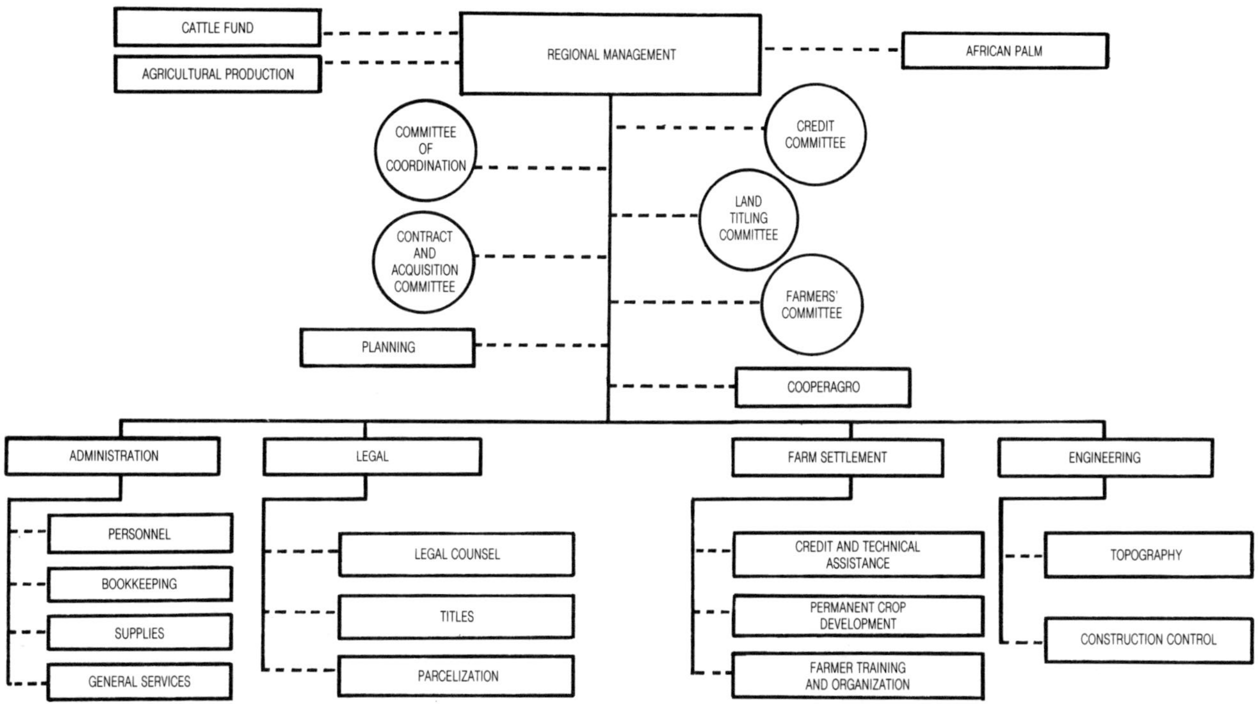

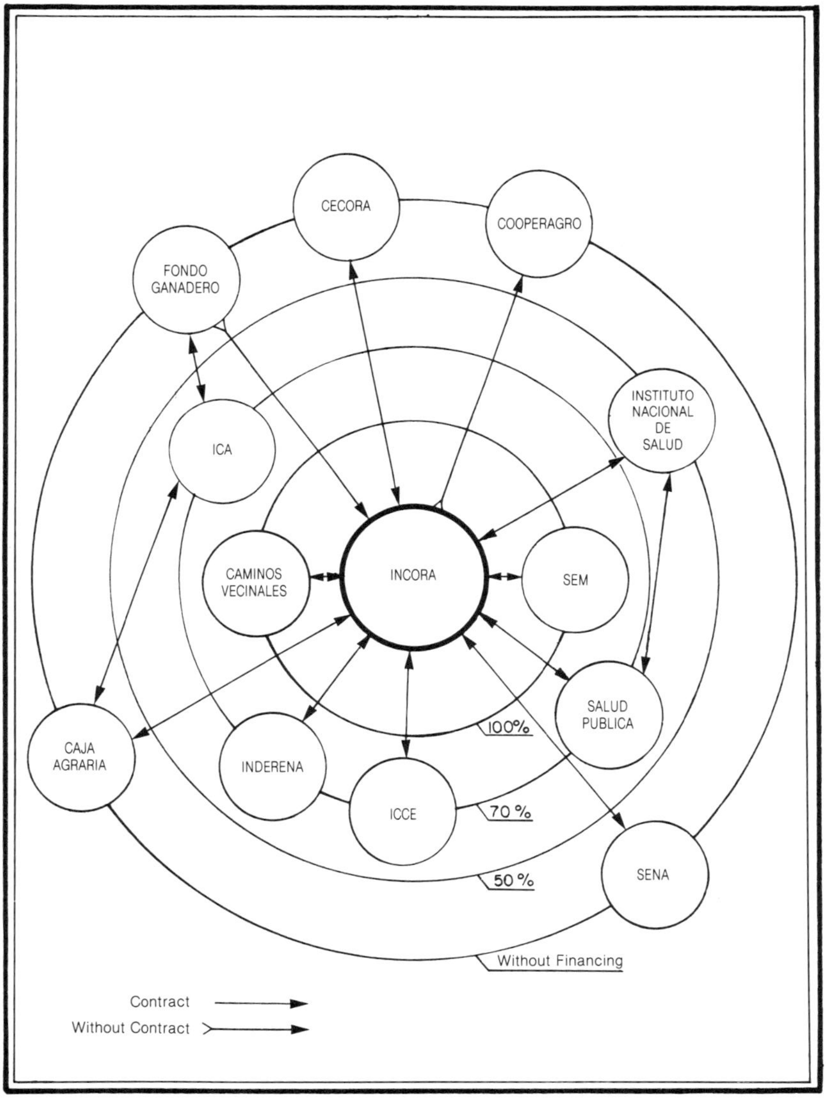

DIAGRAM 4. Project Caquetá, Participating Agencies, Phase 2: Percent INCORA Financed.

SOURCE. Adapted from INCORA diagram, Graphic Arts and Cartology Department, Florencia INCORA Office.

percent). Programs were paid for with funds from the World Bank (40 percent), INCORA (32 percent), the Caja Agraria (14 percent), and the colonos, with the contribution of their land (14 percent).[15]

The economic rate of return on the Project is estimated at 13 percent in the Bank's *Project Performance Audit Report* and at 17 percent in the *Project Completion Report*.[16] The discrepancy between these rates results from the inclusion of family labor at a cost of U.S.$500 per family per year in the *Audit Report*, as compared with a zero value attached to family labor in the *Completion Report*, justified, but perhaps incorrectly, by the high rural unemployment rate in Colombia. Otherwise, both estimates were derived from a weighted average of returns based on Project costs (administration, road and farm development) and Project benefits (increased production of breeding and fattening cattle, rice, corn, yuca, and plantain, plus savings in the transport of cattle and grains facilitated by the Project road development program). Returns were discounted over a period of twenty-three years, the stipulated time for full Project development of costs and benefits. Costs and benefits associated with the health, education, and land titling programs were excluded from the calculations because of the difficulty in quantifying their impact on productivity and income.

Table 9 summarizes Phase 1 accomplishments and costs as originally appraised in 1971, and as actually fulfilled at completion. Halfway through the Project the original targets were revised owing to unforeseen problems, and the termination date was extended two years to September 30, 1976. The new targets, considerably scaled down, were almost completely achieved.

Credit and technical assistance.—As discussed previously, Caquetá farmers typically strive to convert their farms into cattle enterprises, and direct themselves away from the difficult agroclimatic and marketing conditions involved in traditional and cash crop agriculture. Even so, while ranching may be preferable to farming, the tropical climate of Caquetá—characterized by erratic and intense rains and droughts, regular infestations of parasites and plagues, and eroded soils—makes cattle raising (as well as agriculture) a precarious and costly activity. To overcome these environmental difficulties, there would be a need for large public and private investment in technical training and inputs, particularly for those colonos who are inexperienced and occupy the least fertile and most isolated plots.

Once a farmer has made the initial investment to purchase an adequate number of cattle to begin production, in order to assure proper herd development he/she will need to continue to invest

TABLE 9

Caquetá Land Settlement Project (Phase I), 1971–1976

Project activities	Appraisal January 1971		Actual November 1976	
	Number	U.S.$ (million)	Number	U.S.$ (million)
Land titles	4,700		6,000	
Farm development				
Breeding cattle (loans)	4,500	7.52[b]	1,673	8.48
Fattening cattle (loans)	300		141	.14
Cattle (animals)	79,500		28,535	
Roads (km)	380	6.56	164	5.23
Schools	90	.66[c]	60	.412
Health facilities	6		5	.143
Administration		1.62		2.60
Seasonal inputs[a]		5.22		3.38
Total		U.S.$21.58		U.S.$20.385

[a]Includes short-term loans by Caja Agraria and land contribution of the settlers: five hectares of cleared land per borrower.

[b]For breeding cattle and fattening cattle loans.

[c]For schools and health facilities.

Source: *Caquetá Land Colonization Project Completion Report (Loan 739-CO),* World Bank, June 30, 1977.

money and time into the following ongoing management pursuits: (1) meticulous registration of each animal's vital statistics—age, weight, vaccinations, number of births per cow, etc.; (2) proper animal feeding, including adequate intake of mineralized salts, grass, legumes, concentrated feed, and water; (3) pasture upkeep, including appropriate choice and mixture of grasses, weeding, chemical treatments, and systematic rotation; (4) periodic vaccinations against common cattle diseases and monthly baths with disinfectants; (5) construction and maintenance of farm installations—corral, salt trays, loading docks, silos, fences, and (6) regular training on updated methods of animal husbandry. Though ranching is commonly considered "easier" work than farming, in practice, it demands considerable hard work, skill, and financial investment, especially in tropical climates.

When insufficient resources, ignorance or negligence lead to improper management, and livestock development is consequently stunted, the incipient enterprise may become more a burden (cost) than an asset (benefit). In that case, unless the farm produces other sources of steady income to allow for "remedial" investments, the novice rancher may be forced to liquidate his livestock and forego the long-term benefits of cattle raising.

The farm development program of the INCORA/World Bank Project, Phase 1, was designed to assist forty-five hundred established low-income Caquetá colonos to develop viable self-sustaining cattle enterprises by providing them with credit to buy livestock and technical inputs, as well as free technical training. The object was to help motivated but poor farmers to convert their underdeveloped farms into medium-sized ranches, leading, in the short run, to increased capital stock, and in the long run (8–10 years) to increased income and improved living standards.

As it turned out, at the Project's completion only 37 percent (1,673) of the planned number of loans had been distributed. The original appraisal report had underallocated funds for cattle purchase at 1971 Colombian prices by about 42 percent; subsequent sharp price increases (25 percent to 30 percent between 1970 and 1972) further decreased the Project's ability to meet its original target.[17] Moreover, the process of preparing each loan (verifying the applicant's land title, credit standing, and the size and distribution of the farm) and the selection, purchase, and transportation of livestock for distribution, took much longer than expected, slowing progress even more.

During the first two years of the Project (1971–1972), rather than distribute the limited funds among as many needy farmers as possible, INCORA tended to allocate fewer but larger loans to middle-income ranchers who were good credit risks and easily accessible. This can be partly explained by the role of the Banco Ganadero as financial agent for the long-term credit program—a bank that is accustomed to handling large loans for "middle" and "upper" level ranchers throughout Colombia. During a World Bank audit mission of Caquetá, Banco Ganadero officials informed the visitors that they believe "it is not economical to initiate cattle production with less than 40 animals,"[18] even though, with limited Project funds, at 40 head per colono only 713 loans would have been possible.

This was clearly unacceptable, given the Project's original objectives and targets. Therefore, in 1973, World Bank and INCORA officials overrode Banco Ganadero policy by stipulating that henceforth cattle loans would not exceed fifteen animals and would not be given to any applicant whose total herd exceeded twenty-five animals after receipt of the loan. After 1973, 83 percent of long-term loans were allocated to owners of medium-sized farms (50–160 hectares), most of whom had low incomes, though they were not as poor as Caquetá farmers who had smaller and less developed plots. The average loan value was Col.$86,472 (U.S.$3,051 at the 1974 exchange rate), distributed as follows: 82.6 percent—cattle; 9.6 percent—technical inputs; 2.1 percent—housing improvements, and 5.7 percent—life and accident insurance.[19]

In addition to the long-term credit program for breeding cattle, the Phase 1 Project planned to make three-hundred short-term loans for fattening cattle. INCORA provided CECORA (its national cooperative affiliate) with funds for short-term credit, and CECORA was to allocate those funds to COOPERAGRO, its Caquetá "subsidiary," for cattle purchase and distribution among Caquetá colonos on a profit-sharing basis. One hundred forty one, or less than half of the planned loans, were actually made because there were political differences between the two cooperatives CECORA and COOPERAGRO.[20] Apparently, COOPERAGRO's leadership in the early 1970's was highly policized, intent on using the organization as a lobby for peasant rights against private and government abuse. CECORA was tied to national agrarian policies that were turning more and more away from agrarian reform, especially after the successful ANUC-supported land invasions of 1972 and 1973. CECORA refused to provide COOPERAGRO with the full funding it had received from INCORA for short-term credit; consequently, the Project's attempt to promote Caquetá's only farmer cooperative was undermined, and COOPERAGRO's influence in the region diminished.

In order to facilitate cattle distribution and loan control, the Project area (1.4 million hectares for Phases 1 and 2) was divided into nine credit zones (map 5), each with a credit chief and several credit supervisors. During Phase 1 and now under Phase 2, the supervisors have fulfilled a dual function as technical extensionists and loan officers. They are required to teach animal husbandry methods and proper pasture management as well as to supervise the investment and amortization schedules of a select number of bor-

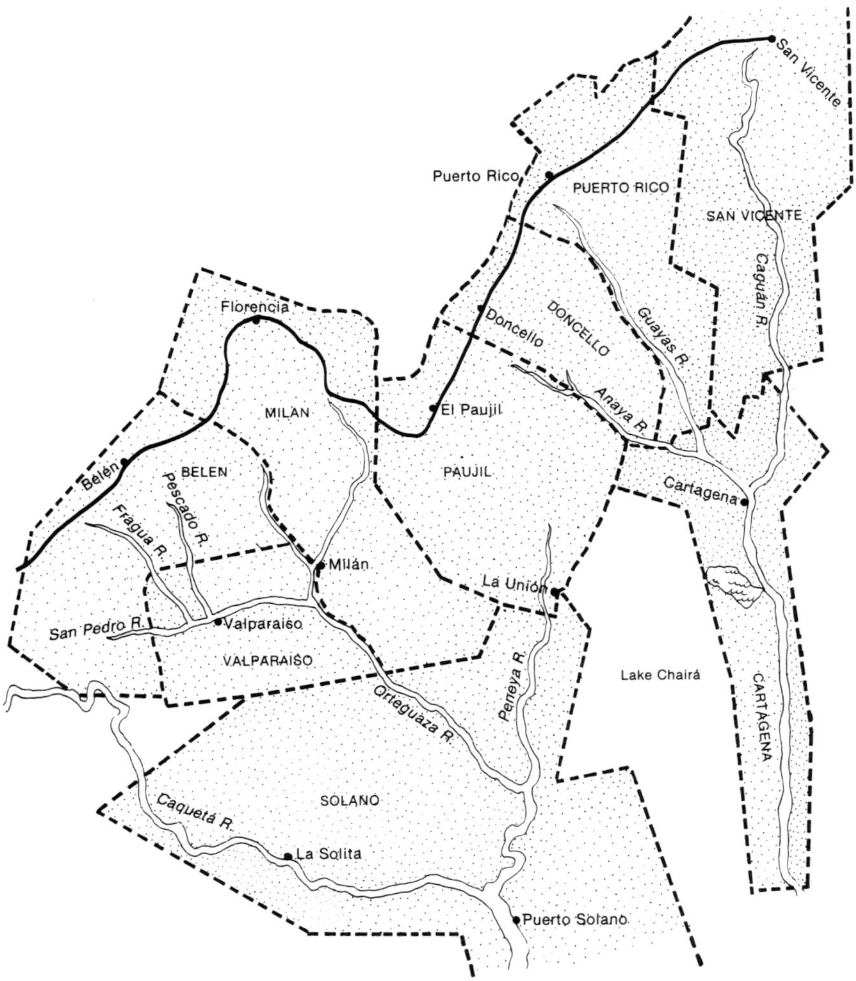

MAP 5. Project Caquetá: Credit Zones. SOURCE. Adapted from INCORA diagram, Graphic Arts and Cartology Department, Florencia INCORA Office.

rowers (from 40 to 100) in their credit zones. On average, each borrower is visited three times per year, though "problem" cases (those not obeying credit regulations) are visited more frequently, and often the most isolated farmers are visited less frequently.

Additional technical assistance is provided by INCORA's professional veterinarians and zoologists (from seven to nine during Phase 1) and one agronomist. Originally the professionals resided in the credit zones so that assistance would be readily available and accessible to credit borrowers. Because of the difficult living and working conditions in the smaller towns, however, and the consequent high turnover rate, it was decided that the professionals should reside in Florencia and visit the zones for one- or two-week shifts on a rotational basis. Details on the technical assistance program are presented in the section on Phase 2.

Phase 1 has had very few credit default cases (0.1 percent of total loans) in comparison with the previous Supervised Credit program. Having learned from past errors, Phase 1 supervisors and administrators were careful to choose the most reliable colonos among the low-income applicants for credit, i.e., established farmers with pasture ready for use, who seemed to be well adjusted to Caquetá's climate and lifestyle. New arrivals or farmers who were very poor and had not yet prepared their farms to receive cattle were not considered. Furthermore, once the loans were approved, subsequent regulations were rigorously enforced. Borrowers who committed one or more of the following errors were recommended for "liquidation" so that their animals could be transferred to more reliable and "worthy" families: (1) consistently ignored INCORA credit recommendations on farm management; (2) did not invest credit funds according to the recommended development plan; (3) sold cattle without prior permission, thus undermining long-term herd development, or (4) did not pay loan quotas on time.

In addition to more vigilant supervision, the relatively good credit terms of Phase 1 have contributed to an excellent repayment record. Borrowers received credit at 8 percent interest (lower than the national inflation rate), and were given an initial three-year grace period followed by a seven-year amortization schedule, with quotas increasing in size each year as the borrower becomes more able to pay. Furthermore, the price of cattle in Colombia, though gradually increasing throughout the seventies, did not experience its greatest jump until 1975–1976, so that Phase 1 borrowers received their cattle at relatively low cost (on average Col.$4,200 per animal) compared with Phase 2 borrowers (on average Col.$8,600 per animal). Thus, in a matter of a few years the original animals (not counting their off-spring) doubled in value, making loan payments, which are fixed, quite manageable for most of the Phase 1 borrowers.

Road development.—At appraisal, the Phase 1 Project planned to construct 380 kilometers of penetration and access roads (linking existing roads with river ports and newly settled areas), all with gravel surface, at a total cost of U.S.$6.56 million (Col.$118 million), or U.S.$17,222 per kilometer. After various problems became apparent during the first two years of the Project, the planned targets were reevaluated and scaled down by more than 50 percent. At the Project's completion, 164 kilometers had been constructed (43 percent of the appraisal estimate) at a total cost of U.S.$5.23 million (Col.$148 million*), or U.S.$29,499 per kilometer (58 percent more than the $/km. appraisal estimate).[21] Map 6 shows INCORA roads built in Caquetá from 1963 to the present, including those constructed during Phase 1.

When the Project was appraised, both INCORA and World Bank planners failed to give sufficient attention to the unique problems of road development in Caquetá, and Colombia generally; problems which caused construction to be much more time consuming and costly than anticipated.[22]

First, machinery and most materials had to be imported from other regions of Colombia, or from the United States, over a mountainous and hazardous road connecting Caquetá to Huila. Even those materials available in Caquetá (gravel, stone, and wood) had to be transported long distances within the region, at high cost. Second, during Phase 1 an urban construction boom in Colombia and a quasi-black market on imported intermediary goods created a shortage of construction materials, upped the prices, and caused delivery delays. Third, a nationwide shortage of qualified building contractors in Colombia, exacerbated by the urban construction boom, drove bids unusually high and made it difficult to attract experienced, qualified contractors to marginal areas such as Caquetá. In order to keep within the budget, INCORA accepted the lowest bids, usually from inexperienced small contractors with weak financial backing. Fourth, owing to Caquetá's nine months of heavy rain, most work had to be completed during the three-month summer season, making it physically impossible to complete the road system as planned. Furthermore, heavy rains quickly deteriorate the roads unless they are rigorously maintained. Fifth, Caquetá's hilly terrain

*The devaluation of the Colombian peso (from 18 pesos per U.S. dollar in 1970 to 31 pesos per U.S. dollar in 1975) explains why road construction costs increased in pesos from the appraisal estimate but decreased in dollars.

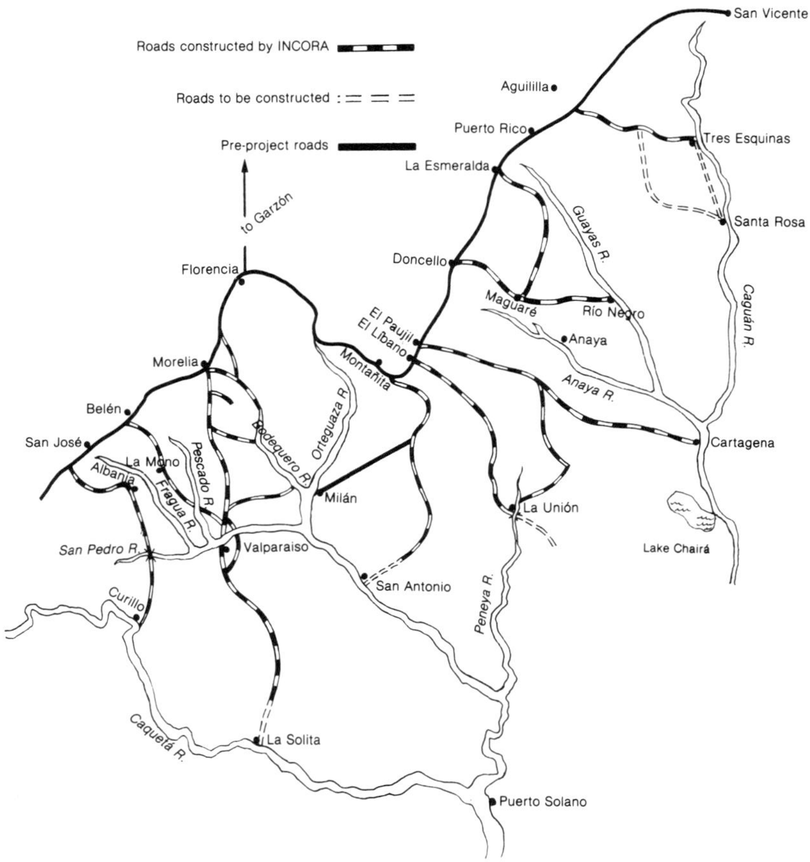

MAP 6. Project Caquetá: Roads, 1963–1980. SOURCE. Adapted from INCORA diagram, Graphic Arts and Cartology Department, Florencia INCORA Office.

requires considerable earth moving; its sandy soils and deeply seated white clays must be removed or countered with more resistent substances to prevent the roads from disintegrating and cracking. Not having anticipated these environmental difficulties and accompanying expenses, INCORA and the contractors were ill prepared, technically and financially, to deal with them. Finally, labor (especially specialized labor) is scarce in Caquetá, so that construction projects are likely to be plagued by human error unless they are continually inspected, and permanent inspection is costly.

All of these factors contributed to the drastic reduction in appraisal targets and the high increase in costs per kilometer of road constructed. While some of the problems were unavoidable, others could have been avoided or more effectively resolved with better planning. For instance, if careful research had been undertaken at appraisal time, including studies of previous construction efforts in Caquetá, the difficult soil, weather, and labor conditions would have been foreseen and contractors would probably have submitted more realistic, though higher, bids. Also, the failure of the Colombian government to cooperate with INCORA by speeding up the delivery of funds and materials as well as assuring the quality of the competing bidders, was a major and unnecessary impediment to progress. The World Bank could have used its influence to obtain better government cooperation. Similarly, despite verbal promises from the Ministry of Public Works to provide for road maintenance from its department, Camino Vecinales, in practice, funds for that purpose were never made available.

In sum, the Caquetá road development program did not receive the priority attention it merited as a government sponsored effort aimed at providing important social and economic benefits to a deprived region, but rather, was neglected in favor of more prestigious development in the urban centers. The tasks were difficult to begin with, owing to natural impediments, but became far more difficult because of INCORA and World Bank planning errors, and a lack of commitment by the central government in Bogotá. Nevertheless, to the extent that road construction during Phase 1 was successfully completed, it was highly appreciated by the affected public (under Project Caquetá 1, see the section on Road Development for a list of benefits).

Though it is difficult to accurately determine the number of families that directly benefited from the Phase 1 road program, sufficient information has been collected from interviews and land studies to make a reasonable calculation.[23] By dividing the average hectare size per farm by the total number of hectares affected per kilometer of road, the number of farms or families benefited per kilometer can be calculated. Taking an average of 1,600 hectares of land (16 km^2) affected per kilometer of road, and an average farm size of 80 hectares, the total number of families benefited (affected) per kilometer of road is twenty. Multiplying twenty families by 164 kilometers, the total number of families benefiting directly from Phase 1 road development is 3,280. Again, this is a rough estimate based on averages. Indirect beneficiaries (not calculated, but would include hundreds more) include more distant farmers who also make use of the new roads, though less frequently and without having the value of their land appreciate to any significant extent.

Health and education.—Of total Project funds, 2.7 percent (U.S.$555,000) financed the construction of sixty rural primary schools (two classrooms each) and five health facilities (four clinics and one center); equipment and staffing were provided by the Ministries of Health and Education. A small percentage of funds also financed the adult Rural Training programs (Capacitación Campesina), part of the Farm Settlement section.

In order to provide permanent decentralized health services to needy rural families and small town residents, INCORA, together with the Public Health Department of the Ministry of Health, constructed four small health clinics providing first aid, maternity care, and drugs, and one larger health center equipped to handle more severe and complicated health problems. Each health facility is located more than 100 kilometers from Florencia. According to a study made in 1977 by an INCORA sociologist on the Phase 1 health program, 118 rural communities averaging nine families each have benefited, based on physical proximity, from the five health facilities. Adding these rural families (1,062 families, to total approximately 7,500 individuals) to the population (8,050) of the small towns where the facilities were built, the total sum of potential beneficiaries comes to 15,550 (a rough estimate).[24]

The study mentions several other important factors on the quality of health care offered: (1) none of the facilities are staffed with a full-time doctor (the Center has since received a doctor); (2) the clinics' inadequate supply of instruments and equipment does not allow even simple tests and operations to be performed; (3) more adults are attended than children, despite a greater incidence of illness and death among the latter, and (4) all but one of the facilities are underused vis-à-vis available first aid, maternity, counseling, and pharmaceutic services (on average, 150 patients are attended per month).[25]

To some extent the clinics are underutilized because potential users are discouraged by their inadequate services and personnel. Other discouraging factors are the long distances that the more isolated rural families must travel to reach the clinics, widespread fear and ignorance of medical treatment, and insufficient outreach and promotion. To encourage more visits from children, the study suggests that special infant and childcare programs be established that would inform parents about the importance of regular preventive health care for themselves and their offspring. So far, such information has been disseminated only on a casual basis.

At appraisal, the Project plan was for INCORA and ICCE (Instituto Colombiano de Construcciones Escolares) to build ninety primary schools using free labor and wood provided by the beneficiaries. The planners felt that by engaging the community in "self-help" construction work, farmers would learn the skills of cooperative, communal work, become more unified, and feel a special commitment to their school once completed.

As it turned out, it was unrealistic to assume that farmers had the time to commit to community works, especially during peak clearing and harvesting periods; most were too poor to pay outside laborers to manage their farms while they worked for free building schools. Furthermore, the distances between the farms and the construction sites varied from five minutes to one and a half hours, making it difficult to obtain equal cooperation from all parties. If the farmers had been paid for their labor and construction had been limited to slack farming periods the plan might have eventually succeeded. Instead, in order to keep to the planned time schedule and budget, it was decided to scale down the original target to sixty schools and finance outside labor with Project funds. Problems also occurred when the agreement between INCORA and ICCE broke down because ICCE was not able to carry out its financial responsibilities. INCORA had to engage independent building contractors to carry out construction and this further delayed progress.

The sixty schools are concentrated in the more developed, accessible rural areas; only six of them are located in the three most isolated credit zones—Cartagena, San Vicente, and Solano (see map 7). Because there exists a great shortage of schools in the newly colonized areas, applications from these zones are being given priority during Phase 2. Still, rural educational needs far exceed Project plans, and colonos feel considerable resentment when their children are denied access to schooling, especially if promised assistance does not materialize.

Another major problem, as discussed earlier, is the shortage of qualified rural teachers. Once the schools are constructed, whether by INCORA, ICCE, or local communities, the Ministry of Education is responsible for providing equipment, teaching materials, maintenance, and teachers. To date, these services are sorely deficient, partly because of inadequate financing from the national budget and local mismanagement, and partly because of the weak power base of the rural communities in need. As a result, these communities are usually suspicious of government institutions (INCORA, ICCE, the Ministry of Education), leading to poor colono-government relations and further inaction.

In addition to the Phase 1 health post and school construction projects, health and education mini-courses were offered by INCORA's Rural Training department, a division of the Farm Settlement section. The department staff included: one sociologist (the

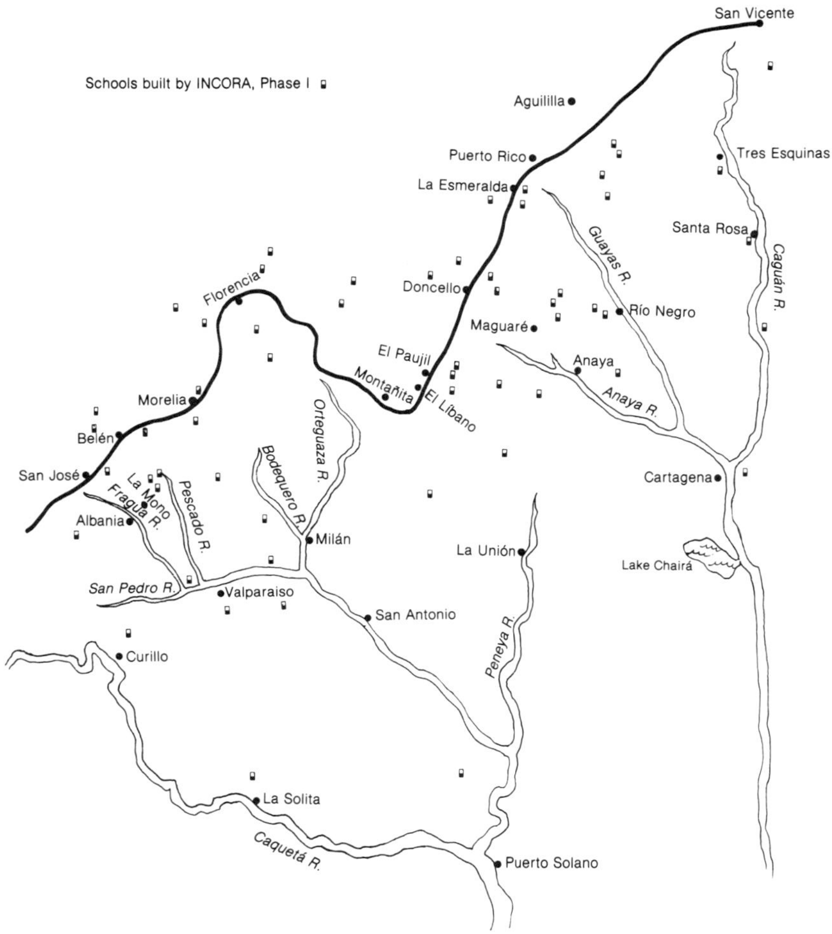

MAP 7. Project Caquetá: Schools. SOURCE. Adapted from INCORA diagram, Graphic Arts and Cartology Department, Florencia INCORA Office.

department chief), one part-time medical doctor, one nurse, three social extension workers, and one driver. The staff rotated visits to different rural communities, either to individual farms or to planned communal meetings, giving mini-courses and informal talks on first aid, farm and house management, childcare, and community organizing. The medical personnel carried out vaccination campaigns against tetanus and yellow fever as well as general physical and dental checkups.

These programs aimed at raising the standard of living of the colonos by supplying information on their basic needs (nutrition, hygiene, shelter, literacy), and by demonstrating the least costly methods to satisfy those needs. Much of the work was focused on family and home life, especially the tasks normally carried out by women. The principal shortfall of the program, as during Project Caquetá 1, was its inability to reach large numbers of colonos on a consistent, follow-up basis; limited to a seven-person staff and a part time work schedule, the Rural Training programs touched only the surface of the basic needs problem.

Phase 1 evaluation.—The World Bank and INCORA evaluation reports on the Land Settlement Project, Phase 1, express general satisfaction with the Project's accomplishments and impact on regional development. Indeed, despite the myriad of problems discussed earlier, Project Caquetá is considered a "model" colonization and rural development project in Colombia and even on an international scale. "The Caquetá Land Colonization Project is demonstrating, probably for the first time in South America, that a squatter can be assisted to settle permanently and establish a farm providing a reasonable living for himself and his family. The project has already shown the feasibility of productive land use in the Amazon basin."[26]

Concurring with the above World Bank point of view, INCORA's general manager states: "In general, we share the Bank's point of view on the Project's implementation and impact, which has been a success, becoming one of INCORA's most effective lines of work."[27]

As demonstrated earlier, it is difficult to calculate how many Caquetá settlers actually benefited from the Project's programs; rough estimates of potential beneficiaries (from schools, health posts, roads) and definite beneficiaries (recipients of credit and land titles) are shown in table 10. The coverage rates (percentage of total

TABLE 10

Caquetá Land Settlement Project (Phase I), Summary of Benefits, 1971–1976

Program	Number of families benefited	Percent of total rural population[a]
Credit	1,814[b]	9.0
Land titling	4,700	23.5
Roads	3,280[c]	16.4
Schools	1,000[d]	5.0
Health clinics	2,220[c]	11.1

[a]Estimated at 20,000 rural families in 1975.

[b]Total number of loans for breeding and fattening cattle.

[c]See p. 92 for the methodology used to arrive at these estimates.

[d]Calculated using an average of 50 children per school and three school-age children per family.

population affected per program), while not particularly impressive in absolute terms, are apparently quite good in comparison to previous government sponsored colonization efforts in Colombia and elsewhere.

As to the quality of the Project programs, we have already seen that each program suffered from major inadequacies: poor road maintenance, insufficient personnel and equipment for both the schools and health facilities, too little and unsatisfactory technical and social extension work, etc. Some of these shortfalls are being corrected in Phase 2 as we shall see. It is still too early to determine the full impact of the credit program on colono productivity and income, though a preliminary evaluation is possible, as discussed later.

But first, to bring the Project's status up to date, I will continue with a section about Phase 2 of the Caquetá Land Settlement Project, currently in progress. Since I conducted my research in Caquetá during Phase 2, and very little evaluative work has been done on the Project since 1976, the following section leans heavily on personal observation as well as on interviews with INCORA staff and local rural families.

Phase 2, 1976–1980

Since both the Colombian government and the World Bank were pleased with the results of Caquetá Land Settlement Project 1, they agreed to extend the Project with a new World Bank Loan (CO-1118) for U.S.$19.5 million, to begin disbursement June 30, 1975 and complete disbursement five years later in mid-1980. Similarly to Phase 1, the lending term for the second phase is twenty years, including four years' grace at 8.5 percent interest, with the borrower (Republic of Colombia) assuming responsibility for foreign exchange risk. The total Project cost, U.S.$37.1 million, will be financed 53 percent ($19.5 million) by the World Bank, 32 percent ($12.1 million) by the government, and 15 percent ($5.5 million) with settlers' land and labor contributions. The projected Project expenditures per program basically continue the same priorities as Phase 1: farm development (44 percent of total cost); road development (35 percent); health and education (7.6 percent); forestry and erosion control (2 percent); administration (11 percent); except that the budgets of the road development and health and education programs were substantially increased both absolutely and proportionate to other programs.[28]

Approximately U.S.$19.5 million, 62 percent of total Phase 2 expenditures (excluding settlers' contributions), constitute a direct government subsidy to INCORA. These grant funds (originating from the World Bank loan and the National Treasury) will finance the costs of road, school, and health clinic construction, erosion control, technical assistance, and project administration. The remaining 38 percent of Phase 2 expenditures (U.S.$12.1 million) will be financed from a twenty-year, interest-free government loan to INCORA and allocated to the repayable credit component of the Project.

The Phase 2 government subsidy to INCORA, distributed equally among all rural Caquetá families (estimated at 22,000), comes to almost U.S.$900 per family. Taking into consideration both Phase 1 and Phase 2 government grants (a total of U.S.$31.3 million), the subsidy per rural Caquetá family increases to U.S.$1,400, and to over U.S.$7,000 when counting only credit recipients. If the value of land grants (colonized baldío land) were considered, the government subsidy element would be even greater. As it is, these cost estimates demonstrate clearly the high economic opportunity cost involved in government supported colonization projects, especially, as explained in this chapter, when even these substantial per-family subsidies are insufficient to cover the costs of minimum development and basic needs programs.

Financial management.—In designing Phase 2, certain important changes were made in the financial management of the Project. First, while World Bank funds were directly channeled to INCORA during Phase 1, under Phase 2 the Colombian government insisted that loan payments first be sent to the Treasury Ministry in Bogotá in order to maintain firmer control over the entry of foreign exchange. Second, the Banco Ganadero no longer manages the long-term credit program, having been replaced by the Caja Agraria. According to INCORA officials in Florencia this change was a national decision provoked, on the one hand, by the Caja's financial difficulties and its urgent need for new accounts, and on the other hand, because the Banco Ganadero had essentially monopolized control over the credit program during Phase 1, diverting attention away from INCORA's leading role in the program.[29] Third, subloan (INCORA loans to Caquetá settlers) interest rates were raised from 8 percent during Phase 1 to 15 percent, plus 1 percent for life insurance, for Phase 2. Despite this increase the real interest rate remains negative in financial terms due to Colombia's high inflation rate, averaging more than 20 percent yearly since 1975.[30]

Another financial matter of importance concerns the method of disbursement of the World Bank loan employed during Phase 1 and currently under Phase 2. It is World Bank policy (worldwide) to disburse loan payments only *after* the borrower has invested money into the Project, according to agreed upon appropriations. Once a portion of total Project funds has been allocated and spent, the documented statements of expenditure are submitted by the beneficiary (INCORA) via the borrower (Republic of Colombia) to the World Bank in Washington for review. Upon approval, the borrower is reimbursed for the sum corresponding to the Bank's proportion of financing per investment expended.

For example, in the case of Phase 2 financing, if INCORA-Caquetá plans to spend Col.$100 million in a given year, the Colombian government will dispatch 30 percent of that sum (its financial obligation for most Phase 2 programs) in 12 monthly disbursements, equaling Col.$2.5 million per month. INCORA-Caquetá then invests this money in Project programs, and once a substantial bill has accumulated (about Col.$20 million), a statement of expenditures is sent to the Treasury Ministry in Bogotá for review and then to the World Bank for approval. The World Bank then dispatches 70 percent of the money expended (its financial obligation) to the General Treasury of Colombia for review and registration and upon final approval it is sent to INCORA-Caquetá for Project use. The disbursement process and accompanying delays are shown below, as explained to me by the INCORA statistical advisor in Caquetá:

A B C
INCORA → Treasury Ministry → World Bank →
D
General Treasury of the Republic of Colombia → INCORA

A. 2–3 months delay before bill has accumulated.
B. Approximately 2 months delay for revision.
C. Approximately 1 month delay for revision.
D. Approximately 1–2 months delay for revision.

Thus, if INCORA sends the statement of expenditures in March (accumulated since January), the Bank reimbursement will arrive approximately five months later in July, or seven months after funds were first expended.

Both the management changes and the disbursement process mentioned above have caused serious financial problems for Phase 2 development, namely, long delays and constant shortages. The Colombian government and the World Bank are both at fault; however, the former justifies its actions on account of national budget shortages and balance of payments difficulties which require centralized control, while the latter considers its disbursement policy necessary to avoid money squandering and corruption by local agencies, such as has occurred in other World Bank-financed projects. The impact of these financial problems on specific Project programs, as well as methods used to resolve them, are discussed further in this section under program headings.

The appraised, revised, and completed targets of the Caquetá Land Settlement Project 2 are shown in table 11. The targets and costs of the revised plan remain true to the original plan except for the farm loans, which have been scaled down by 30 percent because of rising cattle prices and process delays, and for the farm supply stores, which have been eliminated and their funds absorbed into the costs of the new and improved INCORA administrative centers.

Phase 2 investments did not begin until April 1976, and are supposed to be completed by December 31, 1980, so that the targets so far accomplished (September 1978) should, according to the current plan, be equal to more than half of the total revised targets for the 4.9 year Project. Nevertheless, as shown in the table, all pro-

TABLE 11

Caquetá Land Settlement Project (Phase II), 1975–1978

Project activities	Appraisal[a] May 1975	Revised[b] 1978	Actual[c] September 1978
Farm development			
Breeding cattle (loans)	3,200	2,263	802.0
Fattening cattle (loans)	800	511	33.0
Road development			
Roads (kilometers)	200	201	135.0
Bridges	4	4	3.4
Administrative centers	11[d]	5[e]	2.7
Schools	30	30	8.0
Teaching materials	500	500	500.0
Health facilities[f]	12	12	3.7
Aqueducts	9	9	2.0
Water supply	81	81	10.0
Sewage systems	9	9	—
Sanitary units	9	9	4.0
Anti-malaria solution (tons)	58	58	14.0
Farm supply stores	3	3	—

[a]Total cost of Project, U.S.$31.9 million (U.S.$1 = 40 Col. pesos).

[b]Total cost of Project, U.S.$31.9 million.

[c]Cost to date, U.S.$13.8 million.

[d]Three centers, five houses for INCORA personnel.

[e]Two new centers, three improved centers, no housing.

[f]Two centers, ten clinics.

Source: INCORA trimester report, September 1978, Planning Office, Florencia, and World Bank Appraisal Report, May 1975.

grams except road development, teaching materials, and the administrative centers are considerably behind schedule, though expenditures to date already equal 43 percent of total projected costs. It is unlikely that Project appropriations will be sufficient to complete even the revised targets; refinancing and an extended termination date are presently being negotiated by the World Bank, INCORA, and the Colombian government.

In designing Phase 2, World Bank and INCORA planners incorporated new or improved programs to correct deficiencies encountered during the development of Phase 1. Some of these changes concern expansion of the health and education programs: provision of five hundred sets of German-designed teaching materials for rural primary schools; an agreement with SEM to provide funds for the non-toxic anti-malaria solution Baygon, and a program to improve hygienic conditions with water supply and sewage systems. Others concern the credit program: fattening cattle to be sold directly by INCORA or through COOPERAGRO (not CECORA); long-term loans not to exceed fifteen cows and one bull per beneficiary, and specific allocations made for thirteen professionals to provide technical assistance to farmers as well as special funds made available to ICA to develop pasture, cattle, and plantain experimental programs at ICA's experimental farm, Macagual. Still others concern road development and erosion control: a financial agreement with Caminos Vecinales for road maintenance and the purchase of heavy equipment; a contract with a consulting firm to handle the design and supervision of road construction, and an erosion control program designed to protect roads, rivers, and farms from future devastation by erosion. In addition, the World Bank instructed INCORA to establish an evaluation and monitoring unit in Caquetá to study such topics as farm budgets, herd development, and deforestation, using a random sample of settlers as informants. Finally, before signing the loan agreement, the World Bank obtained assurances from the Colombian government that funds would be made available to INCORA and other participating institutions to meet the full cost of the Project.

Credit and technical assistance.—According to appraisal plans, the Phase 2 credit program would allocate 3,200 long-term breeding cattle loans and 800 short-term fattening cattle loans to Caquetá colonos meeting the following conditions: (1) have no access to other sources of credit; (2) have at least 10 hectares of land cleared and under pasture; (3) possess less than 25 head of cattle, and (4) own a farm of between 30 and 200 hectares.

The credit program was designed to assist low income rural families with medium-sized farms to develop viable herds of cattle as means to attaining higher incomes and a "reasonable" standard of living. The program's objectives are essentially the same as under Phase 1, except that more attention has been placed on limiting loans to sixteen animals per beneficiary, and on giving priority to credit applicants in the more isolated credit zones.

As of October 1978 (2.7 years into Phase 2), 827 cattle loans had been distributed throughout the nine credit zones, equal to 20 percent of the original four-year credit target and 30 percent of the revised five-year credit target. Therefore, as of October 1978, loan distribution was more than 20 percent (one year) behind the revised schedule. The average size of loan between 1976 and 1978 has been fourteen head of cattle worth Col.$118,000, plus Col.$24,000 for farm and house improvement and life insurance, equaling on the average, Col.$142,000 (approximately U.S.$4,000 in 1976) per loan.[31]

According to the credit office staff in Florencia, the credit schedule has fallen behind because of inadequate financing caused by persistent increases in cattle prices, delays inherent to the World Bank disbursement policy, and the failure of the national government to fulfill its share of financial obligations. As a result of price increases, the original long-term credit target was scaled down by 30 percent; however, the loans currently in process (on the average, Col.$190,000) even exceed the revised estimates (Col.$143,000). No attempt has been made to exercise national or regional price controls because of the government's reluctance to interfere with "natural" market mechanisms. Furthermore, government funds that have been promised to the program from the national budget are arriving two or three times yearly, instead of monthly as planned.

Without funds in its local account, INCORA cannot process new loan applications nor distribute cattle to applicants who have already been accepted into the program. Consequently, the entire Farm Settlement section stagnates, and rural confidence in INCORA is undermined. It seems that the financial "assurances" obtained by the World Bank from the Colombian government have not served their purpose, and that these assurances were given as a means of obtaining an international loan rather than with sincere commitment to their fulfillment. The financial problem has been exacerbated by the 1978 Colombian presidential election and accompanying personnel and policy changes. This election alone may have pushed the schedule backward by over six months.[32]

The result of inadequate financing, and subsequent stagnation, is that significantly fewer needy rural families can be assisted with credit. On the average, each credit zone has more than two hundred signatures of credit applicants on record, and these records do not represent the true magnitude of need because INCORA officers will not accept applications if they do not expect to receive new funding for their zone in the foreseeable future. Moreover, since the supply of credit is low compared with the demand, INCORA's credit committee can be more discriminative in selecting which applicants are to receive credit. Only the applicants with excellent credit records, land titles in order, reasonably accessible farms, and usually at least 20 hectares in pasture are chosen. The others, considered more risky, are discarded.

During interviews with thirty-five of the credit applicants, I asked them why they had chosen to apply for credit from INCORA and not some other agency. The following answers were given, the first with greatest frequency and the rest with approximately equal frequency: (1) neighbors and friends, satisfied with their INCORA credit experiences, advised them to apply; (2) the four-year grace period is appealing; (3) INCORA services the poor better than other agencies; (4) INCORA loans specifically stress cattle raising; (5) in addition to cattle, INCORA grants loans for farm and housing improvement, and (6) the length of the repayment period is reassuring (10–12 years). Asked why they wanted credit for cattle, they responded, in order of frequency: (1) to make use of subutilized pasture; (2) in order to own their own cattle rather than al partir; (3) to enable better use of their farms as well as more farm income, and (4) to foster greater general well-being. Basically the applicants felt that raising cattle, particularly their own, would allow them to break their dependence on unstable and often uneconomical agricultural activities and would enable better use of their land, averaging 81 hectares per farm. Most applicants interviewed, however, doubted that they would ever receive INCORA credit because their applications had been submitted a year or more before without a positive response. Therefore, they continued to search for cattle from other less favorable sources, that is, the Caja Agraria, Fondo Ganadero, and al partir.

In addition to the above mentioned interviews, fifty INCORA credit recipients (Phases 1 and 2) were interviewed and asked for their opinions on the credit program. Forty (80 percent) responded that they were generally satisfied with the program, although most expressed one or two complaints. Ten (20 percent) responded quite negatively to the program, having experienced serious problems with their loans.

The responses of the recipients indicate that opinions on the INCORA credit program depend largely on the quality of the cattle delivered to each recipient. Those farmers who received healthy, fertile cattle were very satisfied with the program, while those who received poor quality cattle—too young or too old, unfertile, sick, wild—were unhappy with the program.

Most Phase 1 recipients have been able to overcome the difficulties of poor quality cattle by exchanging one cow or bull for another and by natural replacement through the gradual development of their herds. Furthermore, the financial stakes for Phase 1 borrowers are lower because their cattle were purchased relatively cheaply and at a low interest rate, so that the loss of two or three head is not catastrophic. Phase 2 borrowers, on the other hand, are paying high prices for their cattle at double the interest rate. Therefore they suffer greater financial loss when exchanging poorer for better quality cattle (the farmer pays the difference), and are anxious to develop their herds quickly in order to prepare themselves for loan payments in the fourth year. They would also like to reap the advantage of high cattle prices while they last.

In several interviews, credit recipients complained that their INCORA bulls did not "service" well, that is, did not impregnate their cows at a normal rate. Thus the herds developed slowly because the young and nursing cows ready to be "serviced" remained unfertilized.

In the case of one farmer, INCORA had delivered a bull for Col.$19,000 which later turned out to be sterile. Once the recipient realized that his bull was useless he asked INCORA for permission to exchange it, which must be granted by a veterinarian. Months went by before permission was received (until a veterinarian visited the farm, which is quite isolated), at which time the farmer sold the bull for meat at a low price of Col.$10,000. A neighbor was willing to sell him a good bull for Col.$17,000; however, in order to raise the extra Col.$7,000 the farmer was forced to sell two INCORA calves, requiring permission from an INCORA veterinarian once again. INCORA is reluctant to give permission to sell young cows soon after credit is delivered due to its adverse effect on long-term herd development. Nevertheless, permission was finally granted. For the two bulls, minus the sale of the sterile bull, the farmer had spent Col.$26,000, losing two calves worth Col.$7,000 in the process as well as nearly a year's loss of herd reproduction.

In explaining his situation, this particular farmer showed considerable anger and resentment toward INCORA; indeed, he was reluctant to receive us at all. Unfortunately, rather than handle the problem objectively and sympathetically, the INCORA professionals became defensive during the discussion, refusing to acknowledge that INCORA was partly at fault.

Intolerance of this sort is very harmful for it discourages credit borrowers from discussing their problems honestly with INCORA officers. While INCORA staff members, especially the professionals, are generally willing to discuss Project programs critically among themselves, they are reluctant to speak frankly with farmers and their families. This fear or reluctance to "lose face" in front of poor, uneducated farmers demonstrates an attitude of superiority which often creates communication barriers between government officials and the populace at large. Rather than promote mutual respect between INCORA and farmers, these attitudes tend to foster a form of patron-client relationship, causing supposedly benign assistance to become suspect in the eyes of the benefactors.

The problem of livestock quality is difficult to solve given the financial limitations of the credit program. INCORA's purchase method is to advertise its expected demand for animals among large ranchers in Caquetá and other cattle raising regions; sealed bids are received, the lowest bid of animals of decent quality being accepted. The animals are then transported to the appropriate credit zone for random distribution among the new borrowers.

Because of a general shortage of cattle in Caquetá and INCORA's large demand, the credit program is often victim of above-market cattle pricing, forcing the purchase committee to sacrifice quality for quantity. Thus, instead of buying a full corral of grown cows ready for reproduction, as required in Project plans, younger, cheaper cows are purchased and distributed as if they were full grown. Furthermore, the quality of a bull is very difficult to judge from its appearance alone. According to the veterinarians, a machine could be used to verify the fertility of the bulls, but the process is considered to be very expensive and time consuming. INCORA, therefore, is not totally at fault when it sometimes selects infertile bulls; but neither is the colono, who should not be burdened with the consequences of the error. Colonos should be allowed to exchange infertile bulls at no cost to themselves; otherwise they may not be able to recover from initial losses.

Aside from problems related to cattle quality, the following grievances were mentioned in the interviews, though less frequently: (1) high interest rate (Phase 2); (2) credit should include financing of other economic activities besides cattle raising to reduce dependence on one source of income, and (3) technical assistance is insufficient. Among the satisfied borrowers, besides having received good quality cattle, the following positive aspects were mentioned: (1) low interest rate (Phase 1); (2) INCORA allows borrowers to exchange poor for better quality cattle; (3) four years grace is important; (4) credit allows them to improve their farms and their lives, and (5) INCORA's credit is the best option for the poor.

It is too early to know whether Phase 2 borrowers will be able to manage their principal and interest payments as well as Phase 1 borrowers have (see chapter 4 for more detailed discussion). Certainly their credit terms, due to the inflated cattle prices and higher interest rate, are more difficult. On a Col.$150,000 loan, the nine-year amortization plus interest payment schedule will average Col.$40,000 per year (compared with average yearly payments of Col.$20,000 during Phase 1). In order to successfully make these payments, the borrower will need to bring in income from other sources besides cattle sales, allowing him to pay for family and farm costs and simultaneously maintain adequate herd development. The more "diversified" the farm, the better the chances for success. Still, intensive exploitation of the land without fertilizer supplements and crop rotation is not advisable, given Caquetá's natural ecological conditions. Additional factors to be considered are changes in physical, market, and political conditions, family health, and the ability of the colono to manage his farm efficiently.

The last factor mentioned, farm efficiency, brings us to the subject of technical assistance during Phase 2. Phase 2 technical assistance personnel include nine credit chiefs, forty-one credit supervisors, eight veterinarians, two zoologists, and one agronomist. As of October 1978, with 1,986 current status Phase 1 and 2 loans, the ratio of supervisors to borrowers was 1 to 48 and the ratio of professionals to borrowers was 1 to 180 (not counting Supervised or Rotating Fund credit still current from Project Caquetá 1). As mentioned earlier, supervisors are supposed to visit each beneficiary a minimum of three times yearly to administer both technical assistance and loan control. Professionals work in the field on the average ten months out of the year, twelve days and eighteen visits per month, allowing each beneficiary to receive one professional visit per year.

In practice, supervisors tend to meet their quotas more satisfactorily than the professionals, principally because loan control demands more frequent attention and is given higher priority than technical assistance. For example, all the borrowers interviewed were well acquainted with their credit supervisor, but 25 percent had never been visited by a veterinarian while at least 10 percent had been visited by veterinarians several times, more often than their appropriate share.

Asked whether they were satisfied with the technical services provided by INCORA, 60 percent of the farmers interviewed responded favorably, 40 percent negatively. Those who responded positively said they were pleased with the veterinarians' recommendations on animal husbandry and pasture maintenance and made efforts to implement them. A few mentioned that their sick animals had been cured with veterinarian assistance. Among the negative responses, the absence or infrequency of professional visits was cited most often; others complained they were not assisted when assistance was most needed. A few mentioned that they were dissatisfied with the advice given them. For example, veterinarians have sometimes refused to permit animal exchanges, even though the animals are of subnormal quality, and occasionally an unsuccessful treatment is prescribed.

In one case, which I experienced directly, a farmer traveled one Friday afternoon by bus and taxi for more than two hours to the INCORA offices in Florencia because one of his cows was experiencing abnormal labor trouble and he feared both the cow and calf would die if treatment were not provided. Unfortunately, that weekend all but two of the veterinarians were leaving for a conference in Bogotá; since the two who were remaining had not been authorized nor would be compensated for field visits that weekend, the farmer was refused help. Still, the farmer persisted, so eventually the veterinarians gave him some suggestions as to how he might handle the problem by himself. Considering the length and cost of his journey, and the farmer's obvious concern, the professionals showed very little interest in helping; apparently they were preoccupied with the trip to Bogotá. The farmer reacted politely, but it can be assumed he left embittered by the experience.

This brings us to the subject of motivation and commitment among INCORA's technical personnel. Motivation and commitment are interconnected; without the latter the former tends to be low, and vice versa. When the supervisors or veterinarians feel committed to resolving a technical or social problem, they are motivated to tackle the problem thoroughly; on the other hand if they are motivated to carry out good work because of rewarding incentives, their commitment toward their work responsibilities generally intensifies.

Unfortunately, in Caquetá, motivation and commitment tend to be low among both the supervisors and the technical professionals. This stems from several factors, the three most important being: (1) work is too routine and boring; (2) financial and training rewards are inadequate, considering the difficult working conditions, and (3) often farmers do not follow technical advice and the supervisors and veterinarians feel helpless to change the situation.

Among the credit supervisors motivation generally diminishes the longer they have worked, and more so when their experience is limited to one credit zone for several years. Supervisors respond to work monotony by giving less to their work as each year passes, until only the minimum requirements are fulfilled. The newer supervisors, fresh out of school, tend to meet their duties with much greater enthusiasm, especially the challenges of orienting themselves in the jungle, befriending the farmers, and surviving difficult climatic and living conditions. However, as time goes by, the hardships become more of a burden than a challenge and even the small rewards, principally the generosity and friendship of the colonos, are less appreciated.

In addition to the physical deprivations and monotony of their work, the supervisors feel resentful that they are not included in the decision-making processes in Florencia and Bogotá, even when they know and understand the situation of the colonos better than anyone. Furthermore, many of them are anxious to undertake additional training to upgrade their technical skills; Project-financed training for supervisors is limited to occasional seminars given by ICA and INCORA professionals in Florencia.

Some envy and resentment exists between the supervisors and the professionals, first because the latter are granted greater training opportunities and carry more authority in decision-making, and second, because the supervisors feel that the veterinarians are not sufficiently responsive to colono needs. The supervisors believe that they should be trained to carry out duties normally reserved for the professionals (granting permission for animal exchanges, purchasing cattle, simple operations, vaccinations, etc.) so that their visits to farmers would become more useful and the shortage of professionals would be felt less acutely.

In sum, it seems that the INCORA supervisors are committed to their work and to the colonos they represent when they first join the Project; however, their motivation gradually wanes and this adversely effects their commitment.

The INCORA professionals often feel unmotivated because they are dissatisfied with the nature of their work as technical assistants to poor farmers. They are not, for the most part, committed to what could be called self-sacrificing work. They believe their work is too physically demanding, having to spend weeks at a time walking, visiting, eating, and sleeping in the countryside under uncomfortable conditions. They also dislike the idea of working for a government agency with few chances for economic and professional mobility. After having spent five years studying to become professionals, they believe they deserve better opportunities. The veterinarians find their work additionally frustrating when their technical suggestions are not carried out, which is attributed to colono stubbornness and ignorance.

Most of the professionals want to work for themselves as soon as possible—in a clinic, on a ranch, or in a business—and are saving from their salaries toward that end. Certainly if they were given additional incentives (scholarships, higher salaries, more equipment) motivation would increase; however, since most professionals are "buying time" until they can work for themselves, low commitment levels are to be expected.

Work in Caquetá is difficult: hygienic conditions are poor; the cultural life is minimal; the climate is often oppressive; transportation is very time consuming; and the colonos' ability to provide good food and housing is minimal. Consequently, even if the material and educational incentives were greater, the technical personnel must additionally feel some social commitment to their work if they are to adapt themselves to the difficulties amenably. This kind of commitment is more present in the supervisors, who often come from rural low-income families themselves, than among the university educated professionals. Nevertheless, it is unreasonable to expect long-term enthusiasm (more than a few years) from any of the INCORA technical assistants, given the marginal lifestyle of Caquetá and INCORA's inability to significantly change it.

As discussed earlier, technical assistance is an essential component of any rural development program, particularly those programs oriented toward low-income farmers who normally lack the resources to pay for formal technical training. We have just seen, however, that technical assistance programs for poor farmers, especially in marginal areas, are frequently troubled with personnel problems stemming from low motivation and commitment.[33] These problems adversely effect the quality and quantity of assistance provided.

A variety of measures can be taken to alleviate staff grievances, once the government agency involved becomes sensitized to the issue. First, if the extension workers and professionals were thoroughly prepared for their work beforehand, receiving specific training about the physical, social, and economic conditions of their assigned areas as well as training on the current and historical situations of small and poor farmers, their quality of work would undoubtedly improve.

Second, to increase motivation, technical personnel should be rewarded professionally and financially for their efforts; hardship allowances should be allocated to technical assistants working under particularly difficult conditions. Without these allowances, extension workers will be likely to visit the more prosperous farmers more frequently than the poor farmers, for there at least they receive some sort of "income-in-kind", that is, good food, gifts (animals, fruit), and a more pleasant atmosphere. To some degree INCORA has implemented income supplements for field work (called *viáticos*) in the form of per diem expenses for professionals and monthly allowances for supervisors. Still, the distribution of visits is not sufficiently controlled to ensure that the neediest farms receive their appropriate share.

Third, both the Project as a whole and personnel self-esteem would benefit if the extension agents were more fully incorporated into the Project's decision-making process. Their input, if solicited frequently, would allow the Project's planners and administrators to keep up with problems and changes occurring in the countryside, and increased interest would encourage extension agents to perform their work more dynamically.

Fourth, ideally, technical workers in difficult areas should be transferred to other projects with better work conditions after three or four years of dedicated service, so that "fresh blood" would enter the hardship areas on a continual basis. In this way, perhaps the period of "challenge" could be sustained before monotony and disenchantment set in. This idea cannot be implemented until the national employment situation for agricultural technicians, veterinarians, and agronomists improves, which, in turn, depends upon the willingness of the government to finance technical assistance for the nation's hundreds of thousands of poor rural families. Once work opportunities open up all over the country, it would be feasible to implement a rotational work plan.

Fifth, measures must be taken to improve the "success rate" of technical assistance. While many colonos take the suggestions of their supervisors seriously and try to implement them, others do not, either because they lack the necessary resources to innovate or because they are satisfied with their own ways of doing things. Just as the technical experts require incentives to carry out their work, the colonos require incentives to innovate. Both the experts and the farmers would profit enormously if the technical assistance program included the provision of free or subsidized farm inputs (seeds, fertilizers, pesticides, tools, etc.) to accompany advice and demonstrations; poorer farmers would feel less reluctant to attempt costly innovative methods, and the experts would see their suggestions more successfully used. So far INCORA only provides low-cost seeds; as for other supplies, the three farm-supply stores which were originally planned for Phase 2 have been scratched. A lack of coordination between Caquetá's government institutes, IDEMA, COOPERAGRO, CECORA, INCORA, ICA, and the Secretary of Agriculture, have prevented a nonprofit, decentralized marketing organization (both for farm inputs and crops) from getting off the ground. As a result, the farmers who implement technical advice tend to be the more prosperous among the credit beneficiaries.

Finally, it would be worthwhile for Project planners to investigate the possibility of training local Caquetá students and farmers to carry out extension work within their own communities. In addition to high school students and farmers, the new university in Florencia, which has recently opened an agronomy department, might provide excellent candidates for INCORA work in Caquetá. Local people not only are better acquainted with the history, culture, and economic conditions of Caquetá, but also have a real stake in seeing local conditions improve. One problem with training and hiring local people to practice extension work in their own communities is that those communities may not respect their abilities as much as formally educated outsiders who carry higher status. This obstacle would likely be overcome if the "paratechnicians" prove their abilities in practice, and are able to communicate their knowledge sensitively, without affectation. In any case, the "paratechnicians" should only supplement, not replace, technical assistance from outside middle-level and professional experts.

The issue of motivation and commitment among staff workers in a development project is very important, but also very sensitive. Sometimes it takes an outside observer, who is interested in knowing all sides of the story, to recognize and analyze the problem. It is best not to place blame on any individual or group, but rather, to suggest feasible methods to overcome apathy and inefficiency when it becomes apparent, or preferably in the planning stages of the project. In the case of the World Bank/INCORA Project in Caquetá, until the government and World Bank administrators in Colombia and Washington, respectively, prove their own financial and social commitment to the Project's programs generally, and to the problem of motivation specifically, it is unlikely that local staff commitment will improve to any significant extent.

In addition to the extension services, the Phase 2 technical assistance program includes agricultural and livestock experimental work in coordination with ICA, as well as the scheduling of minicourses in rural areas by ICA, SENA, and INCORA experts. Under the INCORA-ICA agreement, begun in 1975, INCORA (with World Bank funds) finances 70 percent of three experimental programs on grasses and fodder, meat cattle, and plantain and banana development. ICA has also begun an INCORA-financed program on soils and erosion control, originally assigned to INDERENA. The experiments are carried out on ICA's ranch, Macagual, by two professionals and four agricultural technicians.

The purpose of the agreement is to coordinate ICA's investigative talents with INCORA's overall rural development strategy. After ICA has analyzed the technical characteristics of a region, it performs experiments to test appropriate innovations; then INCORA, SENA, and ICA together disseminate the findings among local farmers through field visits, demonstrations at Macagual, bulletins, and films. As part of the program, seeds of experimental grasses and plantain are distributed at a reduced price.

Each month a group of approximately fifty farmers is brought to Macagual in INCORA jeeps for a day of demonstrations. The day that I participated, three short lectures were given on soils, pasture management, and cacao and plantain cultivation, followed by visits to the experimental plots where cultivation methods were demonstrated. All in all, the farmers seemed very interested and listened attentively. However, according to the ICA professionals, unless the initial visit to Macagual is followed by field visits to individual farms to distribute seeds and monitor the usage of new methods, few farmers will actually implement what they are taught in a single day.

Besides the ICA lectures and demonstrations, SENA, in coordination with Phase 2, has taught thirty-nine mini-courses on cattle raising to 668 farmers and seven courses on agriculture to 114 farmers since 1976.[34] INCORA's veterinarians also give several short courses each year on cattle raising and pasture maintenance as they rotate among the credit zones.

Among the 50 credit recipients interviewed, 28 (56 percent) had attended one or more government-sponsored education course: 21 on cattle raising; 10 on first-aid; 2 on sewing, and 5 on a variety of other subjects. INCORA administered 55 percent of the courses; SENA 32 percent, and the rest were sponsored by INDERENA, ICA, and the Ministry of Health. Among the 35 credit applicants, 37 percent had attended government training courses: 6 on cattle raising; 1 on first aid; 5 on sewing, and 3 on other subjects. SENA taught 53 percent of the courses, and the rest were equally distributed between INCORA and ICA. Asked whether they would like to attend additional training courses, almost all of the farmers (and other family members) responded positively; the preferred subjects are cattle raising (over 80 percent) and sewing (over 50 percent).

Road development.—As of September 1978, 67 percent (135 kilometers) of the road construction and 93 percent (3.7) of the bridge construction planned for Phase 2 had been completed. Expenditures have been kept within the projected budget and construction accomplishments are well within the original and the revised time schedules.

The Phase 2 road development program has succeeded for three principal reasons. First, Phase 2 planners have benefited from the experiences and mistakes endured during Phase 1. Whereas Phase 1 appraisal costs per kilometer were markedly underestimated due to inexperience and insufficient research, Phase 2 appraisal costs are much more realistic. Furthermore, many of the problems encountered during Phase 1 (see discussion on road development, Phase 1) continue under Phase 2, but INCORA is better prepared to handle them. Problematic bidding procedures, scarcity of materials, high inflation, and environmental difficulties were foreseen in the planning stage and contributed to the establishment of more modest goals. Thus the Phase 2 appraisal target is slightly more than half of the Phase 1 appraisal target (201 kilometers versus 380 kilometers) at more than six times the appraised cost (on average Col.$1.9 million per kilometer versus Col.$0.3 million per kilometer).[35]

Second, since the Phase 2 road projects are individually quite large and expensive, INCORA has been able to attract Colombian construction firms from outside of Caquetá with stronger capital structures than local small firms. Consequently, when INCORA payments are delayed, work can proceed for at least six months using private internal funds. This has not been the case for smaller firms, as we shall see later in regard to Phase 2 health and education construction projects. Furthermore, these outside road construction firms continue to employ local workers when available (though scarcity of construction laborers in Caquetá sometimes requires temporary outside recruitment), and at the same time provide more experienced, specialized personnel as needed.

Third, INCORA now employs an engineering consultant firm to assist in analyzing bids and in supervising the progress of road construction. This firm employs qualified, experienced construction engineers; their technical and financial expertise in addition to constant on-the-job supervision have enabled INCORA to meet completion dates and adhere to budget restrictions satisfactorily.

The main problem with the current road development program concerns inadequate road maintenance. The INCORA-built penetration roads are of third, fourth, and fifth category quality.[36] They are narrow, unpaved, often loosely compacted, and constructed with steep embankments. The low quality of the roads, together with Caquetá's long and wet winter season and constant traffic of heavy cargo trucks and buses, make permanent road maintenance essential.

Otherwise the roads become impassable in winter and eventually deteriorate completely.

During Phase 1, both INCORA and the World Bank left the job of road maintenance to the government agency, El Fondo Nacional de Caminos Vecinales, after having obtained assurances in Bogotá that said agency would be allocated adequate funds to maintain INCORA-built roads. As it turned out, adequate funds were not provided, although as long as construction was in progress road contractors were required to maintain each completed segment, and this alleviated the situation.[37]

To avoid further troubles with unfulfilled "assurances," the World Bank and INCORA agreed to sign a specific Phase 2 contract with Caminos Vecinales providing for the equipment required to maintain INCORA-built roads. Under the four-year contract the World Bank finances eleven dump trucks, two bulldozers, two tractors, two motor-graders, two loaders, and two vibrating rollers, all imported at a cost of U.S.$590,000, for use by Caminos Vecinales though remaining the property of INCORA; the Republic of Colombia finances the cost of equipment maintenance, labor, and administration, equal to Col.$27 million (approximately U.S. $770,000). Caminos Vecinales is held responsible for maintaining Project roads according to specified standards established by INCORA and Caminos Vecinales in consultation with the World Bank.[38]

Despite the good intentions of the above-mentioned contract, the delivery of the maintenance equipment has been extremely slow due to several perplexing bureaucratic foul-ups. Only the dumpers and vibrating rollers have been delivered to INCORA and to Caminos Vecinales as planned.

According to INCORA's contract auditor, the motorgraders, loaders, and bulldozers arrived at Colombia in November 1975, February 1976, and March 1978, respectively, but have been held up in the customs warehouses because of delays in filing the necessary import and registration papers. When the papers were finally filed, INCORA was asked to pay the customs storage bill that had been accumulating over several years, but as of January 1979 the bill remained unpaid since Phase 2's budget does not include funding for that purpose. Meanwhile, the equipment has rusted due to moisture and lack of use, so INCORA will need to make repairs before it is even delivered to Caminos Vecinales.

The Fiat tractors, imported from the company ColCaribe, were delivered to Florencia in late 1977, but have not been approved for use because their design and associated parts do not match the original catalogue order. The auditor suspects that the tractors may be contraband because certain of the parts are missing while others are oversupplied and none of the catalogue references match the tractors that arrived. This leads him to assume that ColCaribe delivered excess or "hot" merchandise. Furthermore, ColCaribe has refused to acknowledge INCORA's numerous questions and complaints concerning the delivery, while INCORA's central Supply Division in Bogotá has delayed clarification of the problem for over a year. As of January 1979, the tractors were sitting idly in Florencia.

Since Caminos Vecinales did not receive the equipment promised in the contract, it has been unable to meet its commitment to maintain INCORA's roads in good condition. As a result, many complaints have been voiced by adversely affected communities that have seen their only means of transportation and communication severed due to deterioration. The following three quotes, from three separate letters, the first two from presidents of community action groups (Juntas de Acción Comunal) and the third from INCORA's zone chief in Valparaiso, are examples of these complaints, sent to INCORA's administrative office in Florencia.[39]

> . . . to bring to your attention that innumerable requests have been made before Caminos Vecinales, without having received a positive response on the matter.
>
> It is widely known that the road in question has not been maintained for over two years, that it is totally destroyed, causing harm to the community, being the only means of communication with the outside.
>
> I must inform you, Doctor, that the transport of vehicles has been suspended as a result of the present terrible and dangerous condition of the above cited road.

> Our ambitions for progress are being frustrated; we are about to have our only access to town cut off; as you know, the harvest time is approaching, and if the chaotic situation of the road is prolonged, there will be no way to market our products, our only livelihood. Moreover, many of us farmers hope to meet our financial obligations with INCORA by bringing our goods to Doncello to sell to IDEMA, thus converting this problem of the road into the barometer which indicates the level of well-being or misfortune of the community, and also affects your Entity, for 90 percent of us are INCORA beneficiaries.

> Road Morelia-Valparaiso is in very bad condition, hindering transportation of crops, only source of income for

> farmers in this area of colonization, causing serious economic problems in the region that have adverse repercussions on the progress of our programs. I would appreciate your attention on this matter, before the Director of Caminos Vecinales.

As indicated in the above citations, the problem of inadequate road maintenance is very serious. Nevertheless, to the extent that new roads are being built, and old roads at least minimally maintained, the contribution they make to regional economic development is widely appreciated. Among the eighty-five rural families interviewed, with farms distributed throughout the nine credit zones, 67 percent have benefited to some degree from the INCORA road development program since it began in the early sixties. Those who have not benefited either live in areas where no roads have been constructed, and transportation is limited to river travel and footpaths, or live near roads which were built by the Ministry of Public Works.

Health and education.—The Phase 2 health program is similar to but more ambitious than the Phase 1 program. It combines the INCORA Project and other institutional resources in two joint venture construction projects and an antimalaria campaign, and also includes an internal INCORA rural training program.

In an agreement with the Institute of Public Health, (ISP) the INCORA Project finances 70 percent of the costs of construction and supplying of ten health clinics and two health centers (ISP covers the remaining 30 percent), to be constructed either directly by the Institute or indirectly through subcontracts. In another agreement with the National Institute of Special Health Programs (INPES), INCORA and INPES evenly share the financial cost of water supply and sewerage systems for nine rural towns, as well as pumps or wells for eighty-one primary schools and sanitary units for nine primary schools. INPES usually executes its works directly, often using manpower and material support from local communities. INCORA and the World Bank share full rights, both in agreements to review bookkeeping records, budgets, and construction progress, and to have their financial participation recognized in all public notices.

Both of these construction agreements have experienced serious financial difficulties, slowing progress and preventing deadlines from being completed. The Institute of Public Health and INPES, being government agencies, are subject to the same financial limitations as INCORA; when INCORA does not pay its bills on time, the other agencies' liquidity is quickly drained and construction stalls. As of September 1978, INPES had invested Col.$2,880,149 in two aqueducts, ten wells for schools, and four sanitary units, but INCORA had reimbursed only 33 percent of that sum. The same situation exists with the Institute of Public Health except that in those construction projects it is the small private contracting firm that is owed, and consequently compelled to stall progress. These setbacks are caused by the failure of the Colombian government to disburse the whole sum of funds due INCORA for INPES and ISP projects, within the agreed-upon time limits, and by consequent delays in the release of World Bank funds which follow only after initial Project investments (30 percent) have been made. Without World Bank money, the government lacks the funds to carry out further disbursements, creating a financial "vicious circle."

As mentioned in chapter 2 in the section on Basic Needs (Health), the Phase 2 Project includes an agreement with SEM for the development of an antimalaria program in Caquetá. In the agreement, INCORA supplies SEM with the nonlethal fumigating substance Baygon, and SEM, with funds from the Ministry of Public Health, finances operating costs. The contract specifies that SEM will fumigate, on the average, 7,300 houses per year over four years in the municipalities of Montañita, San Vicente, and Solano, where malaria is most prevalent. SEM also visits over ten thousand homes per year with its own resources, takes blood samples, and prescribes medicine. The figures for 1978 indicate that out of 23,691 blood tests taken, 5,887 or 25 percent, proved positive.[40] For further details on SEM, refer to the chapter 2 section, Basic Needs.

The Rural Training Department of the Farm Settlement Section, described under Phase 1, continues to function under Phase 2 with the same personnel, minus the nurse, who left in June 1978. The director of the department, a young sociologist, hopes to expand his staff with two more social extension workers, an instructor in first aid, and a nurse by the end of 1979. The following table lists the

TABLE 12

Caquetá Land Settlement Project (Phase II), Rural Training in Health, 1976–1978

Health activities	1976	1977	1978[a]
Dental treatment	3,243	1,848	1,378
Vaccination	220	1,308	1,362
Medical consultation	335	514	79
Medical treatment	185	105	28
First aid course	19	21	13

[a]Through September.

Source: Office of Department of Rural Training (Capacitación Campesina), INCORA, Florencia.

health-related accomplishments of the department from 1976 through September 1978. Since the nurse's absence in June 1978, the program has slacked off considerably.

The Phase 2 education program consists of an agreement between INCORA and ICCE to build thirty rural primary schools and to provide teaching materials for five hundred schools throughout Caquetá. Under the agreement INCORA, with World Bank funds, finances 70 percent of the costs of construction subcontracted to local firms and 70 percent of the teaching materials; ICCE, with funds from the Ministry of Education, finances the remaining costs including school furniture and equipment, and the Ministry is responsible for supplying teachers and paying operating costs. As of September 1978, only eight of the thirty schools had been completed. Seven others have been approved and sites of the remaining fifteen are being chosen from community applications submitted to INCORA; priority will be given to the more isolated zones and to the communities with the greatest number of school-age children. The number of applications far exceeds the fifteen that will eventually be chosen.

Table 13 lists the education-related accomplishments of the Rural Training department from 1976 through September 1978. The accomplishments are slim compared with total need, though quite impressive considering the department's small staff and the large geographical area covered. The social extension workers, two women and one man, seem to be very committed to their work, even though it involves strenuous physical activity and repetitive assignments. The male worker, who actually has the title of Community Organizer, has worked for INCORA in Caquetá for over ten years and is well known and well liked throughout the region. The two women workers are also appreciated wherever they go, though they would prefer to concentrate on a few communities over several months, rather than travel continually throughout the year without an opportunity for follow-up work. Their suggestions have not been implemented, for the Project's aims are to reach as many colonos as possible, which prohibits more concentrated assistance.

Conservation.—Areas of rapid colonization, particularly in tropical regions, typically suffer from erosion and minerally depleted soils due to widespread deforestation by new settlers (see chapter 2, the section on Agriculture, for a description of "ecological havoc" in Caquetá). The World Bank and INCORA became aware of these problems in Caquetá during the early seventies and incorporated remedial measures in the design of Caquetá Land Settlement Project 2. Nevertheless, the forestry and erosion control programs have

TABLE 13

Caquetá Land Settlement Project (Phase II), Rural Training in Education, 1977–1978

Education Activities	1977	1977	1978[a]
Courses			
Sewing	6	10	8
Upholstery	—	—	6
House improvement	—	—	6
Lectures			
Rural organization	11	2	—
House/farm improvement	15	67	57
Propaganda			
Leaflets and posters	40	99	93
Movies and slide shows	79	96	52
Radio and newspaper bulletins	8	27	11
Technical bulletins	—	—	6
General bulletins	3	3	—
Photographs for documentaries	2	2	114
Teaching materials	—	—	880[b]

[a]Through September.

[b]The 880 sets include materials for teaching reading, anatomy, math, history, Spanish, and geography; 500 of them are part of the ICCE-INCORA agreement.

Source: Office of Department of Rural Training (Capacitación Campesina), INCORA, Florencia.

been the least successful of all of the Phase 2 programs, principally because of the inept administration of the implementing agency, INDERENA (Institute for the Development of Renewable Natural Resources).

The INDERENA-INCORA agreement encompasses four conservation programs: (1) a nine-month study to identify a suitable pilot project in the *cordillera* (foothills) where socioeconomic effects of antierosion measures could be analyzed, followed by the formulation and execution of an ecologically sound colonization plan for the hillside area; (2) the demarcation and protection of a 20,000-hectare forest reserve to use for experimental study of the natural fauna, flora, and soils within the reserve, and to determine the most appropriate species for planting along eroded river banks; (3) the establishment of several nurseries to house seedlings for reforestation, and (4) a program of technical assistance, in coordination with ICA, to promote the conservation of soils and waterways and to reduce deforestation and overgrazing of settlers' farms.[41] The agreement specifies that INCORA and the World Bank would pay 70 percent of the costs of construction, equipment, supplies, technical personnel, and studies (approximately U.S.$350,000), and that INDERENA would pay the remaining 30 percent of said costs plus 100 percent of the costs of additional personnel and general operations (approximately U.S.$298,000). In the contract, INDERENA is held responsible for the planning and execution of all of the agreed-upon activities.

According to INCORA, the programs never got off to a decent start because INDERENA neglected to hire sufficiently qualified technical personnel. Furthermore, the forest reserve plan was cancelled; after an "appropriate" area had been selected, it was found that a number of colonos had already claimed land within the chosen site and it was too sensitive an issue, politically and socially, to force their eviction; besides, the area was too large to protect it from subsequent "invasions." In 1977, a World Bank mission visiting Caquetá determined that INDERENA had accomplished so little work that a new plan of action would have to be drawn up. Shortly afterward, a research team of INDERENA and INCORA technicians and administrators was given a short orientation tour of Caquetá by plane. The plane crashed, killing the pilot and injuring several passengers. This incident provoked ill feelings about the program, further delaying progress. The nurseries were built, but the seedlings never arrived. Investigative plots were set up in the cordillera, but the equipment to measure the impact of rainfall on the soils under varying conditions (after burning, cropping, grazing) never arrived.

When a Bank mission visited Caquetá in September, 1978, and found that INDERENA had still failed to accomplish its goals, it was decided that the original agreement should be cancelled. INDERENA persuaded the Bank and INCORA to reconsider, admitting that they had committed many administrative errors and were prepared to change. At present, INDERENA maintains responsibility for the nursery and reforestation program; all other programs have been suspended except the antierosion soil studies that are being conducted by ICA.

Project update.—Since my return to the United States from Caquetá in January 1979, I have received many letters from members of the Caquetá INCORA staff which indicate that the economic, social, and political conditions of the region have deteriorated, and that both the Phase 2 Project and Caquetá generally are passing through a critically difficult period. The letters repeatedly mention three interrelated problem areas: (1) the adverse consequences of Caquetá's devastating December 1978–April 1979 summer; (2) the financial crisis of the Project, and (3) the political instability of the region and increased repression.

An INCORA technician describes the 1979 summer, and its consequences in three letters, as follows:

> *February 12, 1979*
>
> Caquetá is in sad shape . . . the jungle burning that is done yearly, this year has spread to the pasture and these poor people can barely protect their corrals and homes from burning also. The summer is particularly harsh this year, the cattle are very thin. . . . I feel sorry for the INCORA borrowers who must take their cattle to other farms for feeding, and even graver, the subsistence crops are being destroyed by the fires. The situation for the next six months will be critical. In the zone of Puerto Rico 400 farms were burned down; it is desolate there.
>
> *April 26, 1979*
>
> The situation for the farmer is critical, food is scarce, the cattle are starving because of the intense summer . . . and then there was a worm plague that destroyed the crops. The cattle are selling at extremely low prices, especially in San Vicente de Caguán.
>
> *June 1, 1979*
>
> The nutritional situation of the farmers is now very difficult, as I told you earlier, the harvests failed and at least ten months will pass before the situation normalizes. Perhaps you could propose that we be sent international assistance from some institution like CARE, to bring food immediately, because it is grave here. . . . with lowered resistance to diseases like malaria, typhus, and even tuberculosis. So far the only assistance has been to provide seeds for pasture . . . the most important need is food, for good health stems from good nutrition. The government officials from Caquetá have traveled to Bogotá to present their grievances before the central government, but from there nothing happens.

A letter from an INCORA zone chief presents further details: "As to the farmers, it pains me to inform you that this year they have suffered the consequences of uncontrolled fires, the majority of the pasture was destroyed, and the crops have been lashed by a worm plague that has destroyed 60 percent of the harvest."

Other letters repeat the same story. It appears that the uncontrolled fires and the worm plague have had dire economic consequences for Caquetá's farmers: burnt grazing land, a sharp decline in cattle prices, a ruined harvest, and severe food shortages resulting in disease epidemics. Undoubtedly the poorest farmers will suffer most due to their dependence upon their harvests for food consumption; though the middle-level farmers with small and medium-sized herds of cattle (typical INCORA credit recipients) are also placed in an extremely precarious situation. They may not be able to make their loan payments if the cattle market remains depressed or if they experience difficulty reseeding pasture that was burned.

Caquetá farmers have no access to insurance against natural catastrophes, nor does the INCORA Project offer guarantees to protect its borrowers from such catastrophes, other than personal accident and life insurance. In different parts of the world, including Caquetá, traditional farmers depend upon high interest "emergency" loans after natural disasters take place, often borrowing from private moneylenders to avoid lengthy loan procedures. This kind of credit arrangement usually leads to long-term indebtedness. In a predisaster insurance program, small yearly payments by farmers would qualify them for emergency low interest loans and technical assistance, immediately after such events occurred (plague, fire, flood, etc.) for which they were insured.

Low interest loans for declared disaster areas are available to farmers in the United States, where such events are quite unusual, but to my knowledge have not been instituted in traditional farm areas of Latin America, where natural disasters take place more frequently. Even as an experiment, it is important that the government of the Intendencia of Caquetá, and particularly INCORA and the World Bank, consider the implementation of a low cost natural disaster insurance plan to protect Caquetá farmers in the years to come. Considering the apathy shown by the local and central governments to date, however, and further financial problems described later, it seems unlikely that the present leadership would be willing or able to initiate this kind of assistance in the foreseeable future.

The present financial crisis through which the Phase 2 Project is passing has been discussed earlier in this chapter, and is updated here by letters from another INCORA technician. The last two letters also describe the national financial and political status of INCORA and other development institutions.

> *May 5, 1979*
>
> The credit program is stagnating . . . cattle will be delivered only to farmers in Cartagena and Belén this year . . . 10 million pesos worth [approximately 60 loans]. All of us are working as always, suffering from adverse climatic and social conditions, sunk into underdevelopment. I am truly bored here, and looking around for work elsewhere.

May 24, 1979

All of the decentralized institutions are in a grave economic situation. INCORA has a deficit of 850 million pesos for 1979 . . . the supply of credit has been curtailed by 80 percent. This has resulted in persecution of public employees, for many are being fired from projects around the country.

July 31, 1979

A few days ago the National Congress met to decide upon the 1980 budget. It looks like INCORA will receive very little, thus our institution suffers from financial collapse due to political whims. On the other hand, other newer rural development institutions like DRI and PAN have been given reasonably good economic backing. We can see clearly that the intention of our government is to elaborate new projects for experimentation, which in reality have the same purpose as the older development programs.

As to Project Caquetá, its progress depends upon the aforementioned situation. The credit program continues to stagnate while unnecessary bureaucratic personnel are being appointed. At present, the policy of INCORA is to appoint people because of political connections rather than professional ability.

In chapter 1, the history of INCORA since its creation in 1961 was described in some detail. Even in the early 1970s, INCORA was losing its power, having former areas of responsibility diverted to newer agencies, such as DRI and PAN. The main motive for the changes was political, to reverse and eliminate the land reform movement and substitute in its place more politically feasible projects like colonization and integrated rural services for small farmers. Apparently the disintegration of INCORA is continuing through the gradual cutback of funds and the replacement of committed, qualified personnel with political appointments. Those who suffer are INCORA's employees and all of the actual and potential rural beneficiaries of INCORA's projects nationwide.

The current political situation in Caquetá is very tense. Guerrilla insurgents (principally the Revolutionary Armed Forces of Colombia, FARC) have been active in Caquetá since the 1950s era of "La Violencia." Their "membership" includes professionals, students, and peasants, particularly young rural men. They exercise significant control over certain areas of Caquetá; the rural community at large lends them passive support by "playing dumb" when questioned by counterinsurgency soldiers.

It is difficult to know whether peasant cooperation stems mainly from fear or from sincere support for the guerrillas' ideas and activities in the region. Both explanations play a part, but in the case of poor farmers, the latter explanation is probably dominant. The guerrillas are appreciated because they protect the rural communities from bandits and cattle thieves, who used to be a big problem and no longer are. In addition, their victims or "hit-list" have included certain large landholders and town merchants who consistently exploited workers and consumers with very low wages and very high prices, and also several policemen who were known to have abused innocent people. The fear stems from the guerrillas' history of "knocking off" anyone (peasant, large landowner, merchant, government official) who cooperates with the police or military in their counterinsurgency activities. Wealthy Caquetá ranchers are subjected to frequent extortion for money and arms; most cooperate and are unharmed, some leave Caquetá out of fear, and a few refuse to cooperate and are killed.

In August 1978, the civilian intendente of Caquetá was replaced by a military colonel; according to rumors the central government in Bogotá had essentially labeled Caquetá "una zona roja," a red zone. Guerrilla assaults intensified in response to the military appointment, and nearly every weekend included some small town. Shops, banks, and drugstores were robbed; violent confrontations took place. INCORA offices in Cartagena were robbed, but no one was hurt. At that time the guerrilla and INCORA had a somewhat benign relationship; neither aggressed against the other. An INCORA engineer who once met with a few insurgents and had a short conversation with them, told me that they believed INCORA represented "a teaspoon of honey in a sea of ice." In other words, though INCORA's activities benefit a few rural communities, its work is insignificant considering the magnitude of the agrarian problem and of rural suffering.

Since I left Caquetá, the counterinsurgency movement has intensified considerably. The following quotes from letters received from three different INCORA employees indicate that the activities of both the insurgents and the counterinsurgents, with the peasantry caught in between, have escalated into a near warlike situation:

> *May 14, 1979*
>
> The situation of public order in Caquetá continues to be very bad; the famous counterinsurgents are torturing

> peasants; for which reason they are abandoning their farms. Last Friday, another assault took place in Belén—the judge, the commander, two policemen, and one guerrillero died. Saturday, a confrontation took place in Florencia with several deaths.
>
> *June 1, 1979*
>
> The public order situation continues as always to be disturbing; the people continue to be unsatisfied with the negligence displayed by local leadership.
>
> *August 8, 1979*
>
> The farmers have been victims of the unrestrained repression of the local military and counterinsurgents; some INCORA borrowers have disappeared, while others have been forced to leave their land.
>
> Furthermore, imagine that they *boletearon*, that is, they threatened the lives of the following INCORA employees if they don't get out of Caquetá: [a veterinarian, a credit supervisor, and an administrator].

These letters and others I have received state that Caquetá farmers are being terrorized by counterinsurgents who are determined to eliminate peasant support for the guerrilla. Terror is taking the form of torture, "disappearances," and the forced abandonment of farms. In response to increased military repression, it seems that the insurgents have widened their sphere of targets; INCORA, to some degree, is now included (the third letter, second paragraph, refers to guerrilla threats).

It is difficult to say whether the three threatened INCORA employees were singled out because of individual "indiscretions" on their part, or because INCORA as a government institution was selected for attack. It may also be that INCORA has cooperated with the new military intendente in recent counterinsurgency efforts, and is enduring the consequences. Or perhaps the threats were made by "stray" insurgents, apart from any premeditated strategy. In any case, the current political situation will undoubtedly affect INCORA's activities in Caquetá, though I have no information about recent changes in those activities that specifically relate to the political climate.

In the short run, INCORA will have to resolve two sensitive problems: (1) how to handle the uneasiness felt by field agents (credit supervisors, social extension workers, veterinarians) working in the midst of violent confrontations, and (2) what measures can be taken to protect at least INCORA borrowers from "unrestrained" military repression. In the long run, INCORA's overall presence in Caquetá will require serious reevaluation in light of current political conditions. It may be that the central government has already decided to gradually curtail INCORA's presence through reduction of funds and personnel. Certainly the reduction of funds, current Project stagnation, and the increased militarization of the "red zone" are interrelated government policies. No one is speculating about what the final outcome shall be; as yet it remains unclear.

Summary

In chapter 2, I discussed the experiences of Colombian rural migrants who have settled on public, marginal land in Caquetá with the hope of establishing viable farm enterprises. It was argued that economic opportunities for Caquetá colonos vary considerably, depending upon the "preconditions" particular to each settler family, i.e., initial wealth, location of farm, technical expertise, access to credit, etc. Nonetheless, nearly all colonos are troubled by unstable earnings, caused by adverse agroclimatic and market conditions, that result in generally poor living standards. In other words, while economic and social mobility are possible in Caquetá, many obstacles lie in the way of their achievement.

In chapter 3, I discussed the efforts of the Colombian Institute for Agrarian Reform (INCORA) to alleviate the aforementioned obstacles by supplying land titles, credit, access roads, and a variety of social services to "eligible" low-income Caquetá settlers. Since 1963, approximately U.S.$50 million has been invested in Project Caquetá 1 and the Caquetá Land Settlement Project, Phases 1 and 2, over half from USAID and World Bank loans.

The stated objectives of INCORA projects nationwide correspond with the objectives of Colombia's Social Agrarian Reform Law 135, 1961, and are similar to the current policy directives of the World Bank. These objectives and directives have led to the adoption of a development approach which aims to raise the standard of living of deprived agrarian regions by increasing farm productivity and income through the use of modern techniques, and by providing a variety of integrated services related to basic human needs; hence, the name "integrated rural development."

In Caquetá the implementation of this development approach has been moderately successful. INCORA and World Bank planners were able to learn from past errors, make subsequent improvements, and expand their programs and budgets according to evident needs.

For instance, several Phase 1 errors and inadequacies were corrected in the appraisal of Phase 2 by enlisting the support of local development-related government agencies for a variety of programs, and by increasing the percentage of Project funding for the health, education, and road development programs.

The INCORA programs have reached a significant portion of the rural population of Caquetá, estimated at 22,000 families in 1978. Between 1963 and September 1978, INCORA granted 17,500 land titles, distributed over 9,000 loans, sponsored over 1,000 mini-courses, built 409 kilometers of roads, and constructed 68 schools and 9 health facilities. In human terms, thousands of farmers received credit and technical assistance at subsidized rates; over 3,000 children were provided with accessible schools; over 8,000 families directly benefited from road construction, and approximately 4,000 rural and small town families now live within reasonable distance of INCORA health facilities. Thus, although most of the INCORA programs fell far short of their original targets, they have still had a strong impact on Caquetá, benefitting thousands of poor rural settlers.

Nevertheless, several basic problems with the projects have not been resolved, or were simply never recognized. One is the accelerating process of land concentration in Caquetá, particularly within the most fertile and accessible areas, as wealthier migrants arrive and purchase the cleared plots of earlier settlers. INCORA has not discouraged this process, and may even stimulate it by enforcing farm size limitations on public, uncolonized land, but not on purchased, privately owned land. Another limitation is the credit-in-kind (cattle) program's coverage of only medium-sized land owners, with 10 to 20 hectares in pasture, essentially excluding the hillside minifundistas, newcomers, and the very poorest farmers. Furthermore, cattle quality is erratic and often poor, placing an unjustified burden on the unfortunate borrowers who receive sub-normal quality animals. Other problems include: (1) low motivation and commitment on the part of credit supervisors and technical professionals; (2) inadequate ongoing technical and social extension work, and (3) an excessive emphasis on cattle raising as opposed to more diversified (hence, more secure) farm development.

Financial problems have plagued INCORA projects since the early sixties; in Phase 2 the situation is especially critical. Nearly all of the agreements with outside agencies (Caminos Vecinales, INPES, ISP, ICCE, INDERENA) are in difficulty because of inadequate financing from the national government in Bogotá, and consequent delays in loan disbursements from the World Bank.

In large part, INCORA's financial troubles in Caquetá result from the inevitable costliness of government-assisted colonization projects as compared to assistance provided to the more developed and populated rural interior. As a result, even when monetary outlays are relatively large, they remain inadequate to cover very high and rising costs.

It appears that these financial problems will intensify in the future because of INCORA's decreasing status vis-à-vis overall government policies and budget appropriations. Newer rural development agencies, particularly the Colombian DRI (Integrated Rural Development), are now in the limelight, while the enthusiasm that originally surrounded the creation of INCORA in the early sixties is almost gone. I repeat a statement quoted earlier in this chapter: "The amount of input and the form in which it is supplied—its 'technical' aspects—are secondary in importance to the quality of commitment and power of the supplying institution."

The present Colombian administration has demonstrated a low level of commitment to INCORA by authorizing a gradual curtailment of its funds and personnel. As a result, INCORA is less able to meet its projected goals and to maintain high level motivation among its staff. The impact of INCORA's diminishing power is very evident in Caquetá, where the Phase 2 Project is stagnating.

This is the basic problem involved in government-sponsored rural assistance projects; their programs and beneficiaries are too dependent upon the political decisions of fickle government administrations. While long-term commitment is the essential ingredient for the success of any integrated rural development project, that is precisely the ingredient which is most often lacking.

In the next chapter, I analyze the impact of the INCORA credit and technical assistance program, Phases 1 and 2, on the productivity and income levels of selected INCORA borrowers. Their current (1978) economic situations are compared with their preloan situations and also to the current productivity and income levels of similar rural families who have not received INCORA credit. The World Bank has assessed the economic life of the Caquetá Land Settlement Project at twenty-three years (1972–1995), fifteen years of loan amortization for Phase 1 and 2 borrowers followed by eight years of "free" herd development. Consequently, the statistics and evaluative statements presented in chapter 4 indicate the probable outcome of the credit program at full development, but are not definitive.

Notes

1. Instituto Colombiano de la Reforma Agraria, *Cinco años de reforma agraria* (Bogotá: INCORA, October 1967), pp. 5–7.

2. The material covered in this section, and throughout Chapter 3, is largely based on INCORA and World Bank published and unpublished reports as well as informal interviews with INCORA personnel (see Bibliography for list of reports). Material which is based on my interviews with Caquetá farmers is clarified as it is presented in the text.

3. Information collected from the INCORA legal advisor of the Legal Section, Florencia, Caquetá, December 1978.

4. Ralph Leon Roberts, "Migration and Colonization in Colombian Amazonia: Agrarian Reform or Neo-Latifundismo." (Ph.D. dissertation, University of New York, Syracuse, 1975), Abstract.

5. Information collected from the INCORA credit manager, Farm Settlement Section, Florencia, Caquetá, December 1978.

6. Instituto Colombiano de la Reforma Agraria, *Proyecto Caquetá 1* (Bogotá: INCORA, Oficina de Divulgación, May 1972), p. 15.

7. Ibid., pp. 14–16 and table on Summary of Investments, p. 30.

8. International Bank for Reconstruction and Development (World Bank), *Caquetá Rural Settlement Project Appraisal Report No. 501a–CO*, Annex 2, "The Status of Bank Group Operations in Colombia (as of March 31, 1975)" (Washington, D.C.: World Bank, May 1975), pp 1–2. The rest of the World Bank loans to Colombia were allocated as follows: 30.5 percent—power; 20 percent—industry; 20.4 percent—transportation; 14.1 percent—water supply; and 3 percent—education.

9. World Bank, *Report: News of the World Bank.* "Rural Development," footnote 1 (Washington, D.C.: World Bank Department of Information and Public Affairs, September/October 1977).

10. For a description and criticism of traditional growth strategies, see: Denis Goulet, *The Cruel Choice* (New York: Atheneum, 1975), and John McHale and Magda Cornell, *Basic Human Needs: A Framework for Action* (New Jersey: Rutgers State University, Transaction Books, 1978). The GNP and growth rate figures used in the text are from the preface to the paperback edition of *The Cruel Choice*, p. XIII.

11. World Bank, *Report*, "Rural Development," pp. 1–2.

12. Judith Tendler, *Inter-country Evaluation of Small Farmer Organizations. A.I.D. and Small Farmer Organizations: Lessons of the Honduran Experience* (Washington, D.C.: Office of Development Programs of the Latin American Bureau of A.I.D., 1976), p. 127.

13. World Bank, *Caquetá Project Appraisal Report*, "Benefits and Justification," pp. 22–23.

14. M.L. Gomez; J. F. Gonzalez; N. I. Laverde; and Z. Torres, "Incidencia socioeconómica del Proyecto de Colonización del Caquetá—etapa 1" Graduate thesis (Bogotá: Universidad Santo Tomás de Aquino, September 1977). See the section, "Evaluación económica del proyecto" for the methodology used to calculate "the effective interest rate" of the World Bank loan to the Republic of Colombia.

15. World Bank, *Project Performance Audit Report: Colombia, Caquetá Land Colonization Project (Loan 739–CO)*, Annex 6 (Washington, D.C.: World Bank, 1978).

16. Ibid., p. 23, para. 61, and in the attached *Caquetá Land Colonization Project Completion Report*, p. A.10, para. .01.

17. Ibid., p. 14, paras. 37–38.

18. Ibid., p. 11, para. 29. The report goes on to say, "From one perspective the Banco Ganadero's view is quite correct; given the required infrastructure and labor, it is much more economical for producers to work with additional cattle, especially in the light of prevailing costs of subloan funds and meat and milk prices. The only justification for limiting loans to smaller size is the desire to assist a large number of producers with the scarce resources available, hoping to provide them with additional loans during future programs."

19. Data collected from the Credit Department of INCORA, Florencia, a summary of Phase 1 credit through October 1978.

20 World Bank, *Project Performance Audit Report*, p. 14, para. 35.

21. Ibid., p. 4, para. 11; p. 7, para. 7; Annexes 5 and 6, and confirmed by the INCORA Engineering Section, Florencia, Caquetá.

22. Ibid., p. 5, para. 13, and World Bank, *Caquetá Project Appraisal Report*, Annex 6. The list of problems that follows in the text is adapted from the above reports and from conversations with the INCORA engineering staff in Florencia, Caquetá, December 1979.

23. In an INCORA Planning Department study of a road begun during Phase 1 and completed during Phase 2, entitled *Evaluación social de la via Albania-Curillo*, January 1978, the author (an economist) determined that the radius of influence of the road was 7.95 kilometers on either side. This figure, though only a rough estimate, is based on extensive interviews in the area, land surveys, and an analysis of the marketing situation; it is similar to estimates calculated by the INCORA Engineering Section.

24. INCORA, *Estudio sobre puestos de salud construidos fase 1* (Florencia: Capacitación Campesina, March 1977).

25. Ibid. Patient attendance averages are based on interviews with medical personnel at each of the INCORA health facilities.

26. World Bank, *Project Completion Report*, p. A.14, para. 10.01.

27. Quoted from a letter from the Acting General Manager of INCORA, Juan José Rodríguez, to the Director of the Operations Evaluation Department of the World Bank, Mr. Shiv K. Kapur; Re: First Caquetá Project, Loan 739-CO, June 1978, p. 1.

28. Data collected from the INCORA Planning Department, Florencia, a summary of Phase 2 accomplishments and costs, original and revised; and from the World Bank, *Caquetá Project Appraisal Report*, May 1975, p. 13. The 1976 exchange rate (U.S.$1 = Col.$34) is used.

29. Government policies vis-à-vis the Banco Ganadero and the Caja Agraria were explained in interviews with the statistical advisor of the INCORA Planning Department, Florencia; the financial difficulties of the Caja Agraria were confirmed in a presentation given by the Caja's General Manager in Florencia, November 1978.

30. World Bank, *Caquetá Project Appraisal Report*, p. 19, para. 6.09.

31. Data collected from the INCORA Credit Department, Florencia, a summary of Phase 2 credit through October 1978.

32. Owing to the 1978 presidential election (the Liberal candidate Turbay Ayala won), and the appointment of a new INCORA director, the INCORA Board of Directors was delayed in making routine decisions on construction bids, emergency funds, hiring new personnel, etc. These delays and the general bureaucratic shake-up slowed progress by over six months on certain INCORA projects and programs nationwide, including in Caquetá.

33. Inadequate government support for rural extension work and low motivation among agricultural and social extensionists is a common problem throughout the underdeveloped world, particularly in marginal areas and in projects directed toward poor farmers. For further discussion on the extension issue, see Tendler, *Inter-Country Evaluation of Small Farmer Organizations*, pp. 106–118, and Tendler, *Piaui: Renters and Sharecroppers* (Washington, D.C.: A report for the World Bank, 1978), pp. 76–78.

34. Data collected from the Rural Training Department (Capacitación Campesina) of the Farm Settlement Section, INCORA, Florencia, Caquetá, December 1978, a summary of rural training activities from 1976 through September 1978.

35. Data collected from the INCORA Planning Department, Florencia, Caquetá, December 1978, a summary of Phase 2 accomplishments and costs, original and revised.

36. According to the engineering staff of the INCORA Engineering Section, Florencia, none of the INCORA-built roads in Caquetá could be considered first or even second category quality. Ideally, they suggest, the roads should be paved with asphalt, one of Caquetá's native resources, to prevent rapid deterioration.

37. World Bank, *Project Performance Audit Report*, pp. 7–8, para. 20.

38. Information taken from the *Caminos Vecinales-INCORA Convenio, fase* 2, June 1975, on file in the office of the Project Manager, INCORA, Florencia.

39. These and other similar letters are on file in the office of the Engineering Section, INCORA, Florencia.

40. Data collected from the SEM (Servicio Nacional de Eradicación de la Malaria) office in Florencia, December 1978.

41. Information taken from the *INDERENA-INCORA Convenio, fase 2*, 1975, on file in the office of the Project Manager, INCORA, Florencia.

4

The Impact of Livestock Credit on Caquetá Farmers

In the previous chapter, the overall objectives and accomplishments of the Colombian Government's rural development and colonization projects in Caquetá since 1962 were discussed. This chapter focuses on the socioeconomic impact of the INCORA/World Bank credit program on selected rural beneficiaries. The findings presented are based on data collected from interviews with eighty-five rural Caquetá families (fifty credit recipients and thirty-five nonrecipients). The interviews were carried out by the writer, together with members of the INCORA Monitoring Unit (Unidad de Seguimiento), between August 1978, and January 1979. The unit members and the writer shared the same resource base and worked side by side over an extended time, though the analysis of their mutual findings was conducted separately.

Sample Selection Process

During the negotiations of the Phase 2 loan agreement, the World Bank recommended that INCORA establish an evaluation and monitoring unit in Caquetá to conduct continuous studies of the socioeconomic impact of Phase 2 programs, focusing on the credit program. The unit would be composed of three professionals and six field agents, and a random sample of beneficiaries would be used as informants. It was presumed that these studies would enable both INCORA and the World Bank to compare actual achievements with stated goals during the program's implementation, indicating the need for remedial measures as errors or setbacks became apparent.

Furthermore, the unit would provide important data and recommendations for future planning, if and when a third phase of the Project was approved.

Originally the Monitoring Unit was planned to evaluate only Phase 2 credit recipients who received credit during the first two years of the program (September 1976–September 1978). According to plan, 1,250 families should have received credit in that two-year interval, though in reality, by September 1978, only 802 families had benefited. The sample for study was selected from the original target universe of beneficiaries.

Employing a universe of 1,250 families, the following formula was applied to select a significantly representative sample:

$$n_i = \frac{k^2 \cdot N \cdot T^2}{k^2 \cdot T^2 + (N-1)E^2}$$

where

n_i = size of sample
N = Universe (1,250)
k = Limit of confidence (1.96 for 95 percent confidence)
T = Typical deviation (29.183 calculated from an estimated sample of 88 families)
E = Limit of error (5.625, or 7.5 percent, of a sample size estimated at 6 percent of the universe).

The equation gives a value of 95.57 for n_i, or a sample size of 96 families.

The 96 families were selected randomly from the total universe (1,250), with a geographic adjustment to assure that the sample number per credit zone corresponded proportionately to the total number of borrowers per zone.

When World Bank and INCORA representatives met in the spring of 1978 to discuss the selected sample and the objectives of the impact study, they realized that it was unrealistic to presume that measurable changes in income and living standards would be evident after only one or two years of credit experience and, therefore, it was a mistake to include only Phase 2 borrowers (beginning in 1976) in the study. Consequently, the original plan was revised to include Phase 1 borrowers as well (beginning in 1972).

To assure a significantly representative and random sample, this major revision in plans would have required a completely new selection process, using a larger universe. Consequently, due to time constraints, it was decided that a nonrandom list of Phase 1 borrowers, selected by the zone chiefs, would simply be added to the original random sample of Phase 2 borrowers, giving a total sample of "mixed" randomness.

The credit chiefs were instructed to choose Phase 1 borrowers based on two criteria: (1) that they generally represent the circumstances and conditions of the zone as a whole; and (2) that they be willing to participate in interviews and keep track of monthly income and expenses in a written register.

For the initial interview schedule, beginning August 1978, the sample included twenty-seven Phase 1 borrowers and twenty-six Phase 2 borrowers, giving a total of 53 families. (The twenty-six, selected from the total random sample of ninety-six, received credit prior to June 1977. The remaining seventy, who received credit after June 1977, will be included in the study at a later time.) Subsequently, eight of the Phase 2 borrowers were eliminated either because they were unwilling to cooperate with the study or because their credit situation was too precarious (probable cancellation of credit or farm relocation). Thus, the final initial interview sample included twenty-seven Phase 1 borrowers and eighteen Phase 2 borrowers, a total of forty-five families. I personally conducted five additional interviews (three Phase 1; two Phase 2), to bring the sample number to an even fifty.

In addition to the interview sample of fifty credit recipients, at the writer's suggestion the Unidad de Seguimiento decided to interview thirty-five farmers who had not received INCORA credit, as a basis for comparison. The non-credit farmers were chosen from lists of credit applicants at the nine regional INCORA Caquetá offices. It was thought that farmers who were interested in receiving INCORA credit (credit applicants) would be more willing to cooperate with the Monitoring Unit than Caquetá farmers chosen at random. In view of time limitations, the credit applicants were selected based on their geographic proximity to the sample credit recipients, allowing both sets of interviews to be conducted in the same general area and time span.

In sum, the findings presented in this chapter are based on interviews with 85 Caquetá rural families: 30 Phase 1 borrowers, 20 Phase 2 borrowers, and 35 nonborrowers. The credit recipients represent approximately two percent of the total "universe" of Phase 1 and 2 INCORA borrowers, 50 out of 2,519 (through September 1978, 1,717 Phase 1 and 802 Phase 2). The Phase 1 sample was chosen by credit chiefs with "representativeness" as a criterion for selection, the Phase 2 sample was chosen randomly with a geographic adjustment and the nonborrowers were chosen based on their desire to receive credit and their geographic proximity to the previously-selected credit recipients. Interviews were conducted by INCORA professionals, credit supervisors, and myself over a period of five months, from August 1978 to January 1979. A sample of the interview form is presented in Appendix 2.

Before the commencement of the interviews, the Unidad de Seguimiento (myself included) met with the Caquetá Project manager to discuss the objectives and plan the chronological activities of the two-year evaluation study. We agreed upon the following objectives and activities:

1. The initial interviews will involve three- to four-hour visits per farmer and should be as informal and congenial as possible, with confidentiality assured. Essential to the success of the interviews will be the ability of the interviewers to obtain the trust of the interviewees.
2. Each family will be issued a notebook and pen to use as a register for daily expenses and earnings, to be kept in as detailed a form as possible, itemized according to articles and value. For example:

August 16

Expenses		Earnings	
1 pound salt	4 pesos	1 day's wages	200 pesos
1 package cigarettes	15 pesos	15 eggs sold	45 pesos
1 ax	150 pesos		

At the end of each month, the credit supervisors will review the notebooks, provide needed assistance, and copy and send the data entries to the head of the Monitoring Unit in Florencia for evaluation. The registers will enable both the farmers and the evaluators to collect reliable, detailed data on rural expenses and income, and to measure and evaluate changes in conditions over time.

3. Every three months, the professionals of the Unit will return to the farms of the participants to review the notebooks personally and discuss the implications of the entries, that is, how to more efficiently invest and spend income; how to improve the development and utilization of farm assets; how to use local resources and income to improve living standards, etc. For example: a farmer, who never before kept a written register of earnings and expenses, now records all of the costs of growing and harvesting 10 hectares of corn as well as the income derived from its sale; he

discovers through simple calculations that the costs exceed income earned. If the cost/benefit analysis turns out to be unfavorable for two or three consecutive years, then the farmer may decide that his efforts and money would be better spent in another activity (a different crop, raising pigs, selling wood, etc.). In this way, the register may influence farmers to make wiser economic decisions (given that viable investment alternatives exist) and, by providing empirical evidence, may contribute to wiser economic planning by INCORA technicians.

4. Subsequent shorter interviews (above six) will be conducted by the credit supervisors to obtain current data on the income, productivity, and living standards of the participants over a two-year period, facilitating an evaluation of the credit program through measurement of change.
5. In addition to the evaluation of the credit program, the Monitoring Unit will conduct impact studies on the road development, health, and education programs, and will monitor the progress of all government institutions participating in the Project programs.
6. In summary, the duties of the Unit will be to collect, consolidate, and analyze detailed information on Project programs for presentation in trimester evaluation reports for INCORA and the World Bank. The reports, including recommendations, will contribute to future modifications and improvements of the Caquetá Land Settlement Project 2, as well as possible subsequent projects.

Aggregate Data on Income

My decision to compare INCORA credit recipients with nonrecipients was based on the assumption that credit is important in explaining long-run positive changes in income and living standards of Caquetá farmers. Nevertheless, when exploring the determinants of change in income, a variety of influential variables require analysis, even when focusing on credit. Otherwise, credit may be given undeserved importance in explaining either positive or negative income changes. Moreover, in an unstable dynamic environment such as rural Caquetá, it would be empirically impossible to isolate the impact of credit from all other intervening factors.

Correlation Tests

In view of the above, before presenting disaggregated data from borrowers and nonborrowers, the income levels of all eighty-five interviewees are considered in terms of several independent variables, including credit. Table 14 ranks average gross annual income in ten

TABLE 14

Study of 85 Surveyed Families, Gross Income Correlated with Seven Independent Variables, 1978

Gross income distribution	Col. 1 Annual mean income[h] (Col.$)	Col. 2[a] Mean farm size (hectares)	Col. 3[b] Mean herd size (head)	Col. 4[c] Mean hectares in pasture	Col. 5[d] Mean hectares in crops	Col. 6[e] Mean percent with credit[i]	Col. 7[f] Mean years on farm[j] (percent)	Col. 8[g] Mean distance to town[k] (percent)
Bottom 10%	31,371	63	16	28	5	25	25	63
10–19	47,247	115	26	46	7	55	—	56
20–29	60,963	120	25	37	7	25	—	50
30–39	74,559	84	23	41	7	55	33	56
40–49	90,675	96	44	45	8	75	36	38
50–59	107,307	103	37	45	9	77	33	78
60–69	132,855	96	49	51	11	63	50	50
70–79	155,583	162	62	80	10	44	33	45
80–89	210,015	127	79	85	9	75	36	13
Top 10%	383,175	177	104	113	14	89	44	22
	129,375[l]							

[a]Using the rank correlation test, where

$$r' = 1 - \frac{6\,(\Sigma d^2)}{n(n^2 - 1)} \text{ and } z = r'\sqrt{n-1}$$

the correlation has .05 level of significance when $-2.262 < z > 2.262$ and 0.1 level of significance when $-1.833 < z > 1.833$, for a small sample size (less than 30 ranks). Correlating gross income with farm size, $n = 10$, $r' = 0.69$, $z = 2.07$, the correlation is positive at 0.1 level of significance.

[b]$n = 10$, $r' = 0.94$, $z = 2.82$; the correlation is positive at 0.05 level of significance.

[c]$n = 10$, $r' = 0.87$, $z = 2.63$; the correlation is positive at 0.05 level of significance.

[d]$n = 10$, $r' = 0.92$, $z = 2.77$; the correlation is positive at 0.05 level of significance.

[e]$n = 10$, $r' = 0.68$, $z = 2.05$; the correlation is positive at 0.10 level of significance.

[f]$n = 10$, $r' = 0.78$, $z = 2.34$; the correlation is positive at 0.05 level of significance.

[g]$n = 10$, $r' = -0.72$, $z - 2.15$; the correlation is inversely positive at 0.10 level of significance.

[h]Includes an imputed value for products grown and consumed on the farm (Col.$20,235), added equally to each income strata.

[i]Percent of INCORA credit recipients.

[j]Percent of families residing 10 years or more on present farm.

[k]Percent of farms located 15 kilometers or less from the nearest town.

[l]Equals annual mean gross income for the total number of families, including an imputed value for products grown and consumed on the farm. Annual mean *monetary* income (subtracting value of products consumed on farm) equals Col.$109,140.

percentile divisions, from lowest to highest, with 8.5 families per division. Gross income (the dependent variable) is correlated with seven independent variables, chosen based on their probable positive impact on income levels. The statistical rank correlation test for small samples (under 30 ranks) is applied in the table footnotes to determine the level of significance of each correlation.

The footnotes show that four of the seven variables—size of herd, hectares in pasture, hectares in crops, and length of residence on farm—correlate positively with gross income at .05 level of significance. In other words, there is only a 5 percent probability that the compared variables are independent of each other and a 95 percent probability that they are related. Thus, higher income among the eighty-five surveyed farmers is determined in part by larger stocks of cattle, more hectares in pasture and crops, and longer residence on their present farms.

Table 14 also indicates the distribution pattern of gross annual income (monetary and in-kind) and distribution of the four related variables: the highest income average is 12 times greater than the lowest; the largest cattle herd is 6.5 times larger than the smallest; and for hectares in pasture, hectares in crops, and length of residence, the differentials are 4 times, 2.8 times, and 1.8 times, respectively. These figures imply that the differentials in farm assets translate into even greater income differentials. For example, Farmer X may earn 40 percent more monetary and in-kind income than Farmer Y, even though the former owns only 20 percent more cattle and 10 percent more hectares in pasture than the latter.

Two of the independent variables—farm size and percentage of INCORA credit recipients—correlate positively with gross income at 0.1 level of significance. This means that some correlation is probably present (90 percent probability), though the correlations are less strong than with the four variables already mentioned.

Table 14 shows that the largest farm size (corresponding to the top income percentile) is 2.8 times larger than the smallest farm size (corresponding to the bottom income percentile), indicating a positive relation between large farms and high incomes. It is noteworthy, however, that relatively large farms (over 100 hectares) occur throughout the income spectrum. That some poor farmers have large-sized farms is not surprising considering that cheap, unfertile land is relatively abundant in Caquetá. In a separate correlation test, relating farm size to distance from Florencia (Caquetá's capital), I found that the variables are positively correlated at .05 level of significance. In other words, among the eighty-five surveyed families, farm size generally increases as the distance from the farm to Florencia (in kilometers) increases. When large farms are located far into the hinterland, the disadvantages of isolation may cancel the advantages of owning more land. This depends upon the capital and labor resources of the farmer and his ability to overcome high transportation costs.

The distribution of the credit variable, defined by the percentage of INCORA credit recipients in each income percentile, is similar to the farm size distribution in that the largest group of recipients (corresponding to the top income percentile) is 3.6 times greater than the smallest group (corresponding to the bottom income percentile), though high percentages of recipients (over 50 percent) are spread throughout the income spectrum. This correlation test tends to substantiate my assumption that credit positively affects income; however, it also shows that some of the wealthier surveyed families are nonborrowers and some of the poorest are borrowers. Comparisons of these two groups are presented in more detail later in the chapter.

The final independent variable, distance from farm to nearest town (the principal town of each credit zone), shows an *inverse* correlation at 0.1 level of significance. In ranking the distances (percent of farms less than 15 kilometers from the nearest town in each income percentile), I assumed that the most prosperous farms would tend to be located closest to the nearest towns, and thus expected to see a low to high progression as in the case of the other six variables. The figures show otherwise; indeed, the wealthiest farmers (top percentile) live 2.9 times farther away from the nearest town than the poorest farmers (bottom percentile). This somewhat surprising finding has three explanations. First, though some of the more prosperous farmers interviewed live far away from the nearest town, their farms are located close to roads, making transportation less costly and time consuming than for farmers who live nearer to town but must walk long distances before reaching the nearest road. Second, a few of the interviewees with farms adjacent to rivers benefit from more fertile land and easily accessible boat transport, tending to offset the drawbacks of isolation. Finally, as mentioned earlier, the disadvantages of isolation are minimized when the farmers possess sufficient capital and labor to develop successful farms. These explanations question the overall validity of the inverse correlation and, at the same time, demonstrate that location of farms in Caquetá (measured in kilometers from the nearest town) is less important to economic mobility than the other six variables.

In sum, using the rank correlation test to determine the relationship between a variety of farm variables and gross income, it was found that the following variables, in order of correlation strength, are positively related to income: size of cattle stock, hectares in crops, hectares in pasture, length of residence on farm, farm size, and INCORA credit. The distance between the farm and the nearest town was shown to be inversely correlated to income, though several explanations make this seemingly surprising outcome more understandable. This list of independent variables by no means exhausts the determinants of income; other possible related factors are family size, education levels, technical training, initial wealth (before migrating to Caquetá), and general attitudes toward work, progress, the future, etc.

Reliability of Gross Income Figures

At this point, it is important to note that of all the sections in the interview form, farmers reacted most sensitively to questions related to income. This reluctance stemmed from the fear that this information would somehow be used against them, either through increased taxes or, for the thirty-five nonborrowers, through denial of credit due to insufficient need. Consequently, even though confidentiality was assured, the actual income levels of the sample families may in fact be 5 percent to 20 percent higher than the recorded figures. The unspecified income is likely to come from activities other than market sales, i.e., wage labor on other farms or small business transactions (trading of goods, animals, labor) among farmers.

In addition, readers should note that total gross income as shown in table 14 and succeeding gross income tables include an imputed value for farm-grown products consumed at home. This information was not available from the interview findings, though it was possible to arrive at rough estimates through the use of secondary sources on the average quantities consumed per rural family of Caquetá's three principal "home consumption" crops and the writer's own findings on prices to producers. The estimated income values are shown in table 15.

Inasmuch as we have no information to differentiate among the quantities of yuca, plantain, and corn consumed by credit recipients and nonrecipients an estimated value must be added equally to income for both groups. Adding the imputed value of home grown and consumed agricultural products (Col.$20,235) to average gross monetary income figures increases gross income by 13.4 percent and 20 percent for credit recipients and applicants, respectively. Understandably, the value of home consumed agricultural products is greater in proportion to total income for the poorer farmers and these products make up a large percentage of their total food intake.

TABLE 15

Imputed Value for Products Grown and Consumed on Farm, 1978

	(1) Average annual home consumption	(2) Average price to Caquetá producer (Col.$)	(1) × (2) Gross income (Col.$)
	(pounds)	(per pound)	
Yuca[a]	3,100	2.85	8,835
Plantain	3,100	2.00	6,200
Corn[b]	2,000	2.60	5,200
Total	8,200 pounds		20,235

[a]According to the PiDelta Ltda. study on Caquetá, Caquetá families consume on average one pound of yuca per family member per day; the same is true for plantain. That adds up to 365 pounds per year per family member multiplied by an average family size of 8.5, totaling 3,100 pounds per year. Prices for yuca and plantain were obtained from my visits to ten local markets throughout Caquetá.

[b]Of an average harvest of 7 cargas (250 pounds/carga) per hectare of corn, approximately 2 cargas are consumed by the family and for animal feeding. Taking an average harvest of 4 hectares of corn per year, that leaves a total of 8 cargas (2,000 pounds) for family consumption and animal feed. In 1978, Caquetá farmers received, on the average, Col.$650 per carga, or Col.$2.60 per pound.

Taking into consideration the possibilities of error, the general validity of this sample's income figures can be ascertained through comparisons with similar previous sample studies. In a thesis by four Colombian economics students on socioeconomic aspects of the Caquetá Land Settlement Project 1 (see chap. 3, n. 14), the average gross annual income of 142 surveyed Phase 1 beneficiaries in 1977, not including the value of products grown and consumed on the farm, was reported at Col.$97,720 or U.S.$2,714 at the 1977 exchange rate. This compares well with our average gross monetary income figure of Col.$109,140, or U.S.$2,729 at the 1978 exchange rate. In the 1972 PiDelta study on colonization in Caquetá, Phase 1 (see chap. 2, n. 20), minimum family net income was estimated at Col.$16,440 per year, or Col.$40,104 in 1978 pesos, given an average inflation rate of 20 percent from 1972 to 1978. Minimum income, for this study, does not include savings nor the value of subsistence crops. Net income is shown to equal approximately one half of gross income, bringing the estimate of minimum gross income to Col.$80,208 per year. This figure is very similar to the median gross income of our survey of farmers, Col.$78,756 (average of fifth and sixth percentiles, subtracting the value of products grown and consumed on farm, $20,235). Hence, the income findings of both the Colombian graduate thesis and the PiDelta study fall into the same general range of this study's findings, which gives greater credibility to the answers of our respondents than if no comparisons had been possible.

The Socioeconomic Impact of Credit

The standard research design for analyzing the causal relationship between some program or activity (the independent variable) and some desired effect (the dependent variable) is illustrated in the diagram which follows.

	Before	After	
Experimental	X_1	X_2	$d = X_2 - X_1$
Control	X'_1	X'_2	$d' = X'_2 - X'_1$

In this design, the experimental and control groups are assumed to be equal prior to the implementation of the program under evaluation. By using a control group, evaluators are able to observe changes that occur in the absence of the experimental program (d′) and within the experimental group (d) over the same time span. Consequently, when d and d′ are compared, their differences can be attributed, at least in part, to the absence or presence of the independent variable under study.

The research design described above would be ideal for the INCORA credit impact study if complete information were available on conditions "before" and "after" the program's implementation. The interviews provide ample information on borrowers and nonborrowers in 1978 (X_2, X'_2), and other INCORA sources provide adequate information on borrowers prior to receiving credit (X_1). Lacking, however, are economic data on the nonborrowing group during the years before borrowers first received credit (X'_1). Unless we can verify that X_1 and X'_1 ("before" conditions) were generally similar, it would be erroneous to assume that differences between borrowers and nonborrowers in 1978 were due to the credit factor rather than fundamental differences in the initial socioeconomic positions of the two groups.

It is essential to substantiate, therefore, that the two surveyed groups (fifty credit recipients and thirty-five credit applicants) were in a similar socioeconomic position prior to the distribution of INCORA credit to the recipient group. This requirement can be satisfied, in part, by examining the responses of credit recipients and nonrecipients to several survey questions concerning their general social and economic histories. Their responses, reported below, indicate that indeed both groups of families shared similar characteristics before the implementation of the credit program:

1. Geographic areas of origin form similar distributions: 16 percent of the borrowers are native Caqueteños; 40 percent are from

Huila; 21 percent are from Tolima, and 14.5 percent are from Caldas and Quindío. Seventeen percent of the nonborrowers are Caqueteños; 38 percent are from Huila; 21 percent are from Tolima, and 17 percent are from Caldas and Quindío.

2. Upon arriving in Caquetá, 56 percent of the borrowers and 60 percent of the nonborrowers had friends and/or relatives already living in Caquetá, giving proportionately similar ''contact'' advantages for both groups.
3. To better understand their initial economic resources, the interviewees were asked what they brought with them to Caquetá as early settlers: 43 percent of the borrowers brought some money; 58 percent brought tools, furniture, and/or farm animals, and 40 percent brought nothing at all. The nonborrowers responded 38 percent, 55 percent, and 45 percent, respectively for each category, indicating similar ''initial'' resource distributions in each group.
4. Length of residence in Caquetá also shows similar distributions: 38 percent of both groups have lived 15 years or less in Caquetá; 17 percent of the borrowers and 27 percent of the nonborrowers arrived over 25 years ago.
5. Family size, age distribution, and number of adults at home are nearly equal for both groups. The borrowers average 6.4 living children per family and 8.86 persons living permanently at home; 52 percent are 16 years or younger and 80 percent are 31 years or younger. Ninety-four percent of the respondents have at least two adults living at home. The nonborrowers average 5.5 living children per family and 8.25 persons in the home; 51 percent are 16 years or younger and 79 percent are 31 or younger. Ninety-six percent have at least two adults at home.
6. One out of four respondents in each group use some form of contraception to plan their families. The reasons most frequently given for not using birth control were: (1) the man of the house does not approve; (2) pills are unsafe, and (3) lack of knowledge about available methods and where to purchase them.
7. Data on education show that 29 percent of the credit borrowing parents received no schooling, and 38 percent considered themselves to be illiterate. Slightly more nonborrowing parents never went to school (34 percent), however, fewer considered themselves to be illiterate (32 percent). Thus, the illiteracy rate for both parent groups is approximately one-third of the total.
8. As an indication of social participation in the community, respondents were asked whether they were members of the local Junta de Acción Comunal. Of the borrowers, 52 percent, and of the nonborrowers 47 percent responded affirmatively.

Beyond these general social and economic indicators of group homogeneity, question 7 of the interview form provides specific data on cattle-related farm assets for borrowers prior to receiving credit, and nonborrowers shortly after settling on their present farm (the majority, less than five years ago). Responses to this question (see table 26) show that the majority of farmers in both groups were not "initially" engaged in viable ranching activities. Less than 50 percent of them had wire fencing, and 20 percent or less had salt trays, corrals, and loading chutes—all standard equipment for raising livestock. Knowing that in Caquetá the primary key to economic mobility is livestock, we can infer from the above figures that most of the surveyed farmers (in both groups) were earning low incomes prior to credit distribution.

In sum, while our data are insufficient to prove that the "before" conditions of borrowers and nonborrowers were equal, from the indicators that are available, one can at least infer that their conditions were similar.

Assuming similarity of "before" conditions for borrowers and nonborrowers (X_1, X'_1), we can determine the socioeconomic impact of INCORA/World Bank credit by comparing the 1978 "after" characteristics of credit recipients with the 1978 "after" characteristics of nonrecipients. Measurement of change is also possible by comparing the economic and social positions of the recipients prior to and after their experiences with INCORA credit. Still, while emphasizing changes induced by credit, it is important to remember that rural Caquetá is a dynamic, unstable society where a variety of other factors are simultaneously changing and influencing change (i.e., climate, health, prices, land values, farm expertise, etc.). Therefore, credit cannot be analyzed in isolation, but only as it affects the situation of the borrowers in their overall environment.

Land Distribution and Farm Size

In Caquetá, the quality and management of land is more important in determining income than actual farm size (excluding the largest landowners). Nevertheless, because the land is typically unfertile and easily eroded, size becomes important as the farmer begins to exhaust his supply of uncleared jungle for annual crops and especially when he moves increasingly toward ranching, which requires large pasture areas (approximately 1 hectare per adult animal) to raise even moderately-sized herds. When this happens, either the farmer must buy new land from neighbors to accommodate more livestock, or rearrange the distribution of his existing

Table 16

Preloan Land Distribution for 50 Credit Recipients

Area[a] (hectares)	Landholdings			Total area			Mean size of landholding[b] (hectares)
	Number	Percent	Cumulative percent	Hectares	Percent	Cumulative percent	
40–50	4	8	8	185	3.3	3.3	46.2
50–99	21	42	50	1,480	26.3	29.6	70.5
100–149	13	26	76	1,511	26.9	56.5	116.2
150–199	6	12	88	1,005	17.9	74.4	167.5
200–249	5	10	98	1,061	18.9	93.3	212.2
250 +	1	2	100	380	6.7	100.0	380.0
Total	50	100		5,622	100.0		

[a]One hectare = 2.47 acres.

[b]Mean landholding size = 112.4 hectares ($\frac{5,622}{50}$). Median landholding size = 94 hectares (50 percent below, 50 percent above).

farm, exchanging nutrient-depleting annual crop cultivation for perennial crops (plantain, sugar cane) and pasture.

Of the fifty surveyed credit recipient farms, in 1978, the mean landholding size was 125 hectares, and the median landholding size was 102.5 hectares (table 17). Forty-eight percent of the farmers held 26.4 percent of the total land area; the four largest farmers (8 percent of total) held 21.1 percent of the total area. The land distribution curve changed little between the pre- and post-loan years (tables 16 and 17).

Compared to the credit recipients, the mean farm size of the credit applicants was 14 percent smaller (108 hectares) and the median farm size was 20 percent smaller (81 hectares) (table 18). Fifty-seven percent of the farmers held 30 percent of the total land area while the two largest farms (5.8 percent of the total) held 20 percent of the total area, a slightly less balanced land distribution pattern than for the credit recipient group both before credit and after credit (see diagram 5).

Though the difference in farm size for credit recipients and credit applicants is not very great, for farmers expanding into ranching, 20 hectares of additional land with which to plant pasture can be a significant advantage. In exploring the reasons why the credit recipients as a group have more land than the credit applicants, three explanations seem probable:

1. The credit recipients generally have lived longer on their present farms than the credit applicants: 22 percent of the credit recipients have lived less than five years on their farms as compared with 54 percent of the credit applicants; likewise 46 percent of the credit recipients have lived more than ten years on their farms as compared to only 20 percent of the credit applicants. Having arrived earlier, the credit recipients were initially able to claim more uncolonized land than the credit applicants.
2. Confirming the above, more credit recipients colonized,—as opposed to purchased,—their farms (18 percent) than credit applicants (8.5 percent). Thirty-eight percent of the credit recipients bought their farms, and another 38 percent bought part and colonized part; the figures for credit applicants are 60 percent and 23 percent, respectively. Thus, when either deciding to or having to buy land, the majority of the credit applicants were limited as to the amount of land they could afford to purchase and by the amount of land available for purchase, given relatively low land values. Caquetá farmers generally do not have sufficient collateral to purchase land on credit, but rather, obtain the land in

Table 17

Land Distribution for 50 Credit Recipients, 1978

Area[a] (hectares)	Landholdings			Total area			Mean size of landholdings[b] (hectares)
	Number	Percent	Cumulative percent	Hectares	Percent	Cumulative percent	
40–50	2	4	4	90	1.4	1.4	45.0
50–99	22	44	48	1,561	25.0	26.4	70.9
100–149	12	24	72	1,457	23.3	49.7	121.4
150–199	5	10	82	790	12.6	62.3	158.0
200–249	5	10	92	1,040	16.6	78.9	208.0
250 +	4	8	100	1,319	21.1	100.0	329.7
Total	50	100		6,257	100.0		

[a]One hectare = 2.47 acres.

[b]Mean landholding size = 125 hectares ($\frac{6,257}{50}$). Median landholding size = 102.5 hectares (50 percent below, 50 percent above).

TABLE 18

Land Distribution for 35 Credit Applicants, 1978

Area[a] (hectares)	Landholdings			Total area			Mean size of landholdings[b] (hectares)
	Number	Percent	Cumulative percent	Hectares	Percent	Cumulative percent	
10–49	5	14.0	14.0	176	5	5	35.2
50–99	15	43.0	57.0	955	25	30	63.7
100–149	7	20.0	77.0	817	22	52	116.7
150–199	3	8.6	85.6	450	12	64	150.0
200–249	3	8.6	94.2	600	16	80	200.0
250 +	2	5.8	100.0	780	20	100	390.0
Total	35	100.0		3,778	100		

[a]One hectare = 2.47 acres.

[b]Mean landholding size = 108 hectares ($\frac{3,778}{35}$). Median landholding size = 81 hectares (50 percent below, 50 percent above).

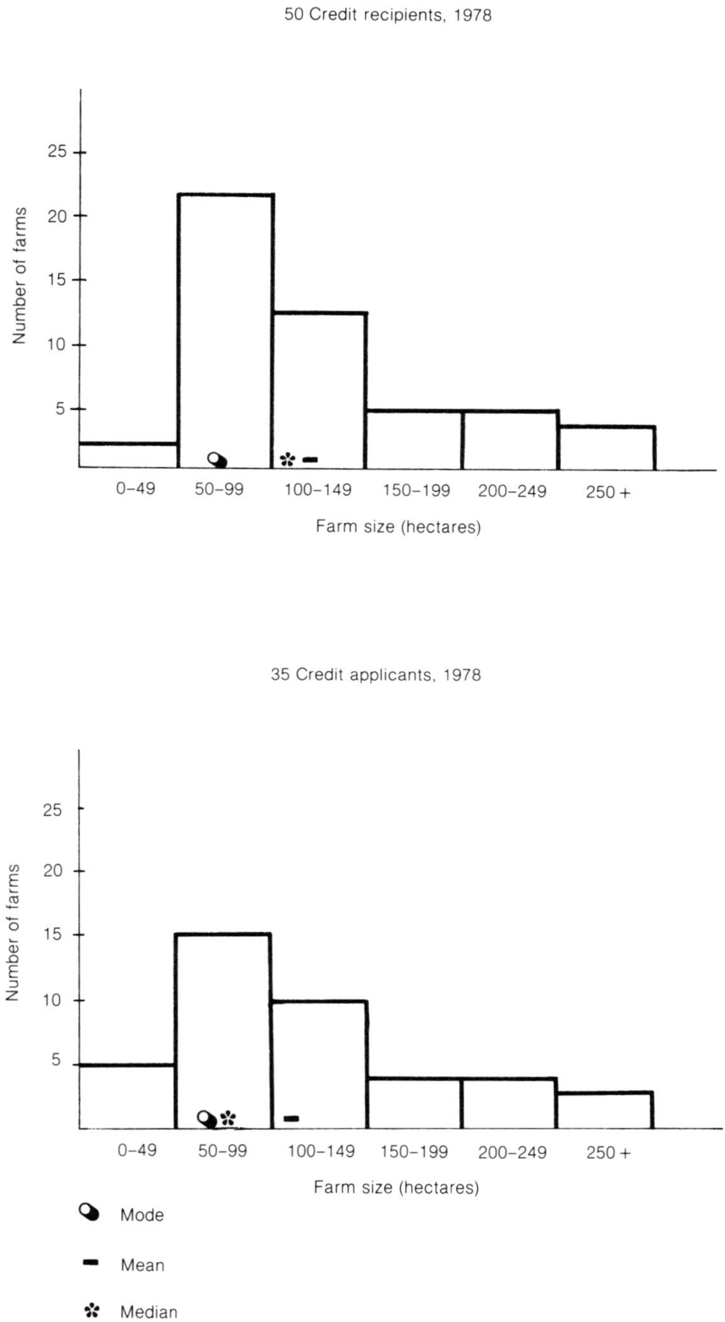

Diagram 5. Farm Size Distribution.

exchange for a combination of assets and cash (hence, interest payments on land do not normally constitute an expense for owners of small and medium-sized farms). Several factors influence in the determination of land values: current average values as calculated by the local tax authorities; what bordering farms have recently sold for; the value of investments made for farm improvements; the need and desire of the farmer to sell his land quickly, and the nature of the relationship between buyer and seller.

3. Tables 16 and 17, which compare the land distribution patterns of credit recipients prior to receiving credit (pre-loan) and after credit (1978), show that the pre-loan median farm size, 94 hectares, was smaller than the post-loan median size, 102.5 hectares, but somewhat larger than the credit applicant median farm size, 81 hectares. The net increase of total farm area for the 50 credit recipients between the time they received credit and 1978 was 635 hectares. This means that, in addition to the initial advantages of the credit recipient group (explanations 1 and 2), the credit factor increased their need to purchase additional land (for grazing the cattle provided through credit) and provided, indirectly, the means to do so (higher gross income).

In short, the median-sized farm of the surveyed credit recipients is 20 percent larger than the corresponding farm of the surveyed credit applicants. Probable explanations are that the credit recipients as a group have lived longer on their present farms; have colonized (as opposed to purchased) a greater percentage of their farms, and, as INCORA credit recipients, have been encouraged to purchase more land for pasture, facilitated by higher gross earnings. Credit does not significantly affect the land distribution curves (comparing pre-loan and post-loan), other than to push the distribution mean upward.

Herd Size and Distribution

Tables 19 through 23 provide data on the size, distribution, and growth of cattle herds for the credit recipient group, "before" and "after" credit, and for the group of credit applicants. Approximately 80 percent of the value of INCORA credit (Phases 1 and 2) is loaned in cattle; therefore, one would expect to observe a significant difference in the mean herd size of credit recipients and nonrecipients, and also in comparing the mean pre-loan and post-loan herd size of the borrowing group. Tables 19–23 demonstrate the quantitative and qualitative character of these differences.

TABLE 19

Farm Animals Inventory on Farms of 48 Credit Recipients, Preloan, 1978

	Preloan			1978						
Farm animals	Farmer-owned	Other[a]	Total	Initial INCORA credit	Total INCORA credit	Farmer-owned	Other[b]	Total	Increase credit %	Increase total %
Cows	232	44	276	653	1,157	136	394	1,687	77	511
Steer	58	18	76	—	210	58	167	435	NA	472
Bulls	14	2	16	46	57	4	11	72	24	350
Calves	96	15	111	107	441	60	133	634	312	471
Subtotal	400	79	479	806	1,865	258	705	2,828	131	490
Horses/mules	89	—	89	18	38	90	6	134	111	50
Total	489	79	568	824	1,903	348	711	2,962	131	421

[a]Cattle from the cooperative CECORA (10), the Fondo Ganadero (14) and profit-sharing al partir system (55).

[b]Cattle from the Fondo Ganadero (283) and al partir (422); horses al partir (6).

TABLE 20

Farm Animals Inventory on Farms of 35 Credit Applicants, 1978

Farm animals	Fondo Ganadero	Al partir	Caja Agraria	Farmer-owned	Total	Pasture use only[a]
Cows	139	320	18	85	562	52
Steer	3	222	—	4	229	41
Bulls	2	7	2	7	18	2
Calves	61	73	4	32	170	19
Subtotal	205	622	24	128	979	114
Horses/mules	—	—	—	66	66	6
Total	205	622	24	194	1,045	120

[a]The owners of these animals pay the credit applicant farmers a monthly fee per head of cattle allowed to graze on their pasture. The farmers, however, are not entitled to any share of the animals' selling price.

TABLE 21

Mean Size Animal Stock Per Farm, Credit Recipients and Credit Applicants Compared

Animals per farm	Credit recipients	Credit applicants	Credit recipients/ credit applicants
	1978	1978	
$\overline{X}$ total number cattle/farm[a]	59.0	28.0	2.1
$\overline{X}$ farmer-owned cattle/farm	5.4	3.7	1.46
$\overline{X}$ horses and mules/farm	2.8	1.9	1.47
$\overline{X}$ pigs/farm	5.4	3.6	1.5
Median total number cattle/farm	54.0	9.0	6.0
	Pre-loan	1978	
$\overline{X}$ total number cattle/farm	10.0	28.0	.36
$\overline{X}$ farmer-owned cattle/farm	8.3	3.7	2.24
$\overline{X}$ horses and mules/farm	1.9	1.9	1.0
Median total number cattle/farm	3.0	9.0	.33

[a]Does not include "use of pasture." $\overline{X}$ = mean.

When we refer to table 19 (the last two columns), we find that by 1978 the credit recipient group had increased its total stock of cattle by 490 percent (from 479 to 2,828), and its initial INCORA stock by 131 percent (from 806 to 1,865). Of the group's total stock of 2,828 cattle, 1,317, or 47 percent, were fully owned (1,059 were offspring of INCORA credit, and 258 were purchased in other ways); 705, or 25 percent, were raised al partir with the Fondo Ganadero and other

TABLE 22

Distribution of Number of Cattle Per Farm, Credit Recipients and Credit Applicants Compared

	Credit recipients, 48 farms							
	Preloan[a]				1978[b]			
Number of cattle	Number of farms	Percent	Cumulative percent	$\overline{X}$/farm[c]	Number of farms	Percent	Cumulative percent	$\overline{X}$/farm[c]
0–9	33	68.7	68.7	2.0	—	—	—	—
10–19	8	16.7	85.4	13.5	2	4.2	4.2	18.0
20–29	3	6.2	91.6	25.0	6	12.5	16.7	24.0
30–44	2	4.2	95.8	42.0	10	20.8	37.5	39.3
45–59	1	2.1	97.9	58.0	10	20.8	58.3	51.2
60–74	—	—	—	—	7	14.6	72.9	66.3
75–99	1	2.1	100.0	90.0	5	10.4	83.3	83.4
100–149	—	—	—	—	5	10.0	93.7	120.0
150–200	—	—	—	—	3	6.3	100.0	170.0
Total	48	100.0			48	100.0		

Continued on next page

TABLE 22 CONT.

Credit applicants, 35 farms

	1978[b]			
Number of cattle	Number of farms	Percent	Cumulative percent	$\overline{X}$/farm[c]
0–9	19	54.2	54.2	4.3
10–19	3	8.6	62.8	13.3
20–29	2	5.7	68.5	20.5
30–44	4	11.4	79.9	40.3
45–59	2	5.7	85.6	50.5
60–74	3	8.6	94.2	67.3
75–99	1	2.9	97.1	88.0
100–149	—	—	—	—
150–200	1	2.9	100.0	286.0
Total	35	100.0		

[a]Includes all preloan cattle.

[b]Includes all 1978 cattle.

[c]$\overline{X}$ = mean.

Note: Credit recipient median pre-loan = 3 head of cattle.
Credit recipient median 1978 = 54 head of cattle.
Credit applicant median 1978 = 9 head of cattle.

private ranchers, and 806, or 28 percent, were loaned INCORA cattle to be paid for over the next decade.

It is interesting that the credit recipients not only increased their stocks through INCORA credit, but also by doubling their total stock of non-credit cattle (from 479 to 963) over the same time span. While non-INCORA farmer-owned cattle actually decreased, the stock of cattle al partir increased nearly nine times. From these figures, one can assume that the credit recipients would have increased their cattle inventories even without receiving INCORA credit, though by much less than they have with credit.

Table 20 shows that the thirty-five surveyed credit applicants raised a total of 979 cattle in 1978. The distribution of cows, steers, bulls, and calves is similar for both credit recipients and credit applicants, cows making up the majority in both cases. We can infer from this that incipient Caquetá ranchers, as a group, prefer to develop their herds through the purchase of breeding cows, rather than steers for fattening and slaughter. While this practice is costly and demanding in the short run, it promises more stability in the long run.

Table 21 compares the mean and median-sized herd per farm for credit applicants and credit recipients. As the final column shows, in 1978 the credit recipients raised, on the average, twice as many

TABLE 23

Herd Development on Farms of 48 Credit Recipients, 1972–1977

	Phase 1					Phase 2	
	1972	1973	1974	1975	1976	1976	1977
Loans (number)	4	8	6	11	1	8	10
Preloan $\overline{X}$ [a] herd/farm	9	4	6	3	—	15.6[c]	14
Initial credit $\overline{X}$ herd/farm	18.5	23	15	14.5	16	15.4	15.7
Total $\overline{X}$ herd/farm	27.5	27	21	17.5	16	31	29.7
1978 $\overline{X}$ herd/farm[b]	72	66	52	36	23	37	29
Percent increase	162	144	148	106	44	19	-2

[a]Includes only farmer-owned cattle. $\overline{X}$ = mean.

[b]Includes only farmer-owned cattle plus INCORA credit.

[c]High value due to one farmer with 90 pre-loan head of cattle.

cattle per farm as the credit applicants. Even more striking, the credit recipient median stock per farm was six times greater than the median for the credit applicant. The large difference between the mean and median-sized herds on credit applicant farms (28 and 9) indicates a very skewed distribution of cattle wealth for that group. This large differential existed for the pre-loan group of credit recipients (10 and 3) as well, but markedly decreased by 1978 (59 and 54), showing that participation in the INCORA credit program had an equalizing effect on the cattle distribution curve.

Table 21 also compares pre-loan credit recipients with credit applicants in 1978. The median-sized credit applicant herd in 1978 was three times larger than the pre-loan recipient herd, though the applicants raised fewer farmer-owned cattle than the recipients. Both groups owned equal numbers of horses and mules.

In sum, while the credit applicant, in 1978, raised three times as many cattle as the credit recipient *prior* to receiving credit, the applicant raised only one-sixth as many cattle as the credit recipient *after* receiving credit. In other words, positive change has occurred with and without credit, though much more rapidly for the borrowing group. Moreover, as shown in table 22 on cattle distribution, INCORA credit has had an equalizing impact on its beneficiaries. We can conclude, therefore, that INCORA credit has both a quantitative (increased herd size) and a qualitative (more balanced distribution curve) impact on cattle wealth.

The last table on livestock, table 23, separates the sample Phase 1 recipients (1972–first half of 1976) from the sample Phase 2 recipients (last half of 1976–1977). As would be expected, the earliest recipients have increased their animal stocks many more times than the recent recipients. Taking the group as a whole (1972–1976), the annual herd increase averages out to 27 percent. The herds of 1977 borrowers have remained essentially stagnant due to natural developmental delays. Finally, table 23 reminds us of the long-term nature of the INCORA/World Bank credit program, and that the definitive economic impact of credit on Caquetá borrowers will not be known until the full costs and benefits of the program are established. According to World Bank estimates, the development period of Phases 1 and 2 will last from 23 to 26 years, ending in the late 1990s.

Use of Farm Land

Table 24 presents data on land use for the sample fifty credit recipients, before and after credit, with net changes summarized in the last two columns (see diagram 6 for a schematic of land use). Prior to the credit program, 33 percent of the total farm area was devoted to pasture and 7 percent to crop production; 60 percent was unused land, either uncleared jungle or secondary growth (*rastrojo*). In 1978, after from one to six years with INCORA credit, the distribution of land use had changed as follows: 53 percent of the land was in pasture (61 percent increase); 5.8 percent was in crop production (17 percent decrease); and 41.2 percent was unused (31 percent decrease). In terms of change in total land area, the sample group "gained" 632 hectares between the two studied time periods, representing a total land increase of 11.2 percent.

Between the pre-loan years and 1978, large areas of jungle were cleared and planted with artificial grasses, while rastrojo was cleaned and used as natural pasture. In addition, 632 new hectares of land were bought or claimed (baldío) and converted into grazing land. The decrease in hectares devoted to annual crops (52 hectares in total) is not significant, especially considering constant seasonal variations in crop cultivation. Figures showing that only thirty-seven out of fifty farmers were involved in annual crop cultivation prior to credit, as opposed to forty-five out of fifty after credit, probably do not reveal a real increase, but rather, differ owing to the time of year when the information was collected. Figures on perennial crop cultivation show little change, other than that six more farmers grew plantain or sugar cane in 1978 than before (pre-loan). In short, while substantial change has occurred in the use of land for cattle raising, the use of land for agriculture has remained essentially stagnant.

TABLE 24

Use of Farm Land on Farms of 50 Credit Recipients, 1978

Land use	Preloan				1978				Change	
	Total hectares	Percent of total area	Number of farms (out of 50)	Median hectares/ farm	Total hectares	Percent of total area	Number of farms (out of 50)	Median hectares/ farm	Net[d] change in hectares	Percent increase (decrease)
Natural pasture	389	6.9	20	14.0	851	13.6	42	11.0	+ 462	119
Artificial pasture	1,459	25.9	45	21.0	2,465	39.4	48	44.0	+ 1,006	69
Annual crops[a]	259	4.6	37	5.0	207	3.3	45	2.5	– 52	20
Perennial crops[b]	133	2.4	41	2.5	158	2.5	47	2.8	+ 25	19
Fallow land[c]	1,095	19.5	48	17.0	762	12.2	45	12.0	– 333	30
Uncleared jungle	2,287	40.7	49	30.0	1,811	29.0	50	15.5	– 476	21
Total	5,622	100.0			6,254	100.0			+ 632[e]	

[a]Corn, yuca, rice.

[b]Sugar cane, plantain, cacao, coffee, pineapple.

[c]Rastrojo—not in productive use.

[d]Sixty percent of farms increased in size, 30 percent decreased in size, and 10 percent remained the same size.

[e]632 hectares = 11.2 percent increase in total area.

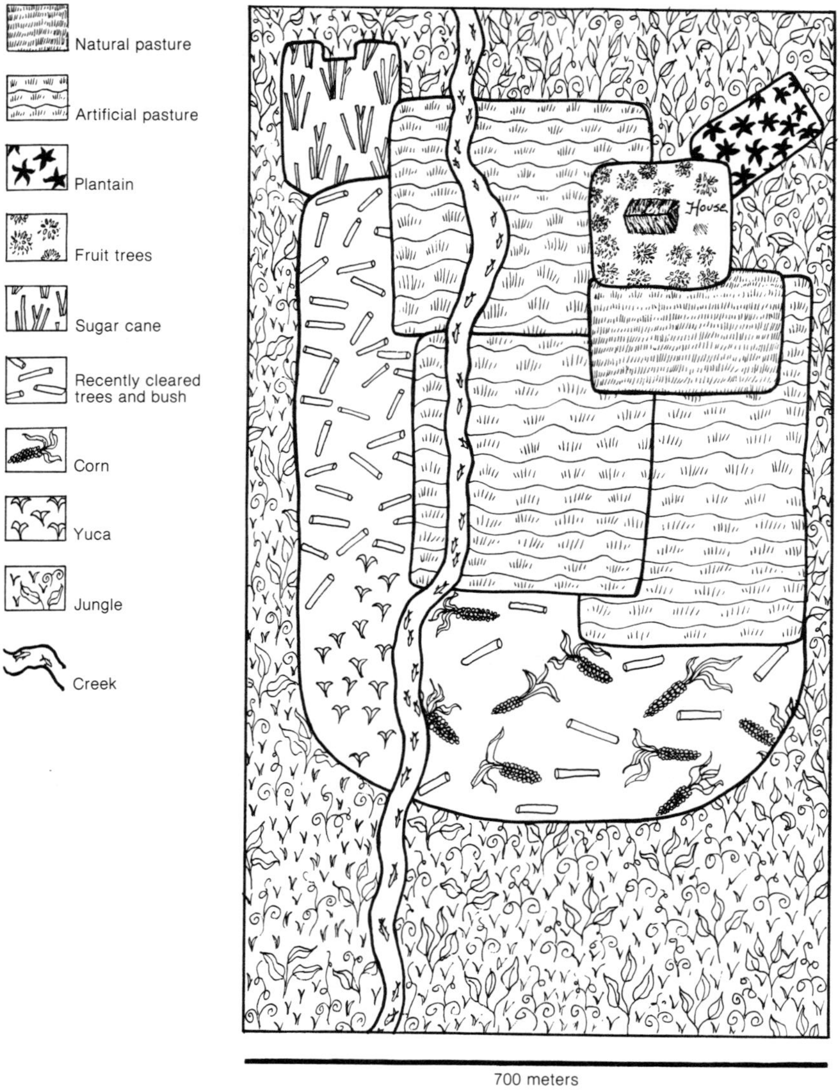

DIAGRAM 6. Medium-Sized Caquetá Farm, 100 Hectares

Relating the data on land use to data on cattle stocks (tables 18 and 20), it is possible to calculate the degree of under-use and over-use of pasture, prior to credit and after credit. Taking aggregate figures, the pre-loan sample of borrowers averaged 5 hectares of pasture per adult animal (1,848 hectares, 368 adult livestock), and comparing median hectares of pasture per farm (35) to the median number of cattle per farm (3), they averaged 11.6 hectares per animal. Even on typically poor Caquetá land, 1 to 1.5 hectares of pasture should be able to support one adult animal. The pre-loan borrowers, therefore, held very large areas of unused pasture, basically because they could not afford to purchase more cattle nor share the expenses of raising more cattle al partir. In 1978, after becoming INCORA credit recipients, the same fifty borrowers, in aggregate figures, averaged 1.5 hectares of pasture per adult animal (3,316 hectares, 2,194 adult livestock), and in median terms, averaged 1 hectare per animal (55 hectares, 54 cattle). As their herds grew, the farmers used previously neglected pasture and opened up new grazing land to prepare for future growth.

The ratio of 1.0 – 1.5 hectares per adult animal indicates generally adequate pasture use, allowing for poor soils, lack of artificial fertilization, the common use of low-nutrient natural grasses, and labor shortages. Nevertheless, these aggregate figures, when separated farm by farm, would undoubtedly reveal over grazing on the fullest stocked farms (over 75 head) and under-use of pasture on the poorly stocked farms (under 30 head). If new grass and legume species were introduced and farmers were able to hire help for frequent weeding and proper rotation, then more animals could be supported on a given space, thus conserving land and increasing productivity at the same time. The other major problem, that of unused pasture, will only be solved as additional sources of livestock become available, or when farmers are given incentives to convert unused land for crop cultivation.

Comparisons between tables 24 and 25 on *Use of Farm Land* for credit recipients and applicants, respectively, provide further insight into the impact of INCORA credit on productive uses of farm land. In 1978, the non-borrowing group devoted 54 percent of its farm land to productive use (47 percent in pasture, 7 percent in crop cultivation), and 46 percent to nonproductive use (33 percent in uncleared jungle and 13 percent in rastrojo). Comparing these distribution percentages to those for credit recipients in 1978, the latter devoted 6 percent more of their land to pasture than the former, 5 percent less to nonproductive uses, and 1.2 percent more to crops. Considering the entire farm area, these differences are not very significant.

In comparing median hectares per farm devoted to each use category, the credit applicants resemble the credit recipients (1978) in crop cultivation (6.2 hectares versus 5.25 hectares) and in unused land (30 hectares versus 27.5 hectares), but have 40 percent fewer hectares in pasture (35 hectares versus 55 hectares). This latter difference is basically because of the considerably smaller median-sized farm of the credit applicant (81 hectares) as compared to the credit

TABLE 25

Use of Farm Land on Farms of 35 Credit Applicants, 1978

Land use	Total hectares	Percent of total area	Number of farms (out of 35)	Median hectares per farm
Natural pasture	365	10.0	24	10.0
Artificial pasture	1,391	37.0	35	25.0
Annual crops[a]	136	3.5	32	3.5
Perennial crops[b]	135	3.5	34	2.7
Fallow land[c]	501	13.0	31	11.0
Uncleared jungle	1,224	33.0	34	19.0
Total	3,752	100.0		

[a]Corn, yuca, rice.

[b]Sugar cane, plantain, cacao, coffee, pineapple.

[c]Rastrojo—not in productive use.

recipient (102.5 hectares). The credit recipient's additional 20 hectares have nearly all been converted to grazing land, particularly in recent years as INCORA herds have grown.

In terms of pasture use, in aggregate figures the credit applicants averaged 2.2 hectares of grazing land per adult animal (1,756 hectares, 809 adult livestock). When median hectares of pasture per farm are compared with the median number of cattle per farm (9), however, the stocking rate comes to nearly 4 hectares per animal. The majority of credit applicants, therefore, have large areas of excess pasture (similar to pre-loan credit recipients). Their need for more livestock, to make good use of this excess pasture, explains why they have all applied for INCORA credit in the last few years.

In sum, though the median credit recipient owns 20 more hectares of grazing land than the corresponding credit applicant, proportionate to total farm area, each devotes approximately one-half of the total to pasture. This indicates that, irrespective of credit, Caquetá farmers tend to convert jungle to pasture on a consistent annual basis, to accommodate existing livestock or with the hope of acquiring more livestock in the future. The credit recipients must accelerate this process, as more pasture is needed to feed their larger and growing herds. Finally, although both sample groups have large areas of land devoted to pasture, on the average the credit applicants use only a fraction of the total while the credit recipients use nearly 100 percent.

As for crop cultivation, the only impact that INCORA credit may have is to inadvertently discourage agriculture by overtly encouraging cattle raising. Still, generally negative agroclimatic and market conditions in Caquetá influence farmer decisions on crop production more than their need for additional grazing land. Only if INCORA were able to reverse these unfavorable conditions by concentrating financial and technical assistance on agriculture (versus ranching) might farmers decide to invest more of their resources in crop cultivation.

Farm Installations

Data on farm installations (table 26) were discussed earlier in the chapter when establishing the general similarity of initial conditions for the entire sample of 85 rural families. We found that, initially, a small minority of both groups (credit recipients and credit applicants) owned cattle-related installations (salt trays, corrals, loading chutes), though the percentage of credit applicants with these installations slightly exceeded the corresponding percentage of credit recipients.

If we return to the research design described at the beginning of this section, data from table 26 permit us to calculate d $(X_2 - X_1)$ and d′ $(X'_2 - X'_1)$, and to compare the two to determine the rate of change with and without credit.

These figures show that a large percentage of farmers in both sample groups acquired new farm installations, particularly salt trays, corrals, and wire fencing, between the initial period and 1978. Nevertheless, the net increase of the credit recipient group for three cattle-related installations—salt trays, corrals, and loading chutes—was from 33 percent to 51 percent greater than the net increase of the credit applicant group. Net increases for the other three installations—sugar mills, water pumps, and fencing—were more similar, though slightly higher for the credit recipient group.

The credit recipients, having acquired credit in cattle that developed into larger herds over the years, and having received additional INCORA monies to invest specifically in cattle-related farm improvements, were nearly all motivated to construct those installations considered essential for adequate livestock management. Indeed, if they had not built corrals, fencing, etc., they might have risked credit cancellation for disobeying INCORA instructions. As for the moderate increases in farmer-owned sugar mills and water pumps, one can infer that at least a few farmers have improved their economic positions sufficiently to invest in nonessential technological improvements.

Income Sources, Levels, and Distribution

Earlier in the chapter, the gross income levels of the total surveyed sample were reported as correlated with seven independent variables

TABLE 26

Installations on the Farm

a. 50 Credit Recipients and 35 Credit Applicants Compared

	Initially[a]				1978			
Installations	Number of credit recipients	Percent of total	Number of credit applicants	Percent of total	Number of credit recipients	Percent of total	Number of credit applicants	Percent of total
Sugar mill	2	4	2	6	15	30	10	29
Water pump	1	2	—	—	4	8	—	—
Salt trays	5	10	7	20	50	100	27	77
Corral	5	10	5	14	50	100	23	66
Loading chute	1	2	5	14	35	70	11	31
Fencing	23	46	11	31	50	100	31	89

TABLE 26 CONT.

b. Impact of Credit on Farm Installations

Installations	d (Percent increase with credit) Credit recipients	d′ (Percent increase without credit) Credit applicants	d − d′ (Difference in percent increase)
Sugar mill	26	23	3
Water pump	6	—	6
Salt trays	90	57	33
Corral	90	52	38
Loading chute	68	17	51
Fencing	54	58	4

[a] *Initially* for credit recipients is just before receiving credit; for credit applicants it is the year when they arrived at their present farms.

to determine the direction and strength of their relationships (see table 14). We found that herd size, hectares in pasture, hectares in crops, length of residence on farm, farm size, and INCORA credit correlated positively with gross annual income. Then, in comparing the conditions and assets of credit recipients to nonrecipients, we found that the credit recipient group raised significantly larger herds, had somewhat larger farms with considerably more hectares in pasture, and owned more cattle-related farm installations than the credit applicant group. It is reasonable to conclude that INCORA credit has had a positive impact on several important economic determinants of gross income. In other words, INCORA's credit-in-kind program has enabled poor colonos to acquire those economic assets which, in the long run, are the key to upward economic mobility in rural Caquetá. While this generalization holds true, it nevertheless is clear that the nonrecipient group has also improved its economic position over time, though improvement is slower and less equally distributed.

We would expect the average INCORA recipient to take in a higher gross annual income than the average nonrecipient, given similar pre-loan backgrounds. In the following sections, the quantitative and qualitative character of this differential is discussed (tables 27 and 28), followed by discussion of the sources of gross income (tables 29 and 30), total annual expenses (tables 31 and 32), and net farm income levels (tables 33 and 34) of borrowers and nonborrowers. Finally, net income is related to average expenditures and loan payments to determine the level of savings, indebtedness, and living standards of both surveyed groups.

TABLE 27

Distribution of Gross Income for 50 Credit Recipients, 1978

Income bracket (Col.$)	Families			Mean annual income per family[a] (Col.$)	Percent total income in each bracket	
	Number	Percent	Cumulative percent		Percent	Cumulative percent
25,000– 75,000	11	22	22	51,702	7.5	7.5
75,001–125,000	15	30	52	94,241	18.8	26.3
125,001–175,000	9	18	70	136,786	16.3	42.6
175,001–225,000	6	12	82	197,280	15.7	58.3
225,001–275,000	2	4	86	243,715	6.4	64.7
275,001–325,000	3	6	92	311,142	12.3	77.0
325,001–375,000	1	2	94	343,755	4.5	81.5
375,001–425,000	1	2	96	394,347	5.2	86.7
425,001 +	2	4	100	503,211	13.3	100.0
Total	50	100		151,211[b]	100.0	

[a]Includes imputed value for products grown on farm for home consumption (Col.$20,235).

[b]Col.$151,211 is the mean gross income; the *median* gross income is Col.$115,335.

TABLE 28

Distribution of Gross Income for 35 Credit Applicants, 1978

Income bracket (Col.$)	Families: Number	Families: Percent	Families: Cumulative percent	Mean annual income per family[a] (Col.$)	Percent total income in each bracket: Percent	Percent total income in each bracket: Cumulative percent
25,000– 75,000	17	48.5	48.5	46,874	22.4	22.4
75,001–125,000	7	20.0	68.5	89,486	17.6	40.0
125,001–175,000	8	22.8	91.3	147,257	33.1	73.1
175,001–225,000	1	2.9	94.2	213,435	6.0	79.1
225,001–275,000	1	2.9	97.1	236,235	6.6	85.7
275,001 +	1	2.9	100.0	507,391	14.3	100.0
Total	35	100.0		101,668[b]	100.0	

[a]Includes imputed value for products grown on farm for home consumption (Col.$20,235).

[b]Col.$101,668 is the mean gross income; the *median* gross income is Col.$74,035.

Sources of Gross Income for 50 Credit Recipients, 1978

	Number of families	Income[a] Col.$	Income[a] Percent	Annual mean (Col.$)	Annual median (Col.$)
Monetary income					
Livestock and by-products[b]	47	5,215,956	69.0	110,976	73,608
Agricultural products[c]	32	1,082,136	14.3	33,816	20,496
Outside labor[d]	9	27,408	.3	6,852	4,500
Wood	4	223,284	3.0	24,816	12,000
Subtotal		6,548,784	86.6	130,976[e]	95,100[f]
Nonmonetary income					
Products grown and consumed on farm	50	1,011,750	13.4	20,235	20,235
Total	50	7,560,534	100.0	151,211[e]	115,335[f]

[a]Data on gross income were collected for a six-month period (post-harvest), and then doubled to equal annual gross income. The value for home grown and consumed products (yuca, plantain, and corn) was derived as explained in the text.

[b]Includes sale of cattle, chickens, pigs, eggs, milk, and cheese.

[c]Mainly sale of corn, rice, and some sugar cane.

[d]Paid work on outside farms and ranches.

[e]Does not equal the sum of the above figures, rather the total income (column 2) divided by 50 families.

[f]Does not equal the sum of the above figures, rather the median gross income value for all 50 families.

Note: Given the 1978 exchange rate of approximately 40 Colombian pesos to one U.S. dollar:

	U.S.$ Gross	U.S.$ Net
Annual mean income per family	3,780	2,179
Only monetary income	3,274	1,673
Annual median income per family	2,883	1,437
Only monetary income	2,378	931
Median income per capita	360	180
Only monetary income	297	116

TABLE 30

Sources of Gross Income for 35 Credit Applicants, 1978

	Number of families	Income[a] Col.$	Income[a] Percent	Annual mean (Col.$)	Annual median (Col.$)
Monetary income					
Livestock and by-products[b]	23	1,125,420	31.6	48,936	32,004
Agricultural products[c]	25	1,121,016	31.5	44,844	18,696
Outside labor[d]	11	194,124	5.5	17,652	12,000
Wood	1	24,000	.7	24,000	24,000
Others[e]	7	385,596	10.8	55,080	26,004
Subtotal		2,850,156	80.1	81,433[f]	53,800[g]
Nonmonetary income					
Products grown and consumed on farm	35	708,225	19.9	20,235	20,235
Total	35	3,558,381	100.0	101,668[f]	74,035[g]

[a]Data on gross income were collected for a six-month period (post-harvest), and then doubled to equal annual gross income. The value of nonmonetary income was derived as explained in the text.

[b]Includes sale of cattle, chickens, pigs, eggs, milk, and cheese.

[c]Mainly sale of corn, rice, and some sugar cane.

[d]Paid work on outside farms and ranches.

[e]One sale of home; one sale of car; two small storage businesses; one help from working children; one bus driving; one sales from hunting.

[f]Does not equal the sum of the above figures, rather the total income (column 2) divided by 35 families.

[g]Does not equal the sum of the above figures, rather the median gross income value for all 35 families.

Note: Given the 1978 exchange rate of approximately 40 Colombian pesos to one U.S. dollar:

	U.S.$ Gross	U.S.$ Net
Annual mean income per family	2,542	1,687
Only monetary income	2,036	1,181
Annual median income per family	1,851	1,233
Only monetary income	1,345	727
Median income per capita	231	154
Only monetary income	168	91

TABLE 31

Total Annual Expenses for 50 Credit Recipients, 1978

Expense items	Number of families	Total Col.$	Percent of total	Annual mean Col.$	Mean for items 1, 2, 3 (percent)	Annual median Col.$	Median for items 1, 2, 3 (percent)
Food	50	2,323,200	33.0	46,464	68.9	38,400	74.0
Clothing	50	713,028	10.0	14,216	21.2	9,300	17.9
Health care	50	334,176	4.8	6,684	9.9	4,200	8.1
Subtotal		3,370,404	47.9	67,409	100.0	51,900	100.0
Education	17	72,420	1.0	4,260		2,400	
Recreation	34	471,120	6.7	13,856		5,400	
Subtotal		543,540	7.7				
Veterinary drugs and salt		630,624	9.0	12,870		10,800	
Hired labor		1,397,316	19.9	29,111		25,200	
Supplies		138,540	2.0	4,469		1,980	
Miscellaneous		68,748	1.0	11,458		3,600	
Transportation		179,796	2.6	5,800		5,040	
Subtotal		2,415,024	34.5				
Interest payments —Phase 1		257,730	3.7	8,353		8,591	
Interest payments —Phase 2		440,000	6.2	22,770		22,200	
Subtotal		697,730	9.9				
Total		7,026,698	100.0	Phase 1 134,933[a] Phase 2 149,350[a]		Phase 1 117,707[b] Phase 2 131,316[b]	

[a]Does not equal the sum of the above figures, rather the total amount of expenses for Phase 1 and Phase 2 borrowers, divided by 30 families and 20 families respectively.

[b]Does not equal the sum of the above figures, rather median expenses for the 30 Phase 1 borrowers and 20 Phase 2 borrowers, respectively.

Note: Given the 1978 exchange rate of approximately 40 Colombian pesos to one U.S. dollar:

Annual mean expenses per family	U.S.$
Phase 1	3,373
Phase 2	3,734
Total credit recipients	3,554

Annual median expenses per family	U.S.$
Phase 1	2,943
Phase 2	3,283
Total credit recipients	3,113

Food, clothing, health care	U.S.$
Mean per family	1,685
Median per family	1,298
Median per capita	162

TABLE 32

Total Annual Expenses for 35 Credit Applicants, 1978

Expense items	Number of families	Total Col.$	Percent of total	Annual mean Col.$	Mean for items 1, 2, 3 (percent)	Annual median Col.$	Median for items 1, 2, 3 (percent)
Food	35	1,231,200	38.0	35,177	68.3	31,200	75.4
Clothing	35	309,024	9.5	8,829	17.2	7,200	17.4
Health care	33	246,528	7.6	7,471	14.5	3,000	7.2
Subtotal		1,786,752	55.1	51,477	100.0	41,400	100.0
Education	12	58,116	1.8	4,843		1,260	
Recreation	15	204,768	6.3	13,651		3,600	
Subtotal		262,884	8.1				
Veterinary drugs and salt	26	191,136	5.8	7,351		4,914	
Hired labor	29	658,500	20.3	22,707		15,408	
Supplies	20	138,528	4.3	6,926		3,420	
Transportation	24	208,836	6.4	8,702		5,382	
Subtotal		1,197,000	36.8				
Total		3,246,636	100.0	92,761[a]		71,863[b]	

[a]Does not equal the sum of the above figures, rather the total expenses (column 2) divided by 35 families.

[b]Does not equal the sum of the above figures, rather the median expense amount for all 35 families.

Note: Given the 1978 exchange rate of approximately 40 Colombian pesos to one U.S. dollar:

	U.S.$
Annual average expenses per family	2,319
Annual median expenses per family	1,797
Food, clothing, health care	
Average per family	1,287
Median per family	1,035
Median per capita	129

TABLE 33

Distribution of Net Farm Income for 50 Credit Recipients, 1978

Income Bracket Col.$	Families			Mean annual income per family[a] Col.$	Annual per[b] capita income Col.$
	Number	Percent	Cumulative percent		
Low income:					
0[c]	12	24	24	—	—
1–25,000	10	20	44	11,392	1,424
25,001–50,000	7	14	58	37,740	4,718
Medium income:					
50,001–75,000	3	6	64	64,279	8,035
75,001–100,000	7	14	78	85,718	10,715
High income:					
100,001–150,000	3	6	84	135,903	16,988
150,001–200,000	2	4	88	162,913	20,364
200,001–250,000	3	6	94	222,046	27,756
250,001 +	3	6	100	367,253	45,907
Totals	50	100		66,937[d]	8,367

[a]Net farm income = gross monetary income minus farm expenses (veterinary drugs and salt, hired labor, transportation, supplies, miscellaneous) minus interest payments (Phase 1 and Phase 2 annual averages).

[b]The surveyed group have an average of eight persons per family.

[c]These families have negative net income; that is, their farm expenses exceed their gross income. One can presume that they are paying for both farm and personal expenses partly on credit, at least during 1978.

[d]Col.$66,937 equals the *mean* net income; the *median* net income is substantially lower, Col.$37,248. Similarly, median per capita income, Col. $4,656, is lower than the average, Col.$8,367.

TABLE 34

Distribution of Net Farm Income for 35 Credit Applicants, 1978

Income Bracket Col.$	Families			Mean annual income per family[a] Col.$	Annual per capita income[b] Col.$
	Number	Percent	Cumulative percent		
Low income:					
0[c]	6	17.1	17.1	—	—
1–25,000	11	31.4	48.5	13,355	1,669
25,001–50,000	4	11.4	59.9	36,334	4,542
Medium income:					
50,001–75,000	7	20.0	79.9	59,173	7,397
75,001–100,000	2	5.7	85.6	92,576	11,572
High income:					
100,001–150,000	3	8.6	94.2	117,806	14,726
150,001–200,000	1	2.9	97.1	159,432	19,929
200,001 +	1	2.9	100.0	427,156	53,395
Totals	35	100.0		47,233[d]	5,904

[a]Net farm income = gross monetary income minus farm expenses (veterinary drugs and salt, hired labor, transportation, supplies).

[b]The surveyed group have an average of eight persons per family.

[c]These families have negative net income; that is, their farm expenses exceed their gross income. One can presume that they are paying for both farm and personal expenses partly on credit, at least during 1978.

[d]Col.$47,233 equals the *mean* net income; the *median* net income is substantially lower, Col.$29,088. Similarly, median per capita income, Col. $3,636, is lower than the average, Col.$5,904.

Gross income

In tables 27 and 28, we find that the mean annual gross income of the fifty credit recipients (CR), Col.$151,211 (U.S.$3,780), is nearly 50 percent higher than the mean annual gross income of the thirty-five credit applicants (CA), Col.$101,688 (U.S.$2,542). The difference in median income levels, 58 percent, is even greater.

In terms of income distribution, the lower 52 percent of the CR earn 26.3 percent of total income, and the upper eight percent earn 23 percent of total income. In comparison, for CA, the lower 48.5 percent earn 22.4 percent of total income and the upper 8.7 percent earn 27 percent of total income. These figures indicate a very similar income distribution pattern for both credit recipients and nonrecipients. However, if the imputed value for products grown and consumed on the farm were subtracted from gross income, leaving only monetary income, the income curve would show a slightly more egalitarian distribution pattern for CR (approximately 4 percentage points). A similar distribution indicator, that of comparing mean income levels with median income levels, confirms the same trend. The CR median equals 72.6 percent of the mean, while the CA median equals only 66 percent of the mean (excluding products grown and consumed on farm), again a difference of a few percentage points.

As stated earlier, INCORA credit has had an equalizing impact on its borrowers, enabling the poorest recipients to improve their economic positions more markedly and quickly than similar colonos without credit. The data on gross income distribution reaffirm this equalizing impact, which, though modest in the short run, could be significant in the long run.

Sources of income.—Tables 29 and 30 illustrate the sources of gross monetary and nonmonetary income for credit recipients and nonrecipients, respectively. Several interesting comparisons emerge:

1. Of the recipient families, 94 percent derived income from the sale of livestock and by-products, equaling nearly 70 percent of total income earned. On the average, the CR earned 56 percent more than the CA from 1978 livestock sales.
2. The credit applicants received 31.5 percent of their total income from the sale of agricultural products, though the distribution of income earned per farmer was very uneven. The credit recipients derived only 14.3 percent of their total income from agriculture; however, the value of their median gross agricultural sales (Col.$20,496) was greater than the corresponding value for credit applicants (Col.$18,696).

3. More nonrecipients than recipients depend upon wage work on outside farms as well as auxiliary small business activity to make ends meet.
4. The imputed value for farm grown and consumed yuca, plantain, and corn, applied equally to all farmers, represents approximately 13 percent of total gross income for recipients and substantially more, nearly 20 percent, for nonrecipients.

Annual Expenses

During the interviews, the respondents were asked to approximate their average monthly expenditures on personal and farm-related items. It soon became clear that monthly approximations were not always appropriate, depending on the item in question. Consumer goods purchased on a frequent, regular basis, principally food, were more accurately quoted as per week, whereas items that were purchased only a few times per year and irregularly, such as clothing, drugs for the family, and farm supplies, or purchased according to agricultural "peaks" and "valleys", such as fertilizers and hired labor, were more accurately quoted on an annual or semi-annual basis. Veterinary drugs and salt and education, recreation, and transportation expenses corresponded best with monthly accounting. Accordingly, farmers responded to different expense items as per week, month, semiannually, or annually. Subsequently the results were calculated to obtain across-the-board annual averages.

Annual expense approximations are presented in tables 31 (credit recipients) and 32 (credit applicants). We see in the first column that almost 100 percent of the families purchase food, clothing and drugs from outside sources, showing that both surveyed groups are clearly involved with the market economy. In addition, 34 percent of both groups have expenses related to their children's education. Data on the last personal item, recreation, are not very reliable due to the vague definition of recreation, especially in rural areas, as well as to the reticence of respondents to answer truthfully. However, in general, more credit recipients spend money on such items as alcohol, travel, and entertaining than nonrecipients. Looking at farm expenses, nearly all of the recipients hire outside labor and purchase veterinary supplies, while 20 percent to 25 percent of the credit applicants do not. Equal percentages of both groups spend money on transportation and general supplies. The value of family labor is not included.

Caquetá farmers, both INCORA borrowers and nonborrowers, frequently borrow from the Caja Agraria, principally to pay for pre-harvest and harvesting costs. These loans range in value from Col.

$5,000 to Col.$100,000, at 18 percent interest annually, and normally must be repaid within eighteen months. Caja Agraria interest payments are not included as an expense item in tables 31 and 32 since less than half of the applicants and many fewer recipients were paying back Caja loans at the time of the survey. Nevertheless, Caja interest payments represent a significant additional annual expense for a substantial number of Caquetá farmers (on the average, Col. $9,000 in 1978).

For credit recipients, the interest paid on Phase 1 and Phase 2 INCORA loans is included as an additional expense. The 30 Phase 1 borrowers pay 8 percent annual interest, charged on the amortization of principal over a gradually increasing seven year payment schedule. Interest accumulated during the initial three year grace period is charged in the first payment year. The earliest interest payments for surveyed Phase 1 borrowers began in 1975.

The mean loan value for the thirty Phase 1 borrowers, Col.$94,300, requires a total interest payment of Col.$58,469 over seven years. Interest payments range from a low of Col.$1,509 in the first year to a high of Col.$15,090 in the last year, giving an average value of Col.$8,353 per year. Median loan value and interest charges do not vary significantly from these averages. The median annual interest charge, Col.$8,591, equals approximately 7 percent of the median total annual expenses calculated for surveyed Phase 1 borrowers.

Phase 2 credit recipients must pay 15 percent annual interest on their loans, spread over a nine year amortization payment schedule after an initial four year grace period. Interest is charged on outstanding debt, decreasing over time, except for interest accumulated during the grace period which is distributed over the nine year schedule and charged as a percentage of amortized principal.

The mean loan value of the twenty Phase 2 borrowers surveyed, Col.$151,800, requires a total interest payment of Col.$204,931, averaging Col.$22,770 per year. The median interest payment is slightly lower at Col.$22,200, which equals 17 percent of Phase 2 borrowers' median total annual expenses. Interest payments for these borrowers first come due in 1980.

The "Percent of total" figure for interest payments shown in column 3 of table 31, a value equaling nearly 10 percent of total expenses, was calculated by multiplying the number of borrowers in each loan group by their respective median annual interest payments and then adding the two group figures together. Understandably, the 10 percent figure falls in between what Phase 1 borrowers must pay (7.2 percent of total expenses) and what Phase 2 borrowers must pay (17 percent of total expenses).

Comparing tables 31 and 32, one observes that the percentage of total expenses spent on each group of items (excluding interest payments) is similar for credit recipients and applicants: approximately half on food, clothing, and health care; slightly over a third on farm expenses, and the remainder on education and recreation.

Where the important differences between the two groups emerge is in comparing their average and median annual monetary expenditures per item. These expenditures are summarized in U.S. dollars in the note at the bottom of each table. The average credit recipient spends a total of U.S.$3,554 per year; 47 percent of the total is spent on basic food, clothing, and health needs. The average credit applicant spends 35 percent less in total, U.S.$2,319, 55 percent spent on food, clothing, and health care. Using median figures, the credit applicant spends 42 percent less on the sum of all items, but only 20 percent less than the recipient on basic food, clothing, and health care.

These expense differences are significant, though less than the already mentioned variances in gross income. Differences are less marked for expenditures on basic need items essential for survival. Median per capita expenditures on food, clothing, and health care, using an average family size of eight, are very low for both groups. This is especially true when we consider an annual inflation rate of over 20 percent on many basic need items. The median credit recipient spends U.S.$162 per year, or just U.S.$3.25 per week per capita, while the median nonrecipient spends U.S.$129 per year, 20 percent less, or just U.S.$2.50 per week per capita. This money goes toward the purchase of food items which are not produced on the farm: oil, vegetables, salt, coffee, meat, beans, chocolate, etc., plus clothing, drugs, and medical consultations. When a member of the family falls ill, money normally spent on food or clothing must be used to buy drugs; alternately, when new clothing must be bought for school, boots for work, etc., drugs and food are sacrificed or bought on credit. Families earning below the median income depend almost entirely on home-grown foods, a basic diet of yuca, plantain, panela, and occasional milk and eggs. This applies even to many families with good-sized herds, who view their livestock as security for the future, requiring poor diets, clothing, and housing conditions in the present.

Net Income

The net farm income figures in tables 33 and 34 show both the distribution curve and level of purchasing power for the two sample groups under study. The tabulated values equal gross monetary income less farm expenses and interest payments, leaving net farm income for food, clothing, health care, education, recreation, travel, and house improvement. Once these subsistence expenses are deducted, one is left with disposable income from which INCORA loan principal payments may be subtracted. By juxtaposing these net income figures with average annual personal expenses (tables 31 and 32) and loan payments (Phases 1 and 2), we can gauge average levels of savings and indebtedness.

Both tables have been divided into three income strata—low, medium and high—to make clearer the distribution of wealth within each group; they should not be viewed as absolute indications of low or high income levels or living standards.

The average credit recipient earns a net monetary income of Col.$66,937, or approximately U.S.$1,673. However, 62 percent of the recipients have annual net incomes below the average. The median recipient family earns Col.$37,248 annually, which comes to U.S.$931, or U.S.$116 per capita. Of the 50 families, 24 percent did not earn any disposable income in 1978; that is, according to their own responses, on-farm expenses plus interest payments exceeded gross monetary income. Whatever consumer purchases were made were bought on credit, or perhaps through barter.

Subtracting annual average and median food, clothing, and health care expenditures from corresponding net farm income levels, we find that these basic need expenses exceeded monetary income by Col.$472 for the average recipient and by Col.$14,652 for the median recipient. In other words, after on-farm expenses and annual interest payments, the average credit recipient earned just short of the income necessary to cover essential personal needs at low consumption levels, while the median recipient incurred substantial debt to pay for these items. Only the upper 38 percent of credit recipients earned sufficient monetary income to cover farm, interest, and basic need costs. In practical terms, this means that over 60 percent of the recipients are purchasing subsistence items on credit, and that approximately three out of four go into debt to pay for "non-essential" items such as education, recreation and house improvement.

Of the fifty borrowers interviewed, all but twelve will have begun to pay back their INCORA Phase 1 and Phase 2 loans by 1980. Given an average Phase 1 loan of Col.$94,300, the loan principal payment comes to Col.$4,715 in the first year, Col.$9,430 in the second and third years, Col.$14,145 in the fourth year, and just under Col.$20,000 in the final three years. The Phase 2 principal payments will be substantially higher: on an average loan of Col.$151,800, the first two payments will be Col.$7,590 and for the following seven years will vary from a low of Col.$15,180 to a high of Col.$30,360. (Interest payments were already deducted as part of annual expenses.)

Given a median net farm income level of Col.$37,248, and a negative median disposable income of Col.$14,652 after food, clothing, and health care expenditures, it is clear that the borrowers must begin to sell their assets, mainly livestock, to make the aforementioned loan repayments. Taking 1978 livestock prices, the first Phase 1 principal payment could be made from the sale of 2.5 cows (worth Col.$8,000/cow), the second and third payments from the sale of three cows, and so forth, depending upon future livestock prices.

The burden of these loan payments for the individual borrowers will depend upon their ability to sustain long-term normal rates of herd development. According to the herd development figures in table 23, as of 1978 the 1972, 1973, and 1974 borrowers had increased their herds annually by seven or eight head, the 1975 borrowers by six head, and the recent 1976 borrowers by only three head. Therefore, for instance, the 1972 and 1973 Phase 1 borrowers, making their third and second payments, respectively, in 1978, forfeited over one-third of the value of one year's average herd development to make the payments. This is a steep but still manageable cost which will probably not threaten future herd development. However, Phase 2 borrowers will face a substantially greater debt burden, for unless the price of cattle continues to rise sharply (which is very uncertain), they will be forced to forfeit a dangerously large share of their annual herd growth to repay their loans, particularly after the first two years.

As explained in the section on annual expenses, Phase 2 borrowers are further disadvantaged because their interest due is charged on outstanding debt, rather than on the amortization of principal (as for Phase 1), resulting in high interest expenses in the first few years when the borrowers are least able to pay. Though INCORA officials have expressed serious doubts about this payment schedule, when the Caja Agraria took over the administration of INCORA funds in 1976, their system of interest paid on outstanding debt was accepted.

The object of the INCORA loans is to promote long-term herd development as a means for securing higher incomes in the future. Most of the Phase 1 borrowers and middle-and upper-income Phase 2 borrowers will succeed in repaying their loans and still end up with considerably larger herds than when they began repayment. Assuming these conditions, higher disposable incomes will follow. Nonetheless, given the rising costs of basic need items and the instability of future earnings, it is probable that the low-income Phase 2 borrowers will not be able to sustain loan repayments and simultaneously develop their herds at an acceptable rate. Barring unexpected improved earnings, these farmers will be forced into cattle decapitalization and/or will have their credit liquidated due to default or breach of contract obligations concerning the premature sale of INCORA cattle.

Table 34 presents the distribution and level of net farm monetary income for the thirty-five surveyed credit applicants. The average credit applicant has a net annual income of Col.$47,233 (U.S.$1,181), 30 percent lower than the average net income of INCORA borrowers. The applicants' median income, Col.$29,088 (U.S.$727), is 22 percent lower than the borrowers' median income. Using the same income strata for each group, 60 percent of the credit applicants earn low incomes versus 58 percent of the credit recipients; 26 percent of the credit applicants earn medium incomes versus 20 percent of the credit recipients; and 14 percent of the credit applicants earn high incomes versus 22 percent of the credit recipients.

Subtracting average and median food, clothing, and health expenditures from corresponding net farm income levels, the average credit applicant in 1978 was in debt by over Col.$4,000 and the median applicant by over Col.$12,000. Thus, after farm expenses, annual interest payments, and basic need expenses (but before loan principal repayments), the median credit recipient was Col. $2,000 more in debt than the median applicant. As shown in gross income tables, the applicants' better net income position results, not from higher earnings, but rather from lower expenses and, more important, no interest payments.

When the INCORA loan principal repayments are considered, the level of indebtedness of the recipient group becomes even graver. In other words, judging from all of the figures thus far presented on gross income, net farm income, annual expenses, and debt payments, the credit recipients have not and will not improve their disposable income levels substantially until their INCORA debts are paid.

Nonetheless, the recipient families have increased their farm assets substantially (livestock, installations, pasture) since receiving INCORA credit, and in 1978 were in a markedly better asset position than the nonrecipients. To what extent the total group of recipients will be able to sustain these improvements, cover their loan repayments, and eventually increase their disposable income as well, cannot be determined for at least another decade. As mentioned earlier, one of the key elements in determining the final outcome will be the future price of cattle throughout Colombian markets.

We do know that the rate of delinquency on Phase 1 loans has been very low. INCORA separates delinquency into three categories: delinquent debt up to six months, debt currently undergoing legal examination, and uncollectable or "bad" debt. As of October 1978, 36 percent of the total Phase 1 loan portfolio had been repaid and only .2 percent of remaining outstanding debt was delinquent by more than six months, none of which had been classified as uncollectable. As of the same date, only 2.5 percent of the Phase 2 loans had been repaid, still too soon to make a statement on delinquency.

Default loans that pass into the "uncollectable" category, are liquidated. In most cases, INCORA recovers the value of the loan plus legal fees through the acquisition of farm assets, such as animals, crops, supplies, and installations; however, in rare cases the farm itself may be taken away from the debtor. When this occurs, the farm is auctioned to the highest bidder; proceeds are used to cancel bad debts and pay legal fees and any additional funds are remitted to the evicted farmer.

Indicators of Living Standards

The data thus far presented show wide variations within and between the two sample groups on most asset variables, and less marked differences between groups for income variables. The living standards within and between these two groups also vary considerably. In general, however, the nutritional, housing, health, and educational levels of the majority of families interviewed are below adequate standards. Living standards of Caquetá farmers generally were discussed in detail in chapter 2, and are briefly reviewed below as they concern the interviewed sample.

Nutrition

We have already seen that per capita expenditures on food are very low for both borrowers and nonborrowers, though on average the former spend 24 percent more than the latter. Although the basic diet of both groups consists of home-grown foods, mainly carbohydrates and some dairy products, the more prosperous families can afford to consume better balanced diets than the low-income families.

To gauge farmer attitudes toward their own nutritional levels, the respondents were asked to comment on whether they considered their families to be well fed. Of the credit recipients, 47 percent responded affirmatively and 53 percent responded negatively. Not surprisingly, the positive responses came mainly from families with net incomes and per capita food expenditures above the group median. They seemed to have a good idea about what constitutes a balanced diet, particularly the need to supplement farm-grown carbohydrates with a combination of eggs, beans, meat, and fish, and most try to serve at least one of these foods daily. At the same time, during difficult periods, farmers mentioned that store-bought items are consumed less regularly. Vegetables, except for onions, are rarely bought at all. The majority of the negative responses came from families who lacked the financial resources to buy the foods necessary for a balanced diet. Many of them mentioned the scarcity and high price of foods containing vitamins and protein, namely vegetables and meat. This was especially true in the more isolated areas, where the local markets do not offer as great a variety of goods as the towns near to major roads and prices are considerably higher due to excess transport costs.

A much larger percentage of the credit applicants (86 percent) responded negatively to the same question. There are three probable explanations:

1. The average credit applicant spends 24 percent less per capita on purchased foods than the average credit recipient.
2. The applicants generally produce fewer consumption goods on their farms, particularly livestock by-products such as milk, eggs and cheese.
3. The credit applicants, being in a position of soliciting credit from an agency (INCORA) that serves low-income farmers, are more likely to emphasize their needs to potentially influential outsiders than would the recipients, who have already been accepted into the credit program.

Housing

The housing conditions of the credit recipients and applicants are compared in table 35. The categories used per house, ordered from poorest to best, are: number of rooms, number of beds, and construction material of the roof, walls and floor.

Close to or more than 50 percent of the families in both groups have two rooms or less, three beds or less, metal roofs, wooden walls, and wooden floors. Beyond these similarities, the two groups differ as follows: fewer credit recipients have one-room houses, and more have four or more rooms in their houses than the credit applicants; 12 percent of the credit recipients have one or no beds versus 20 percent of the credit applicants; 18 percent of the credit recipients have roofs made of palm or cardboard versus 40 percent of the credit

Table 35

Housing Conditions, Credit Recipients and Credit Applicants Compared, 1978

Number rooms	Number credit recipients	Percent	Number credit applicants	Percent	Number of beds	Number credit recipients	Percent	Number credit applicants	Percent	Type roof	Number credit recipients	Percent	Number credit applicants	Percent
1	8	16	9	26	—	3	6	2	6	Palm/				
2	14	28	11	31	1	3	6	5	14	straw	3	6	5	14
3	15	30	12	34	2	12	24	8	23	Card-				
4	7	14	3	9	3	14	28	8	23	board	6	12	9	26
5	3	6	—	—	4	5	10	5	14	Wood	8	16	5	14
6	—	—	—	—	5	4	8	4	11	Metal	30	60	15	43
7	3	6	—	—	6	5	10	—	—	Cement	1	2	1	3
					7 +	4	8	3	9	Tile	2	4	—	—
Total	50	100	35	100		50	100	35	100		50	100	35	100

Continued on next page

TABLE 35 CONT.

Type walls					Type floor				
Chonta	—	—	5	14	Dirt	7	14	9	26
Wood	43	86	29	83	Chonta	—	—	2	6
Clay	4	8	—	—	Wood	39	78	20	57
Cement	3	6	1	3	Cement	4	8	4	11
Total	50	100	35	100		50	100	35	100

[a]Number always refers to number of families.

applicants; none of the credit recipients have chonta walls (bamboo-type material) versus 14 percent of the credit applicants; more credit recipients have clay and cement walls than credit applicants, and 14 percent of the credit recipients have dirt floors compared with 26 percent of the credit applicants.

These figures indicate that, of the two groups, substantially more of the credit applicants suffer from very poor housing and fewer have acquired good housing. Nevertheless, the majority in each group have what can be considered in the region as middle-level housing; that is, they have improved their homes from the rudimentary palm shack with dirt floor to a wood construction with a metal roof, but still lack adequate space, sanitation, and protection from malaria-carrying mosquitoes and heavy rains.

Education and Health

The only other indicators of living standards available from the survey data concern literacy, infant mortality, and common health problems. The differences between the borrowers and non-borrowers in these three areas follow.

Literacy.—The 50 credit recipient families have a total of 138 school-aged children (ages 7–16), of whom 86, or 62 percent, are attending school fairly regularly. The remaining 38 percent either live too far from the closest school to attend, or were withdrawn from school temporarily to help out with farm chores. Of the children seven years of age or older, 35 percent are illiterate (38 percent of the boys and 31 percent of the girls).

The surveyed credit applicants have a total of 85 school-aged children, of whom 45, or 53 percent, are attending school fairly regularly. Of the school aged children, 26 percent are illiterate (30 percent of the boys and 22 percent of the girls). That more of the applicants' children are literate than those presently attending school indicates that some of the nonattenders went to school previously for a year or two and have since dropped out.

In general, the educational levels of the youth (and adults) are similar for both surveyed samples, though the borrowers withdraw their children from school somewhat less frequently than the nonborrowers.

Infant mortality.—Forty percent of the credit recipient families and 54 percent of the nonrecipient families have lost one or more children in their first year of life. Dividing the total number of infant deaths by the total number of births per group, the infant mortality rates of recipients and nonrecipients are 10.4 percent and 14.2 percent, respectively. As points of reference, the United States and India have average infant mortality rates of 0.17 percent and 13.9 percent, respectively.

Asked whether the mother of the house had ever received information or guidance on prenatal and postnatal care, 24 percent of the recipients responded affirmatively, compared to only 11 percent of the nonrecipients. This, in addition to differences in nutrition and sanitation standards, may explain the lower infant mortality rate of the recipient group.

Common health problems.—The surveyed families were asked to list the common illnesses they have suffered from in Caquetá. The answers, shown in table 36, were similar for borrowers and nonborrowers.

Some of the answers probably reflect mistaken identity of symptoms; for instance, high fevers with chills are practically always considered *fiebres palúdicas* (malaria fevers), even though they may actually be symptoms of bad head or stomach flu. Also, diarrhea is

TABLE 36

Common Illnesses in Caquetá
as Experienced by 85 Surveyed Families, 1978

	Credit Recipients percent of total[a]	Credit applicants percent of total[a]
Malaria (fevers)	60	57
Colds	54	54
Gastrointestinal	28	14
Others[b]	14	37

[a]Percent of recipient/applicant families that suffer from these illnesses, with varying degrees of frequency.

[b]Arthritis, polio, skin diseases, kidney problems, ulcers, yellow fever, anemia, backaches.

sometimes so common that it is not identified with any illness, but instead is considered quite normal. The figures do show, in any case, a high incidence of health problems for both groups, caused by inadequate diets, sanitation, and preventive health care, as well as a difficult climate and strenuous work. Asked whether they have used the local health facilities (clinics in the nearest towns), 76 percent of the recipients and 66 percent of the nonrecipients replied affirmatively.

Summary

Data from eighty-five extensive interviews with rural families in Caquetá were measured and analyzed to determine the economic and social impact of the INCORA/World Bank credit program on its beneficiaries. Despite limitations of the selected sample, both in size and method, the families interviewed are generally representative of the total credit recipient and credit applicant populations. The final outcome of the credit program will not be known until the late 1990s, when the loans are repaid and INCORA cattle herds are fully developed. Nevertheless, this interim evaluation is useful for understanding the current state of the program, its successes and shortcomings, and for providing insights on issues relevant to cattle credit programs in colonization areas generally.

The data reveal that INCORA borrowers have increased their farm assets substantially since receiving their initial loans, and at a faster pace than nonborrowers with similar socioeconomic backgrounds. As a result of these improvements, particularly a large increase in the median herd size and better land use, the recipients have increased the volume and value of their annual sales. This, in turn, has led to higher gross annual earnings. Such economic benefits, experienced principally by Phase 1 borrowers, were facilitated by the credit program's four-year grace period and by the marked increase in cattle prices during the mid-1970s.

Despite their increased asset worth, the majority of credit recipients earn very low net annual incomes, a median of U.S.$116 per capita, before loan principal payments. This income does not even cover median basic need expenditures on food, clothing, and health care.

When the programmed loan repayments are further subtracted from their net income, all but the most prosperous families will be forced to sell two, three or several head of cattle (depending upon current cattle prices and individual debt) to cover the annual quotas. And when these loan repayments are included, particularly after the first year, the credit recipient group may be harder pressed to meet basic needs than the applicant group.

Furthermore, unless cattle prices continue to rise above the 15 percent Phase 2 interest rate, and above the inflated prices of essential consumer and farm-related items, the low-income recipients (58 percent of the total) may not be able to make their loan repayments without drastically reducing their herd size. In the case of credit default, the government has the right to confiscate all of the delinquent farmer's assets, including his or her land.

These findings were largely anticipated in the World Bank farm development models formulated at appraisal time and restated in the 1978 *Project Performance Audit Report* (see note 7, chapter 2) as follows:

> An interesting aspect of the appraisal report, brought forth *only within the context of the models themselves*, is that the expected sale of cattle would not have produced sufficient income to cover programmed subborrower loan repayments in a world of stable prices. Accordingly, the appraisal report models *assume* that cattle prices will rise at 15 percent per year due to inflation, although loan repayments remain fixed. Inflation was thus expected to reduce real interest rates to negative levels, thereby permitting planned amortization of the loan. Even under these circumstances, farm disposable income does not rise until the seventh year of development. [Italics added.]

While it is true that the long-term tendency is for Colombian cattle prices to rise at a rate equal to or higher than the national inflation average (diagram 7), since 1950 this overall increase has been characterized by short-term cyclical upward and downward price swings in response to national and international demand and supply of meat and milk (diag. 8). In Caquetá, from 1972 to 1978, the annual rise in cattle prices varied from 7 percent to 49 percent, peaking in 1977. Prices dropped sharply during the summer of 1978 as a result of that year's severe drought, poor harvests, and widespread destruction of pasture by uncontrolled fires, forcing local farmers to sell their livestock quickly and before full development. The negative impact of that summer will be felt for several years to come.

It appears that the World Bank erred in assuming that Caquetá cattle prices would increase steadily for the full length of the planned amortization schedule, ending in the late 1990s for Phase 2 borrowers. Indeed, the international, national, and local conditions that determine cattle prices are too unstable to assume long-term tendencies of any kind, especially when the success of the appraised program hinges upon the correctness of the assumption.

In short, the advantaged borrowers—those with initially larger herds and incomes, or alternately, poor colonos with lower payment

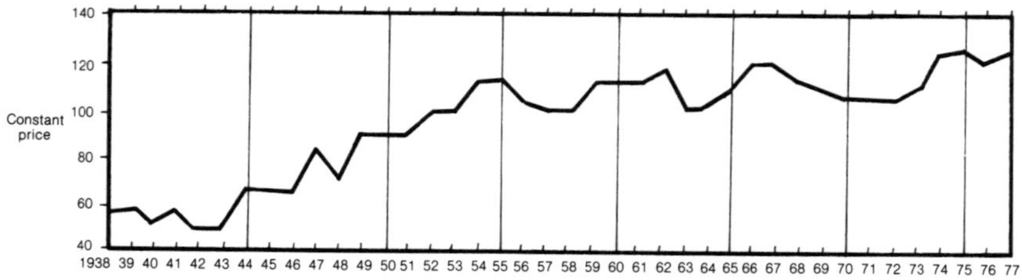

Diagram 7. Cattle Prices in Colombia: Long-Term Tendencies.

Source. Adapted from a chart in Salomón Kalmonovitz, *Desarrollo de la agricultura* (Bogotá: Editorial la Carreta, 1978), p. 176.

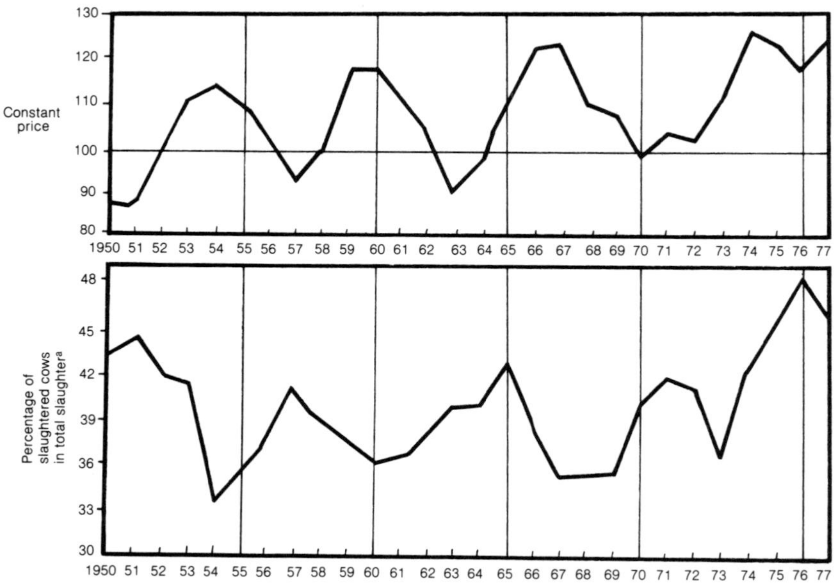

[a] As the percentage of slaughtered cows in the total slaughter increases, the total supply of cattle will decrease, reflecting the rancher's decision to liquidate his assets because of low commercial prices. Note the strong inverse relationship between the supply and price curves.

Diagram 8. Cattle Prices Compared to Supply of Slaughtered Cows.

Source. Adapted from a chart in Salomón Kalmonovitz, *Desarrollo de la agricultura* (Bogotá: Editorial la Carreta, 1978), p. 176,

quotas and interest rates (Phase 1)—will probably experience a long-term net positive impact from their participation in the INCORA credit program. Even these farmers, however, will not experience markedly improved living standards (adequate levels) until their loans are fully repaid, their cash flows increase and stabilize, and a sense of economic security is sustained. The low-income borrowers, particularly in the Phase 2 program, will not fare nearly as well. Indeed, given their low incomes, unstable market and climatic conditions, and the fixed steady increase in annual loan repayments, their long-term prospects appear quite bleak.

We conclude, therefore, that the INCORA/World Bank credit program will succeed in promoting economic and social mobility among its middle-level borrowers by providing them with the assistance required to "take off" and develop their existing potential. Colonos in greater need, however, will find the credit program inadequate and too costly to impel them out of their present poverty.

5

Conclusions and Recommendations

Conclusions

In this work, I have discussed the historical events and debates that led up to the current Colombian government and World Bank emphasis on colonization and integrated rural development strategies as the preferred means of tackling the "agrarian problem." The colonization process and World Bank-funded government assistance programs in Caquetá, Colombia, were analyzed as a case study in order to evaluate the impact of these operations on the economic and social lives of the local rural population. Data and observations collected from primary sources in the field, including farmers, government technicians, and professionals, have permitted an understanding of the perceived successes and failures of government assistance in the area from several vantage points. The conclusions that I draw, after analyzing these varied perspectives, are not clearly positive or negative. The evidence shows that both kinds of change (or lack of change) are present.

The objective of this work has been to understand the underlying tenets and aims of the rural development strategies implemented in Caquetá during the past two decades, to discover whether those aims satisfactorily meet the needs of the affected population, and to make recommendations for change. Where problems and shortcomings exist in the design and implementation of these strategies, I separate them into two categories: (1) those that result from inefficient planning, poor coordination, or local incompetence, and that could be corrected within the framework of integrated rural development; and (2) those that result from the faltering commitment of the national government and powerful interest groups to implement stated objectives, or alternately, from the basic inadequacy of the adopted strategy.

Once the problems are identified and separated, it is possible to make recommendations for change that would either bring current rural development strategies more in line with the needs of the target population, or when necessary, substitute alternative strategies.

Chapter Review

In chapter 1 I presented a brief historical background of agrarian structures and reform in Colombia. It was shown how the contemporary inequalities in land distribution, which foster high rural unemployment, low productivity in basic foods, and intense rural-to-urban migration, are rooted in centuries of imposed policies that have favored a privileged few while thwarting the efforts of rebels and reformers to bring about significant change. Rebel movements, such as the Peasant Leagues of the 1930s, guerrilla defense units during "La Violencia," and militant ANUC actions in the early 1970s, succeeded, nonetheless, in demonstrating the potential power of an organized rural population, and therefore forced Colombia's traditional rulers to debate politically feasible solutions to the agrarian crisis.

In 1961, Colombian Social Agrarian Reform Law 135 was passed and displayed to the world as a model piece of progressive legislation. Its complex articles and decrees promised an overhaul of the established land tenure system to benefit the small producers and landless rural workers. It was the Liberal party solution for eliminating rural unrest and enhancing agricultural productivity simultaneously. However, the ideals and the rhetoric crumbled in the face of powerful opposition by landed interests and the absence of an influential mass constituency to demand that the law be upheld. Subsequent decrees and laws were passed to dilute the strength of Law 135 and its implementing agency, INCORA. Data presented on INCORA accomplishments and land distribution as of 1970–1971 testify to the fact that very few Colombian farmers received land as a result of redistribution (0.45 percent of total farmers received 0.25 percent of total cultivated land). Moreover, the emergence of revolutionary guerrilla groups in the late 1960s and their continued actions throughout the 1970s demonstrate that rural unrest was not eliminated, but only contained temporarily.

Having rejected true agrarian reform as a solution owing to its threat to established latifundismo and capitalist commercial agriculture, the Colombian government was still left with a vacuum in agrarian policy which had to be filled with a policy that would be acceptable to the ruling class, at least minimally sympathetic to certain rural needs, and in line with the requirements of multinational lending institutions. The policy adopted, and currently in use, involves three basic strategies:

1. To encourage large landholders to transform their underused latifundia to commercial use, principally for export, through subsidized credit, technical assistance, and tax incentives;
2. To promote migration to and colonization of the Colombian frontier (the eastern llanos and the southern lowlands), thereby incorporating large abandoned areas into the national economy while providing land and work for a portion of the nation's poor rural population; and
3. To provide a variety of integrated rural services (credit, schools, health clinics, roads, technical assistance, supply stores, etc.) to rural families with small and medium-sized farms in order to raise their productivity and improve their general well-being.

In view of the failures of former attempts to implement stated agrarian policies, it follows that one cannot assume that the abovesaid strategies have or will be carried out in practice. Only empirical evidence can reveal the size of the gap between professed objectives and real accomplishments. Moreover, only through this evidence can one assess the overall validity of the strategies vis-á-vis local and national needs. In the case study so far presented on colonization and integrated rural development in Caquetá, Colombia, I have attempted to provide partial evidence toward the understanding of these questions.

In chapter 2 I discussed the settlement history and socioeconomic conditions of rural colonos in Caquetá. Most Caquetá migrants were pushed away from their areas of origin by land displacement and concentration, unemployment, and rural violence; they were pulled toward Caquetá by the availability of unclaimed baldío land, by its relative tranquillity, and, to a lesser extent, by the promise of government assistance. It was shown that early life on the frontier is almost universally difficult as the migrants struggle to adjust to unfamiliar tropical agroclimatic conditions and isolation. Their dream is to establish viable family-sized farms and to acquire livestock of their own. After long experiences of poverty and unstable earnings, their hope is to secure tangible income-producing assets that can be developed and passed on to their children. Though migration in many cases is a last resort forced by negative experiences in the

Colombian interior, the colonos strive diligently to make the most of their situation, seeking to establish a better life in a new land.

In chapter 3 I described the design and implementation of INCORA programs in Caquetá, aimed at lessening the environmental and institutional obstacles to social and economic mobility presented in chapter 2. The stated objectives and strategies of Social Agrarian Reform Law 135, the World Bank, and the Colombian Government were reviewed generally and then compared to real accomplishments in Caquetá.

In general, the stated objectives of the Caquetá Land Settlement Project, Phases 1 and 2, do address the basic needs of the low-income rural population through plans to provide them with title to adequate land and the means to increase their productivity and income and to improve their living standards. In practice, the achievements realized have been substantial but inadequate.

In spite of repeated failures to reach target goals, INCORA has succeeded somewhat in stabilizing and equalizing land tenure by distributing thousands of land titles to migrants; it has assisted several thousand settlers to acquire livestock and farm installations; and it has sponsored the construction of sorely needed roads, schools, and health clinics. These accomplishments are generally appreciated by the rural community at large; they have made life on the frontier moderately less difficult.

Nevertheless, alongside every achievement there exists an accompanying problem, and for every need fulfilled, there exist still others neglected. These problems, which have in common the obstruction of need fulfillment, should be separated, as indicated earlier, into those which are soluble within the framework of integrated rural development and those which would require a fundamental reworking of current strategies to insure their solution.

Problems Soluble within Current Strategies

The problems that fall into this category have emerged principally as a result of project planning errors and poor coordination among participating government agencies. The following are six major planning errors, made by Colombian and World Bank planners alike:

1. An insufficient emphasis on and investment in primary needs, such as nutrition, hygiene, housing, and education, manifested in the low budget and small staff of the social extension program (Capacitación Campesina), and the failure to establish outreach links with the local Juntas de Acción Comunal.

2. The failure to provide financial and educational incentives to maintain high motivation among INCORA's technical personnel, and of particular importance, the lack of a specific program to include lower-level (credit supervisors and extension agents) participation in decision making.
3. An underestimation of costs, particularly in the road development and credit programs, leading to irregular and often poor-quality construction and cattle, respectively, as well as unfulfilled or much delayed promises made to the community.
4. An excessively high interest rate and price for cattle in the Phase 2 credit program in light of the stated objective to assist low-income farmers, and considering the long-term instability of local market prices and farmer earnings.
5. The lack of some form of financial protection against natural disasters (perhaps a predisaster insurance program tied to low or no interest loans and technical assistance) that, although not the fault of the victims, cripple their ability to develop their farms and repay their loans according to schedule, and the lack of guarantees for farmers who experience initial failures while experimenting with innovative farming, ranching, or marketing methods, thus discouraging the use of such methods.
6. The failure, stemming from an obvious bias toward cattle ranching versus agriculture, to include a plan to provide affordable agricultural credit and technical assistance to the newly arrived and poorer colonos who do not fulfill the present requirements for INCORA credit, and therefore are excluded from direct government assistance.

Besides the above set of planning-related problems and errors, INCORA programs have been seriously hindered by poor coordination with other participating government agencies. In some cases, signed agreements have not been enforced; in other cases, they have not been properly integrated into the total development plan. For instance, though the agreement with SEM to provide the nontoxic substance, Baygon, for fumigation against malaria-carrying mosquitoes is being carried out according to schedule, SEM officials admit that the campaign is severely impeded by the fact that most rural houses cannot be adequately protected due to their poor construction. INCORA credit provides a small allocation for house improvement, which is insufficient to repair or improve construction up to adequate standards, thus undermining the success of the malaria eradication campaign.

A second example of poor coordination is the failure of the Ministry of Education to provide INCORA/ICCE-built schools with a stable supply of well-qualified teachers, resulting in underuse of schools and frustration within the rural communities. Likewise, INCORA has neglected to coordinate the activities of its Rural Training department with the health projects of the local Public Health Institute (Salud Pública), and therefore missed the opportunity to expand distribution of sanitary units and small aqueducts to rural communities.

Finally, the INDERENA/INCORA program for conservation and reforestation has met with myriad problems, not least of which has been a lack of communication between the two institutions on their mutual responsibilities, resulting in nonenforcement of the agreement and sustained inaction. The program's financial problems, however, cannot be blamed on poor project planning or coordination as much as on the lack of national support from Bogotá.

The existence of planning and coordination problems has created a sizable gap between stated project objectives and real accomplishments. Yet solutions to these problems would not require fundamental alteration of the integrated rural development and colonization strategies. A larger budget, a rearrangement of investment priorities, and a stronger commitment to distributing the benefits of credit more equally throughout rural Caquetá, particularly to less advantaged colono families, would go far to correct current project inadequacies. These changes are politically and economically feasible; risks to the established order would be negligible.

Problems Inherent to Current Strategies

A different set of problems, perhaps more important to the long-term fulfillment of rural needs than those already presented, is the product of inherent inadequacies in past and present national agrarian policy. Historically determined, these problems continue unabated. Solutions are therefore more controversial and less feasible in the short run. In brief, these problems stem from the lack of commitment by the government and influential power groups of Colombia to land tenure reform and the equalization of national resource distribution in favor of the rural poor. The currently adopted strategies of integrated rural development and colonization are inadequate substitutes for commitment to these wider policies.

The promotion of colonization in the sixties and seventies, as an alternative to the redistribution and development of large underused private holdings in highly populated rural areas, has required large outlays of government subsidies to provide even minimal benefits to colono families (particularly investment in basic infrastructure). The same quantity of government assistance, properly invested in land reform projects throughout Colombia's interior, would benefit a substantially larger number of farmers and create greater employment opportunities for the mass of landless poor. Historically, the high economic opportunity cost associated with colonization has been justified on political grounds: a means to avoid volatile confrontation with land reform opponents. From the perspective of its original proponents, however, the increasing politicization of colonized areas, particularly a recent upsurge in guerrilla activity, may prove even the political justification for colonization to be unsound.

Although inadequacies inherent to Colombia's national agrarian policy have their greatest impact in the more developed and stratified Colombian interior, including its urban areas, a strong impact is also felt in Caquetá, the focus of this work. Specifically, four major problems evident in Caquetá and resulting from overall national policy, are the following:

1. Waning interest in agrarian reform has led to the gradual curtailment of funds, personnel, and influence of its implementing agency, INCORA. Consequently, INCORA parcelization and colonization projects have suffered nationwide. In the case of Project Caquetá, the national government has not fulfilled its financial responsibilities, causing long delays and great difficulty in meeting planned targets, and low morale as well. The newer government agency, DRI (Integrated Rural Development), now enjoys the limelight that INCORA once enjoyed under former administrations.
2. As a result of the national lack of commitment to land reform, INCORA's local attempts to stabilize and equalize land tenure are only minimally effective. While colonos have been allowed to obtain title to baldío land, there are no guarantees against future land displacement through land sales to wealthier ranchers. No legal limit exists on the amount of land that a private individual may purchase and own. Consequently, the problem of land concentration in the interior of Colombia is spreading to the frontier, diminishing the opportunities of poor migrants to obtain and secure adequate farm units.
3. The problem of highly unstable market prices for primary producer goods, frequently mentioned by Caquetá farmers as their major concern, has not been addressed in any comprehensive national program. IDEMA, the nation's agricultural marketing

agency, has not been provided with the support or the means to offer adequate decentralized services to the countryside, resulting in abuses by commercial middlemen and burdensome transportation costs for isolated farmers. The lack of an effective price support system for small and poor farmers reflects the national government's bias toward urban centers and large-scale commercial agriculture.

4. The present Colombian agrarian policy is essentially government-controlled and directed. The presumed rural beneficiaries are not included in project planning, investment decision making, or the implementation of programs designed on their behalf. More important, poor farmers (colonos, minifundistas, tenant farmers) have neither been encouraged nor allowed to form strong organizations to represent and demand their legal rights. Previous attempts at organization have been thwarted by the state's repressive apparatus. The governing class fears, and rightfully so, that a unified peasant organization with strong leadership would threaten the established order with demands to end latifundismo and exploitative labor relations. This fear is manifested in the present administration's vigorous military campaigns against rural and urban guerrilla groups throughout the nation, including Caquetá. Indeed, within the guerrilla zones, more government resources seem to be devoted to militarization than to economic and social development, even though frequent acts of arbitrary repression practiced during these campaigns actually increase popular support for guerrilla movements.

Unless the present agrarian policy is altered to include small farmer representation in the assessment, planning, and enforcement of development goals, precedent suggests that rural "beneficiaries" will continue to be victims of broken government promises and faltering commitment to the fulfillment of their needs. Built-up frustration of this kind more often than not leads to increasingly violent cycles of rebellion and repression.

Summary

In this conclusion, I have emphasized the obstacles to need fulfillment in Caquetá, while still acknowledging the importance of INCORA accomplishments in the region. The Caquetá Land Settlement Project, as an exercise in integrated rural development and government assisted colonization, has been moderately successful. Of special merit are the Project's credit program, which has enabled a significant number of low-income farmers with medium-sized farms to acquire livestock, and the road development program, which has improved rural-urban communication. Also noteworthy have been certain innovative efforts to coordinate the resources and skills of several local development-related agencies to provide a package of integrated social and economic services to the rural community.

Nevertheless, the Project suffers from several serious planning and coordination problems that have prevented the completion of stated objectives. Still other long-range problems, evident in Caquetá and elsewhere nationwide, stem from the political and economic limitations inherent in current national agrarian policy. This policy determines the direction that regional government programs must take and the resources available to them; it therefore binds the hands of implementing agencies that might otherwise order development priorities differently, and at the same time impedes community participation in the articulation and enforcement of those priorities.

In Caquetá, the limitations of current rural development strategies, and uneven commitment to them, result in programs that exclude the poorest settlers from direct government assistance and bypass certain major obstacles to upward mobility, such as land displacement by wealthy ranchers and unstable prices for cash crops. Ultimately, unless these strategies are strengthened in some ways and changed in others, Caquetá shall no longer serve as a refuge for victims of class barriers and violence in the Colombian interior, but rather, will inherit the very barriers that foster the violence.

Recommendations for Change

I believe that the existing government assistance programs in Caquetá, despite major difficulties, are sufficiently beneficial to justify their continuation. It is also evident, however, that unless the difficulties are mitigated, the benefits of these assistance programs for future participants will be considerably less satisfactory. Suggested recommendations for change that would help to overcome the planning, coordination, and policy problems discussed earlier are presented in this section.

Certain of the following recommendations would simply require a rearrangement of priorities within the existing budget. Others would require additional funding, preferably from the national budget so as not to incur further indebtedness to the World Bank. The latter changes imply cooperation from the national government, which admittedly will only be forthcoming when it is confronted with pressures that cannot safely be ignored. Possible sources of pressure are discussed further on.

Social Extension

The Caquetá Land Settlement Project should continue and accelerate its long-term trend toward increasing the total percentage of Project funds allocated for social services and infrastructure, including schools, health clinics, and extension work. A good way to disseminate information pertaining to better health, nutrition, and hygiene is to employ trained extension workers to organize rural communities around these issues. Rather than have extension workers travel from house to house, they could organize meetings with the established Juntas de Acción Comunal at convenient times, to deliver classes and distribute subsidized inputs, such as vitamins, sanitary units, and written and diagrammed instructions. During these meetings, the community would have a chance to discuss its concerns with government representatives, who, in turn, would pass on the information to their superiors on a regular basis. Extension classes might include such topics as child care, ecology, vegetable gardening, natural fertilizers, craft making for home use and sale, adult literacy, and community organization. Follow-up visits would be important to monitor the impact of these classes and discussions on community well-being. All of this could be accomplished by hiring an adequate number of well-qualified extension workers and by providing them with low-cost inputs that rural families could purchase outright or on credit.

Work Incentives

INCORA's social and agricultural extension agents, veterinarians, and agronomists presently suffer from low motivation, owing largely to the absence of incentives and the deprivations particular to rural work in Caquetá.

In addition to the possible incentives to improve motivation discussed in chapter 3, government workers should be awarded hardship allowances for working in isolated and impoverished areas. Over and above financial rewards, extension agents would appreciate more responsibility in decision making as well as additional opportunities for advanced technical training: classes, seminars, and visits to experimental programs or other INCORA projects throughout Colombia. Motivation would also improve if INCORA technicians were provided with the inputs required to implement their technical recommendations, that is, improved seeds, pesticides, tools, etc., thereby increasing the probability that such recommendations would be positively received and carried out. In short, the object is to reduce the monotony and futility of routine rural visits by making those visits consistently worthwhile for extension agent and farmer alike.

Credit

Interviews with INCORA borrowers and nonborrowers revealed frequent complaints concerning poor cattle quality, insufficient cattle per loan, and too few loans. Phase 2 borrowers often expressed concern over the high cost of their credit, both the principal and interest rate. In other words, farmers would like the existing INCORA credit program to undergo certain changes and at the same time hope for its expansion to satisfy local demand.

One way to reduce the price of cattle without sacrificing quality, or alternately, to improve its quality without increasing the price, would be for INCORA to arrange its purchases prudently and in good time, seeking the best prices from the fairest sources. At present, INCORA cattle are usually purchased in haste and in large quantities at the ''rush'' price offered by large ranchers; some farmers and INCORA technicians even suspect that INCORA purchasers receive a payoff in return for good deals. It therefore appears necessary that knowledgeable outside parties be present during the selection and purchase of cattle for credit to act in an auditing capacity; these might be a competing local rancher together with past and current borrowers.

Furthermore, the credit interest rate should not be set solely according to long-term cattle price criteria, which in fact have an unpredictable history, but also according to the income potential of the majority of borrowers and with consideration of fluctuations in farmer earnings particular to rural Caquetá. After the initial interest-free grace period, the interest rate should gradually be increased to the maximum level as income potential improves.

Finally, it is clear that the demand for INCORA credit far exceeds the supply, even though INCORA's policy has been to distribute fewer cattle per loan in order to provide more loans overall. In order to determine the actual size and character of the current demand for credit, which to date are unknown, it would be useful to conduct a broad representative survey throughout Caquetá. Such a study might provide the basis for increased government funding from Bogotá. Meanwhile, INCORA's policy of loaning fewer cattle to more families seems justified given the limited budget. Indeed, within that limited budget, it would be worthwhile to appropriate even smaller loans (less than ten head of cattle) to poorer colonos with less pasture who are presently excluded from the credit program.

Guarantees

During my field experience, I was impressed by the lack of guarantees or farm insurance against natural disaster, crop failure, and loss incurred through innovation. According to the stated objectives of Social Agrarian Reform Law 135, the state is obliged to provide better guarantees to small farmers, yet the evidence in Caquetá clearly illustrates a breach of that obligation. The absence of these guarantees, in an often unhospitable and unpredictable environment such as Caquetá, invokes the premonition that indeed only the strongest will survive.

To ameliorate this situation, I suggest two possible plans. First, the government, through one of its banks or insurance agencies, could institute an insurance plan to cover major losses caused by insect plagues, drought, fire, or floods, that would be offered at rates corresponding to ability to pay. As a member of the insurance plan, an individual family or group of families would be entitled to emergency low interest loans and technical assistance for basic need expenditures, productive investments, and debt payments until its situation returned to normal.

Second, in order to encourage farmers and ranchers to use experimental methods that would be likely to increase productivity, INCORA would implement a program to insure farmers against possible loss incurred as a result of innovation. The farmer would be loaned the agricultural inputs, including labor costs, required to implement a new method and then would repay the loan from surpluses accrued due to increased yields, or an improved reproduction rate in the case of livestock. If the new method, properly implemented, fails to increase productivity after sufficient attempts, the loan would be cancelled. If the new method actually results in lower productivity, the farmer would be reimbursed for losses incurred. An insurance plan of this sort would undoubtedly stimulate a wider use of technical improvements and would also oblige INCORA, ICA and INDERENA to test the reliability of their experiments before recommending them to individual farmers.

Coordination and Control

The integrated rural development strategy, by virtue of its objective to provide integrated social and economic opportunities and services to rural communities, requires the committed cooperation of as many development-related groups and institutions as possible. In

Caquetá, the INCORA Project has succeeded in enlisting the participation of ten public agencies to carry out its development programs. Contracts between INCORA and each of these participating agencies enumerate and explain their mutual and separate responsibilities toward the completion of specific goals within a defined time period.

Unfortunately, very few of the contracts have actually been enforced according to plan. Perhaps the greatest difficulty has been the delayed disbursement of funds from Bogotá to INCORA and then to the other agencies, or to those agencies directly from Bogotá. Progress has also been impeded by deficient communication and coordination between and among the contracted parties subsequent to the contract signing. Specifically, an ongoing forum is needed, where the discussion of problems encountered during the implementation of long-term projects could take place, along with the coordination of scattered resources to solve these problems. Also needed are effective sanctions to enforce the compliance of written agreements that otherwise are too easily breached. An example of how these suggestions could be used follows.

Imagine that INCORA, ICA, and INDERENA sign a three-way agreement, pooling their resources to design an ecologically sound method of improving pasture coverage in Caquetá. In the contract, INCORA agrees to finance the program and to propagate its findings throughout rural Caquetá; ICA agrees to provide the technical personnel and to undertake appropriate experiments on its farm, Macagual, and on other demonstration plots in several distinct rural areas; and INDERENA agrees to test the new methods for their impact on soil erosion and mineral depletion under normal, flood, and drought conditions. Another contract clause requires representatives from each agency to meet together monthly to give progress reports and to discuss the nature of any problem thus far encountered. Finally, the contract is signed by each participating agency and co-signed by a solvent bank (Banco de la República, Banco Ganadero, or the Caja Agraria) and the Treasury Secretary of the Republic of Colombia.

The additional co-signers will only become important if and when the implementing agencies renege on their agreed-upon obligations. If INCORA delays the disbursement of funds as a result of its own negligence or that of the central government, the co-signing bank will forward funds to make up the deficit, thereby enabling the program to continue, but at the same time will charge a penalty to the party at fault. On the other hand, if ICA or INDERENA misuse INCORA funds or fail to carry out promised experiments and tests without reasonable cause, they will be sanctioned by the Treasury Secretary with a reduction or delay in government appropriations, which will adversely affect local operations until contract obligations are resumed.

This example could easily be applied to other agencies in various agreement combinations. Appropriate sanctions, though unpleasant, should be available to ensure that agreed-upon goals are accomplished. One would hope that as communication and coordination improve with monthly progress reports and discussions, the need to invoke sanctions would correspondingly diminish.

Land Tenure

Historically, colonization advocates have argued that frontier settlement would go far in solving Colombia's tenancy problems by enabling small farmers and landless rural workers from the interior to acquire adequate farm units in the undeveloped frontier regions. Whereas redistribution of land through the parcelization of large private holdings would abuse the sanctity of private property, and therefore provoke strong political opposition, the parcelization of public land in the southeastern lowlands was politically feasible, economically expensive, but in the long run promising, and of great potential benefit to Colombia's rural poor.

In fact, colonization is not an adequate alternative to land redistribution. The hardships and costs that migration and colonization involve limit the number of settlers to a fraction of the total rural population that needs and desires more land. Moreover, as colonization areas become progressively more developed through the efforts of early migrant settlers, they become correspondingly more attractive to large ranchers and entrepreneurs in search of economic opportunities to expand their holdings. Since there is no limit on the amount of land that can be purchased and privately owned, the financially advantaged migrant or absentee owner can amass very large holdings through the purchase of many adjacent smaller holdings—a process that results in the increasing concentration of land ownership.

In Caquetá, as of 1970–1971 (see chapter 2, table 4), 10 percent of the landowners held 57 percent of the total titled land area, while 50 percent of the landowners held only 10 percent of the total area. Ultimately, the only way to prevent further land concentration in Caquetá is to establish legal limits on the amount of land an individual family may own, no matter how the property is obtained. The legal limit for baldío claims (450 hectares) could be extended to include purchased land as well, with smaller limits placed on the choicest landholdings near to major towns and roads.

Meanwhile, two intermediate measures are suggested to stall an avalanche of land sales before the above limits are accepted. First, INCORA should enlarge its Legal Section by hiring several more topographers, and at the same time decrease the bureaucratic steps involved in obtaining a land title. This would allow more colonos to establish legal tenancy in a shorter time period and thereby provide increased protection against forced land displacement. Second, part of INCORA's extension program for low-income farmers should include the dissemination of information on tenancy rights, current land values, and the long-term consequences involved in selling one's farm. It is incumbent upon INCORA to discourage farmers from giving up their land when that action is decidedly against their best interests.

Marketing of Agricultural Goods

Although development programs in Caquetá promote livestock production to a greater degree than agriculture, most Caquetá farmers derive the majority of their income from the sale of agricultural products. The process of marketing agricultural goods is vitally important to low income farmers and considerably important to middle income farmers as well.

Aside from the occurrence of total harvest failure or very low yields, Caquetá farmers are most concerned about the costs involved in marketing their products as well as the level and stability of market prices and the terms of payment. Farmers who live long distances from the central markets are particularly injured by high transportation costs, or, when pressed to sell their produce indirectly through middlemen, by low sale prices. The government marketing agency, IDEMA, is supposed to ameliorate this situation through decentralized purchasing at guaranteed prices. In Caquetá, IDEMA has failed to fulfill these functions. First, its offices and warehouses are all located in towns; second, it usually delays payment from one to three months after the receipt of goods, and third, it has the reputation of favoring wealthy clients over poor ones.

Rather than require isolated farmers to transport their produce to IDEMA's urban-based warehouses, it is more logical to construct IDEMA warehouses in rural areas to which surrounding farmers could bring their produce for temporary storage. Also, IDEMA services would be far more accessible if they were to include mobile purchasing units, that is, buses, trucks, and river barges, to collect produce along roadsides and river banks. Finally, it is essential that IDEMA be assured (by national headquarters in Bogotá) an adequate cash flow permitting it to pay farmers at the moment of purchase, or very shortly thereafter. Otherwise, farmers in urgent need of income to buy food, make loan repayments, pay laborers, etc., will be forced to continue to sell their goods to commercial intermediaries at unreasonably low prices.

Rural Organization

These final recommendations for change are broader in scope and considerably more controversial than those already mentioned. They refer to the need to build an influential peasant-based organization to act on behalf of colono interests before high-level government authorities.

Such an organization is necessary to confront, in a unified and consistent manner, the hypocritical postures and empty rhetoric so common within the political establishment. Government hypocrisy and inconsistency manifest themselves most clearly in rural areas, where failure to effect promised services and structural improvements is the rule, rather than the exception. In Caquetá, the national government has seriously impeded the implementation of its own stated development objectives, programs, and laws by failing to provide adequate corresponding financial and technical support. Without that support, original targets must be constantly reappraised and reduced and newly discovered needs ignored, causing low morale in local programs and communities.

Although promises for reform often succeed in raising the expectations of a rural area destined to receive government assistance, the subsequent failure to deliver that assistance as promised frequently exacerbates long-standing feelings of abandonment and powerlessness among the rural poor. This also results in widespread distrust of government institutions and their representatives, and in considerable suppressed resentment and anger. This negative energy, quite prevalent in Caquetá, needs to be focused and organized into purposeful activity, preferably into the creation of an organization capable of exerting strong pressure on the same political establishment that too often ignores its own stated commitments.

In Caquetá, the rural community might begin to build its own political organization by improving communication among the existing Juntas de Acción Comunal, and eventually, by uniting them into a single, decentralized, rural interest group. From there, each junta would elect one or two representatives to speak, act, and vote on its behalf in coordinated group meetings. Then, a central leadership would be elected from the larger group of local junta leaders to represent the interests of the rural community at large before government authorities and the private sector. In this way the organization would slowly develop into a kind of regional rural union, with an elected leadership, dues-paying members (at minimum cost), frequent decentralized meetings, and specific tasks. Most important, the union would be responsible for assessing the needs of its constituency, for ordering development priorities, and for exerting appropriate pressures to enable the fulfillment of those needs and priorities.

The feasibility of the above plan is unclear. Several obstacles lie in the way. First of all, rural Caquetá is not homogeneous; different communities have distinct needs relevant to their particular physical, economic, and social conditions. Therefore, it would take considerable effort and commitment to arrive at unified platforms and demands. Nevertheless, it seems likely that a dynamic and sensitive leadership could eventually overcome these obstacles. Second, the union members would, within a reasonable period of time, have to be convinced that their organizational efforts were indeed worthwhile; that is, the organization must be able to prove its ability to accomplish concrete benefits for its constituency. This touches on the final and most difficult problem: how to assure that high-level authorities will listen and respond positively to the union's demands. In other words, what kinds of pressures would result in effective action?

It seems reasonable that the best way to attract attention is through unified visible mass action on behalf of specific demands: demonstrations before a government office accompanied by signed petitions asking for the development or expansion of a particular program or service; mass distribution of the union's platform and demands for the purpose of gathering regional and national popular support; financial lobbying in Bogotá by articulate rural spokespeople; political bargaining with current government leaders and future candidates so that, in exchange for delivering the Caquetá rural vote to a particular candidate or party, the rural union obtains a greater voice in decision making and other specific benefits, and possibly strike-boycott actions against certain landowners and merchants guilty of exploitative behavior.

The objective, once again, would be to force government authorities and private individuals to recognize the political power of the rural sector, and to elicit from them a reaction that will bring concrete benefits—better services, more credit, higher wages, more input in development planning, etc.—to Caquetá's poor, rural population. In the case that such peaceful pressures do not lead to positive change or, in fact, provoke more repression and neglect, it would be folly, in light of Caquetá's current political instability, to deny the inevitability of increased political polarization, possibly leading to wider local support for the guerrilla campaigns.

Postscript

Since the completion of this manuscript I have received new material from the World Bank that reports on the progress of the Caquetá Land Settlement Project, Phase 2, through March 1981.[1] Highlights from this material are presented here in a brief overview of recent Project developments.

The INCORA/World Bank Caquetá Project has progressed since 1978 with basically the same activities and problems that are described and evaluated in the text. Recent developments tend to support the author's conclusions and recommendations presented in Chapter 5. Certain of the new data, however, are somewhat surprising and appear to brighten the prospects for INCORA Phase 2 credit recipients beyond the author's original expectations. Guerrilla and army warfare in the region, which has escalated and intensified even beyond the level predicted in the text, could undermine recent social and economic gains in rural Caquetá, depending upon the degree to which INCORA and Project beneficiaries become involved, directly or indirectly, in the conflict.

Overview

The Phase 2 completion date has been extended twice since 1978; the final date for completion is December 31, 1982, two and one half years later than originally planned. Although total Project cost has not been increased since appraisal in 1975 (U.S.$31.6 million in World Bank and government funds), several planned activities were scaled down and the distribution of available funds was revised with substantial changes. Most notably, the road construction costs will have increased by 69 percent over the appraisal estimate by the Project completion date (Col.$2,873,000/km compared to Col.

$1,695,000), representing 45 percent of the total Project cost. Rebudgeted funds to pay for increased road construction costs have come mainly from funds originally designated for the credit program, reducing the productive component of the Project to 37.5 percent of the total cost. The health and education infrastructure projects, antimalarial program, and technical assistance component have retained a similar percentage of total expenditures approved at appraisal, although the targets set for several of these activities have been reduced.

An insufficient and/or slow disbursement of World Bank and government funds from the Treasury of INCORA continues to be a major problem, causing delayed distribution of subloans to farmers and prolonged indebtedness to construction contractors charging high interest penalties. For example, in 1980, the Treasury approved a budget for the INCORA Caquetá Project of Col. $216,623,000, but only disbursed $74,448,000 by the end of the year, 35 percent of the total. Furthermore, disbursements were uneven throughout the year (60 percent transferred in the last quarter), causing production and payment schedule difficulties. The Colombian Treasury places the balance of budgeted funds into a reserve account that may be used by INCORA during the subsequent year, and thereafter are cancelled. World Bank technicians are hopeful that all Project funds will be exhausted by the end of 1982.

Credit

An average of 357 cattle breeding subloans per year will have been made by the completion of Phase 2. A record 501 subloans were made in 1981. The 1978 revised target of 2,300 subloans, which is 72% of the original target, should be met with no problem by the new completion date. Though a strong demand for INCORA cattle continues, loan approvals have been subject to the availability of funds from the Treasury. Supply has consistently fallen short of demand.

As of March 31, 1981, 45 percent of Phase 1 credit recipients had fully paid up their loan obligations. Of the current loan portfolio, 6 percent are past due by less than six months, 2 percent are classified as "problem loans", and 0.2 percent are under judicial proceedings. Ten percent of the Phase 2 recipients have paid up their loans, most of them in advance of scheduled repayment. Only 1.7 percent of the outstanding Phase 2 loans are in arrears, most of them for less than six months.

These low default rates and the evidence of considerable advanced loan repayments by both Phase 1 and Phase 2 subborrowers are encouraging, and indicative of skilled credit management by INCORA and successful herd development by credit recipients. Phase 1 recipients received cattle at low prices and a low 8 percent interest rate, which allowed them to profit later in a high demand, inflationary cattle market. In the text, I predicted that Phase 2 recipients, who were receiving, in 1978, INCORA cattle at double the average cost and interest rate of Phase 1 recipients, would not fare as well and might face economic conditions that would result in substantial default rates. So far this does not appear to be the case, largely because the price of cattle has continued to rise above the subloan interest rate and in line with or above the national annual inflation rate of between 20 and 25 percent. In 1982, Phase 2 recipients will receive subloans at an average value of Col.$250,000, nearly three times the value of average Phase 1 loans. Moreover, as of January 1, 1982, the interest rate will increase from 15 percent to 18 percent annually, including the initial four year grace period. These last INCORA credit recipients, more than any before them, will require sustained high cattle prices during the next decade to be able to pay off their debts without seriously depleting their cattle stocks.

Road Construction and Maintenance

At the time of the Phase 2 appraisal in 1975, INCORA and the World Bank planned that 200 kilometers of unpaved roads and four bridges would be constructed by 1980 at a total cost of Col.$336 million. These goals will be reached, though differing somewhat as to construction location, by the revised completion date in 1982 at a cost of Col.$548 million, 63 percent higher than the original estimate. The large cost overrun occurred because of high inflation in construction supplies and equipment, and difficult topographical and climatic conditions. Some construction sites have also been disrupted by political violence and army occupation.

The road maintenance problem, discussed in detail in the text, continues unabated. A new two year contract between INCORA and Caminos Vecinales was signed in April 1980, for Col.$10 million annually, to provide maintenance for all INCORA-built roads. INCORA has kept its side of the bargain by providing nearly U.S. $500,000 worth of maintenance equipment, however, as of March 1981 Caminos Vecinales in Caquetá had not received any of the approved funds from the national office in Bogotá. The Caminos

Vecinales district manager in Caquetá estimates that Col.$40 million per year (approximately U.S.$800,000) is needed to maintain INCORA roads properly. Considering, therefore, an inadequate budget from the start, and sluggish transferral of even those funds, it is not surprising that very little maintenance has been carried out since 1980. No provisions have been made for road maintenance after Project completion in 1982.

Health and Education

The school, health center, and health clinic construction targets will all be met (less three schools) by December 1982. Water supply and sewerage construction plans, however, were scaled down substantially. The number of aqueducts was reduced from ten to seven, the minor water supply systems (mainly wells for schools) were reduced from 81 to 60, and all nine sewerage systems, with the possible exception of one, have been cancelled. As discussed in the text, the National Institute of Health (INS) has had difficulty all along meeting construction targets, fettered by insufficient and delayed payments by INCORA and its own financial and implementation limitations.

The National Service for the Eradication of Malaria (SEM) is treating a greater number of houses each year, up from 15,187 in 1977 to 28,156 in 1980, at an average cost of U.S.$20 per house. SEM has not yet presented INCORA with an evaluation of its program, and it is therefore unclear how effective the ''Baygon''/insecticide applications have been in controlling endemic malaria in rural Caquetá. The problem of poor house construction in rural areas, that could seriously undermine the efforts of the antimalarial program, needs to be analyzed by both INCORA and SEM in consideration of permanent malaria control.

Forestry and Erosion Control

Major difficulties, described in the text, prevented the INCORA/INDERENA (Institute for the Development of Renewable Natural Resources) contract for forest development and soil erosion control from achieving any of the program's original goals. These problems were never resolved, and the contract was finally cancelled in October of 1980. With growing migration to Caquetá and expanding colonization into the hinterland, using the slash-and-burn clearing method along river banks and into the foothills, deforestation and soil erosion have become increasingly serious problems. INCORA is beginning to plant trees in select areas on a sample number of farms with different classifications of eroded soils. As it gains practical experience from experimentation, INCORA plans to launch a protection and information campaign throughout Caquetá. It is very difficult, however, to place limits on development that may prove ecologically harmful after a relatively unrestricted process of colonization is already established.

Monitoring and Evaluation

The monitoring unit established in 1978 to evaluate the impact of Project programs on rural beneficiaries, particularly the credit program, was disbanded after a few months. The questionnaires and income/expense log notebooks were found to be overly detailed and difficult to maintain and collect on a regular basis. Available data on low default rates and advanced loan repayments tend to indicate successful herd development by many credit recipients; however, INCORA does not have reliable information on changes in rural family incomes nor on changes in basic need fulfillment, such as nutrition, disease, infant mortality, basic and technical education, and house construction, for Project beneficiaries versus unaffected families. It is still unknown whether credit recipients are actually living "better" than nonrecipients. The data and analysis on these questions presented in this study is perhaps the only such effort carried out thus far. The World Bank has asked INCORA to strengthen its Planning Department evaluation activities, using existing data and collecting additional data from a newly designed survey.

It is also important to evaluate the economic return of the Project in aggregate terms. Final data on total Project costs will show that the subsidized infrastructure portion of the Project (mainly road construction) consumed a considerably larger percentage of funds than the productive credit component. INCORA, the World Bank, and the Colombian Ministry of Planning will need to evaluate whether these expenditures, in the national development context, were justified, or whether Project Caquetá should have been designed differently to assure a higher economic return. Subsidized investment in underdeveloped rural areas is important in terms of long-term human and economic development benefits; when there are limited resources it is essential to evaluate where government investment is most needed and for what purposes. The methods chosen for project evaluation in general, both while the project is in process and after completion, should be geared toward analyzing these larger questions as well as questions regarding local impact.

It is still uncertain whether Project Caquetá will have a Third Phase. Although the World Bank is disposed toward negotiating a

Third Phase, and INCORA has already submitted a preliminary proposal, the Project's continuation will depend upon the decision of the new government that takes over in July 1982. That decision will certainly involve the new government's position on the political turmoil in Caquetá, and on the future role of INCORA in the national development framework.

INCORA and Political Warfare in Caquetá

During the field research for this study, the author was aware of frequent instances of guerrilla assaults in various parts of Caquetá, and of an increasingly determined anti-guerrilla response by the military. In 1978 and early 1979, the principal political group carrying out assaults and propaganda campaigns was the Revolutionary Armed Forces of Colombia (FARC), which bases its actions principally in rural areas. Since then, the renowned urban based guerrilla group, the M–19, has also chosen Caquetá as an important strategic region for training, political propaganda, assaults against army and police targets, and financial extortion. In turn, the army and police have launched an aggressive counterinsurgency campaign, including armed occupation of certain highly volatile areas. Violence has become a way of life in many Caquetá towns, and a general sense of insecurity pervades the countryside.

A journalist for the national newspaper, *La Nación*, who spent several harrowing days reporting on guerrilla warfare in Caquetá, wrote this about the situation: "The situation in Caquetá is quite delicate. There is fighting in many areas. The guerrilla is very well armed, and every day the army intensifies its siege against the insurgents in the Orteguaza and Peñas Blancas region. To travel on any river is sure death. The M–19 group has spread throughout Caquetá." (November 6, 1981)

The impact of this political situation on INCORA activities has been significant, but less than one might expect. Project credit supervisors have been withdrawn from some areas (particularly in the Puerto Solano/La Solita zone); INCORA staff have been detained by guerrillas and soldiers, and later released; a few credit recipients have deserted their farms because of the violence; and, in areas under army occupation road construction has been interrupted, causing lengthy delays. Otherwise, it appears that the guerrilla and INCORA have established an unofficial coexistence where neither deliberately interferes with the other's activities. This perhaps indicates that the M–19 and the FARC do not consider INCORA to be an agent of exploitation, which explains why it has not been singled out for assault and financial extortion, as have other government agencies, including the Caja Agraria.

The situation for INCORA is, nevertheless, tense, and undoubtedly the insecure work environment adversely affects staff morale. In fact, given the current political situation, it is somewhat surprising that Project activities have progressed without more serious setbacks and difficulties. This in itself is a sign of success, and underlines the determination of INCORA and local farmers to promote rural development in Caquetá under even the most difficult circumstances.

Notes

1. World Bank, *Supervision Report* (Washington, D.C.: World Bank Latin American and Caribbean Regional Office, July 1981), and discussions with Marc Blanc, World Bank technical officer and supervisor of the Caquetá Project, in April 1982.

APPENDIXES

Appendix 1
Project Caquetá, 1978:
List of INCORA Employees

Farm Settlement

1 Section chief (veterinarian)
1 Section secretary
1 Credit chief
1 Credit assistant
8 Veterinarians
2 Zoologists
1 Agronomist
1 Permanent crop advisor
1 Sociologist
2 Social extensionists
1 Rural organizer
9 Zone chiefs
41 Credit supervisors (agricultural extensionists)
8 Zone secretaries
1 Driver
9 Manual workers
1 Maintenance man
6 Janitors
5 Plant caretakers

100 Total

Engineering

1 Section chief (engineer)
1 Engineer
1 Secretary
2 Work inspectors
4 Drivers

9 Total

Health

1 Medical doctor

1 Total

Administration

1 Project manager (economist)
1 Secretary to project manager
1 Section chief
1 Planning advisor (accountant)
1 Budget advisor (economist)
1 Statistical advisor (engineer)
1 Personnel assistant
3 Secretaries
1 Warehouse chief
1 Warehouse assistant
1 Warehouse aide
1 Accounts payable supervisor
1 Accounts payable clerk
1 Chief of general services

1 Mechanic
1 Workshop assistant
1 Carpenter
5 Drivers
6 Maintenance men
3 Gardeners
3 Janitors
36

Legal

1 Legal advisor
1 Legal assistant
1 Investigator
1 Secretary
1 Chief of calculation and design
4 Graphic artists
2 Precision topographers
15 Compass topographers
7 Assistant topographers
8 Commission chiefs
41 Total

Appendix 2
Sample Interview Form
(Translation Follows)

INSTITUTO COLOMBIANO DE LA REFORMA AGRARIA "INCORA"

PROYECTO CAQUETA

ENCUESTA SEGUIMIENTO USUARIOS DEL CREDITO

FICHA SOCIOECONOMICA PARA SEGUIMIENTO DE PRESTATARIOS

I. INFORMACION GENERAL

FECHA:____________________

1.1. ZONA DE CREDITO______1.2. SECTOR______1.3. CODIGO_____________

1.4. LUGAR DE NACIMIENTO DEL JEFE____________________________________

1.4.1. DEL CONYUGE____

1.5. FECHA DE ESTABLECIMIENTO EN LA FINCA____________________________

1.6. FECHA DE LLEGADA AL CAQUETA_____________________________________

1.7. COMO OBTUVO LA FINCA? 1.7.1. COMPRA DE MEJORA__________________

1.7.2. FUNDADA________1.7.3. MIXTA__________1.7.4. OTRA________

1.8. ESTA TITULADA? 1.8.1.SI___1.8.2. NO_____1.8.3. EN TRAMITE______

1.9. AREA TITULADA_____________1.9.1. AREA SIN TITULAR______________

1.9.2. AREA TOTAL EL LA FINCA____________________

1.10. DISTANCIA DE LA CASA A LA CARRETERA MAS CERCANA

1.10.1. KM______1.10.2. TIEMPO______1.10.3. CUAL?______

1.11. DISTANCIA DE LA CASA AL RIO NAVEGABLE

1.11.1. KM______1.11.2. TIEMPO________

1.12. DISTANCIA DE SU FINCA A LA POBLACION MAS CERCANA

1.12.1. KM______1.12.2. TIEMPO________

1.12.3. CUANTO TIEMPO GASTABA ANTES DE ESTAR LA CARRETERA ?

II. ASPECTOS SOCIALES_________

2.1. NUMERO DE HIJOS______2.1.1. VIVOS______2.1.2. MUERTOS_________

2.2. NUMERO DE PERSONAS QUE DEPENDEN ECONOMICAMENTE DE USTED________

2.3. COMPOSICION FAMILIAR

#	PARENTESCO JEFE	SEXO M	SEXO F	EDAD	EST. CIVIL S C U.L.	ESTUDIOS PRI. SEC.	ESCRIBE LEE	OCUPACION PRINCIPAL
1								
2								
3								
4								
5								
6								
7								
8								
9								
10								

III. CARACTERISTICAS DE LA VIVIENDA

3.1. PAREDES__________3.2.TECHO___________3.3. PISO______________

3.4. # DE CUARTOS_____3.5. COCINA SEPARADA? 3.5.1.SI___3.5.2 NO__

3.6. LETRINA? 3.6.1.SI___3.6.2.NO___3.7. DE DONDE TOMA EL AGUA?__

__________3.7.1. COMO LLEVA EL AGUA A LA CASA?__________________

3.8. HA MEJORADO LAS CONDICIONES DE LA VIVIENDA EN LOS ULTIMOS

AÑOS? 3.8.1. SI____3.8.2. NO____3.8.3. EN QUE ASPECTOS______

____

IV. CONDICIONES DE VIDA

4.1. CUANTAS CAMAS TIENE EN SU VIVIENDA?_________________________

4.2. CUANTAS LAMPARAS TIENE EN SU CASA?__________________________

4.3. TIENE RADIO? 4.3.1. SI______ 4.3.2 NO______

4.4. TIENE MOLINO? 4.4.1. SI______ 4.4.2. NO______

4.5. QUE CLASE DE ESTUFA UTILIZA?___________________

4.6. QUE CLASE DE PLANCHA UTILIZA?__________________

4.7. TIENE DUCHA O BAÑO EN LA VIVIENDA? 4.7.1. SI______4.7.2. NO______

5. CUANTO GASTA APROXIMADAMENTE USTED Y SU FAMILIA MENSUALMENTE EN:

5.1. ALIMENTACION______5.2. VESTIDO_______

5.3. DROGA HUMANA______5.4. DIVERSION_____

5.5. EDUCACION_________5.6. DROGA VETERINARIA Y SAL______________

5.7. OTROS INSUMOS_____5.8. JORNALES______

5.9. GASTOS EN TRANSPORTE_______5.10. OTROS________________________

6. EXPLOTACION AGRICOLA

CUANTAS HECTAREAS TIENE EN:

6.1. PASTOS NATURALES___________6.2. PASTOS ARTIFICIALES_________

6.3. PLATANO________6.4. YUCA_________6.5. MAIZ__________________

6.6. ARROZ__________6.7. CAÑA_________6.8. OTROS CULTIVOS________

6.9. RASTROJO_______6.10. TOTAL AREA INCORPORADA__________________

6.11. MONTAÑA_____________6.12 AREA TOTAL_________________________

7. INSTALACIONES DE LA FINCA

INSTALACIONES	INICIAL SI NO No.	ACTUAL SI NO No.	
TRAPICHE			
MOTOBOMBA			
SALADEROS			
BEBEDEROS			

CORRAL						
BRETE						
POTREROS						
CERCAS KM						

8. GANADERIA

8.1. MOVIMIENTO GANADERO TOTAL

CATEGORIA		INCORA				FONDO GANADERO				CAJA AGRARIA				OTROS			
		I	C	P	V	I	C	P	V	I	C	P	V	I	C	P	V
	No.																
VACAS	$																
NOVILLAS	No.																
VIENTRE	$																
NOVILLAS	No.																
LEVANTE	$																
	No.																
TERNERAS	$																
NOVILLOS	No.																
LEVANTE	$																
NOVILLOS	No.																
CEBA	$																
	No.																
TOROS	$																
	No.																
EQUINOS	$																
	No.																
PORCINOS	$																
	No.																
TERNEROS	$																

9.- FUENTES DE FINANCIACION DIFERENTES A INCORA

CLASE DE PRESTAMO	FECHAS OTORG. VTO	VALOR PRESTAMO	SALDO	VALOR MOROSO	PAGO INTERESES	AMORTI ZACION
CAJA AGRARIA						
BANCOS						
FONDO GANADERO						
OTROS						
TOTAL						

10. EDUCACION Y SALUD

10.1. CUANTAS PERSONAS DE SU FAMILIA ASISTEN A LA ESCUELA?________

10.1.1. HOMBRES______ 10.1.2. MUJERES_______

10.2. DISTANCIA DE LA CASA A LA ESCUELA EN: 10.2.1. TIEMPO_______

10.2.2. KM_______

10.3. HA RECIBIDO USTED O ALGUN MIEMBRO DE SU FAMILIA CURSOS DE CAPACITACION? 10.3.1. SI____10.3.2. NO____10.3.3. QUE CLASE DE CURSO?__________________________________

10.3.4. CUANTO DURO EL CURSO?______________________________

10.3.5. QUE ENTIDAD LO DICTO?______________________________

10.3.6. EN QUE FECHA RECIBIO EL CURSO?_____________________

10.3.7. QUE CURSO LE GUSTARIA RECIBIR?_____________________

10.3.8. EN QUE MESES DEL AÑO SE LE FACILITA LA ASISTENCIA? __________________________10.3.9. QUE TIEMPO PODRIA DEDICAR AL CURSO?_________________

10.4. QUE HOSPITAL, CENTRO O PUESTO DE SALUD LE QUEDA MAS CERCA? ____________ 10.4.1. DISTANCIA EN TIEMPO___________________

10.4.2. KM___________10.4.3 HA UTILIZADO ESTOS SERVICIOS?

10.4.3.1. SI____10.4.3.2. NO_____10.4.3.3. PORQUE_________ __________10.4.4. FECHA DE LA ULTIMA VISITA________________

11. INGRESOS

11.1. POR GANADERIA EN LOS ULTIMOS SEIS MESES

CATEGORIAS	UNIDAD	CANTIDAD	VALOR	OBSERVACION
NOVILLOS CEBADOS				

VACAS			
CRIAS			
OTROS			
UTILIDADES DE GANADO AL PARTIR			
LECHE			
CUAJADA			
SUBTOTAL			

11.2. RECIBE INGRESOS POR VENTA DE PRODUCTOS DE CAZA? 11.2.1. SI___

11.2.2 NO______11.2.3. CUANTO______

11.3 RECIBE INGRESOS POR VENTA DE PESCADO? 11.3.1. SI____________

11.3.2. NO______11.3.3. CUANTO______________________________

11.4 VENTA DE PRODUCTOS AGRICOLAS ULTIMOS SEIS MESES

PRODUCTOS	UNIDAD	CANTIDAD	VALOR	OBSERVACIONES
MAIZ				
ARROZ				
PLATANO				
YUCA				
OTROS				
SUBTOTAL				

11.5 VENTA PRODUCTOS MADEREROS EN LOS ULTIMOS SEIS MESES

PRODUCTOS	UNIDAD	CANTIDAD	VALOR	OBSERVACIONES
ARBOLES				
TABLONES				
OTROS				
SUBTOTAL				

11.6. OTROS INGRESOS

INGRESOS	UNIDAD	CANTIDAD	VALOR	OBSERVA - CIONES
JORNALES JEFE				
JORNALES FAMILIA				
OTROS INGRESOS				
SUBTOTAL				

11.7. TOTAL INGRESOS ____

12. OBSERVACIONES:

____

____

____

____

____

____

____

ENCUESTA SEGUIMENTO USUARIOS DEL CREDITO

ANEXO 1

INFORMACION GENERAL

1. TENIA FAMILIARES O AMIGOS YA ESTABLECIDOS EN EL CAQUETA CUANDO UD. LLEGO?

   SI_____NO_____QUE AYUDA LE PRESTARON?______________________________

   ____

2. QUE ARTICULOS Y DINERO TRAJO UD. AL LLEGAR A SU FINCA? HERRAMIENTAS

   ____________MUEBLES____________DINERO_____________OTROS_________

SALUD

1. DE CUALES ENFERMEDADES SUFRE LA FAMILIA CON MAS FRECUENCIA?_________

   ____

2. UD. CONSIDERA QUE SU FAMILIA ES BIEN ALIMENTADA? SI_____NO_________

   PORQUE?____

   ____

3. LA SENORA HA RECIBIDO INFORMACION SOBRE EL CUIDADO DE LOS NIÑOS?

   PRE-NATAL: SI_____NO_____POST-NATAL: SI_______NO_________________

   UD. CREE QUE ES NECESARIO?____

4. EMPLEAN UDS. MEDIOS ANTICONCEPTIVOS PARA PLANIFICAR LA FAMILIA?

   SI________NO_______MEDIO____

EDUCACION

1. QUE PIENSA UD. DE LA EDUCACION QUE RECIBEN SUS NIÑOS EN LA ESCUELA?

   ____

2. UDS. (LOS PADRES) COLABORAN CON EL (LA) MAESTRO (A)? SI____NO_____

   ____

INCORA

1. SE SIENTE UD. SATISFECHO CON LOS SERVICIOS DE CREDITO QUE EL INCORA LE HA PRESTADO?

   SI________NO________PORQUE____

   ____

2. SE SIENTE UD. SATISFECHO CON LOS SERVICIOS SOCIALES - PUESTOS DE SALUD, ESCUELAS, VIAS?

   SI________NO________PORQUE____

3. CON LOS SERVICIOS TECNICOS - VETERINARIOS, DIAS DE CAMPO, CURSOS, ETC?

   SI________NO________PORQUE____

   ____

4. CON LA TITULACION DE TIERRA?

   SI________NO________PORQUE____

   ____

5. QUE OTROS SERVICIOS PIENSA UD. QUE LE PUEDE PRESTAR EL INCORA?_____

   ____

ASPECTOS PERSONALES

1. UD. PERTENECE A UNA ASOCIACION CAMPESINA? SI__________NO__________

   JUNTA DE ACCION COMUNAL______ASOCIACION DE USUARIOS________________

   COOPERATIVA__________________OTRO____________________________________

   QUE TRABAJO REALIZA EN ELLA?____

   ____

2. CUALES ACTIVIDADES OCUPAN SU TIEMPO FUERA DEL TRABAJO? MERCADO____

   ______MISA__________DIVERSIONES____

   VIAJES______________OTRAS____

3. EN GENERAL, UD. Y SU FAMILIA ESTAN CONTENTOS AQUI EN EL CAQUETA?

   SI__________NO__________PORQUE____

   ____

ENCUESTA PARA SOLICITANTES DEL CREDITO

ANEXO 2

INFORMACION GENERAL

1. TENIA FAMILIARES O AMIGOS YA ESTABLECIDOS EN EL CAQUETA CUANDO UD.

   LLEGO? SI_____NO____QUE AYUDA LE PRESTARON?________________________

   ____

2. QUE ARTICULOS Y DINERO TRAJO UD. AL LLEGAR A SU FINCA? HERRAMIENTAS ______MUEBLES____________DINERO____________OTROS____________________

SALUD

1. DE CUALES ENFERMEDADES SUFRE LA FAMILIA CON MAS FRECUENCIA?_________

   ____

2. UD. CONSIDERA QUE SU FAMILIA ES BIEN ALIMENTADA? SI_____NO_________

   PORQUE____

   ____

3. LA SEÑORA HA RECIBIDO INFORMACION SOBRE EL CUIDADO DE LOS NIÑOS?

   PRE-NATAL: SI____NO____POST-NATAL: SI____NO____

   UD. CREE QUE ES NECESARIO?____

4. EMPLEAN UDS. MEDIOS ANTICONCEPTIVOS PARA PLANIFICAR LA FAMILIA?

   SI_____NO_____MEDIO____

EDUCACION

1. QUE PIENSA UD. DE LA EDUCACION QUE RECIBEN SUS NIÑOS EN LA ESCUELA?

   ____

2. UDS. (LOS PADRES) COLABORAN CON EL (LA) MAESTRO (A)? SI____NO_______

   PORQUE____

CREDITO

1. UD. HA SOLICITADO CREDITO DEL INCORA. PORQUE SOLICITO A INCORA Y NO

   OTRA ENTIDAD?____

   ____

2. PORQUE LO NECESITA? EN QUE LO INVERTIRIA?________________________

____

3. INCORA, ADEMAS DE PRESTAR CREDITO, HA CONSTRUIDO ESCUELAS, PUESTOS DE SALUD, Y VIAS, TAMBIEN OFRECE SERVICIOS VETERINARIOS Y CURSOS SOBRE CULTIVOS UD. Y SU FAMILIA HAN BENEFICIADO DE ESTAS CONSTRUCCIONES Y ESTOS SERVICIOS? SI____NO____CUALES______________

____

4. UD. PIENSA QUE EL CREDITO OTORGADO LE DARA UNA MAYOR PRODUCCION EN LA FINCA? SI_____NO_____PORQUE______________________________

5. CREE UD. QUE PODRIA CUMPLIR CON LAS OBLIGACIONAS DEL CREDITO? SI_____NO_____PORQUE____

ASPECTOS PERSONALES

1. UD. PERTENECE A UNA ASOCIACION CAMPESINA? SI________NO____________

JUNTA DE ACCION COMUNAL______ASOCIACION DE USUARIOS________________

COOPERATIVA______________________________OTRA____________________

QUE TRABAJO REALIZA ON ELLA?______________________________________

____

2. CUALES ACTIVIDADES OCUPAN SU TIEMPO FUERA DEL TRABAJO? MERCADO_____

_________MISA________________DIVERSIONES_________________________

VIAJES_______________________OTRAS______________________________

3. EN GENERAL, UD. Y SU FAMILIA ESTAN CONTENTOS ON EL CAQUETA?

SI__________NO__________PORQUE____________________________________

____

Translation of Interview Form

Colombian Institute of Agrarian Reform "INCORA"
Project Caquetá

Monitoring Interview Form for Credit Recipients
Socioeconomic Data on Monitored Borrowers

I. General Information Date:
1.1. Credit zone 1.2. Section 1.3. Credit code 1.4. Birth place of head of family 1.4.1. Of spouse 1.5. Date of settlement on farm 1.6. Date of arrival in Caquetá 1.7. How did you obtain the farm? 1.7.1. Purchase of land and improvements 1.7.2. Colonized 1.7.3. Combination (purchased and colonized) 1.7.4. Other 1.8. Do you have legal title to your farm? 1.8.1. Yes 1.8.2. No 1.8.3. In process 1.9. Area of legally owned land 1.9.1. Area without legal title 1.9.2.Total area of farm 1.10. Distance from the house to the closest road 1.10.1. Kms. 1.10.2. Time 1.10.3. Which road? 1.11. Distance from the house to a navigable river 1.11.1. Kms. 1.11.2. Time 1.12. Distance from your farm to the nearest town 1.12.1. Kms. 1.12.2. Time 1.12.3. How long did it take before the road was built?

II. Social Aspects
2.1. Number of children 2.1.1. Alive 2.1.2. Dead 2.2. Number of people who depend on you for economic support 2.3. Family composition: Relationship to head of family, Sex (M,F), Age, Civil Status (single, married, common law marriage), Schooling (primary, secondary), Writes, Reads, Principal occupation

III. Characteristics of the Living Space
3.1. Walls 3.2. Roof 3.3. Floor 3.4. # of rooms 3.5. Separate kitchen? 3.5.1. Yes 3.5.2. No 3.6. Latrine? 3.6.1. Yes 3.6.2 No 3.7. Where do you get your water from? 3.7.1 How do you carry water to the house? 3.8.Have you made improvements in your living space in the last few years? 3.8.1. Yes 3.8.2.No 3.8.3. In what ways?

IV. Living Conditions
4.1. How many beds do you have? 4.2. How many lamps (kerosene) do you have? 4.3. Do you have a radio? 4.3.1. Yes 4.3.2. No 4.4. Do you have a mill? (for grinding corn/yuca/rice) 4.4.1. Yes 4.4.2. No 4.5. What kind of stove do you use? 4.6. What kind of iron do you use? 4.7. Do you have a shower or bathroom? 4.7.1. Yes 4.7.2. No

5. Approximately how much do you and your family spend monthly on: 5.1. Food 5.2. Clothing 5.3. Drugs for people 5.4. Entertainment 5.5. Education 5.6. Veterinary drugs and salt 5.7. Other supplies 5.8. Wages for workers 5.9. Transportation 5.10. Other

6. Agricultural Development. How many hectares do you have in: 6.1. Natural pasture 6.2. Artificial pasture 6.3. Plantain 6.4. Yuca 6.5. Corn 6.6. Rice 6.7. Sugar cane 6.8. Other crops 6.9. Cleared, unplanted jungle (rastrojo) 6.10. Total area in use 6.11. Jungle 6.12. Total area

7. Installations on the farm: Sugar mill, Water pump, Salt trays, Drinking troughs, Corrals, Loading chutes, Grazing fields, Fencing(kms.) (Owned when first settled on farm: Yes, No, Number; Owned now: Yes, No, Number)

8. Cattle raising. 8.1. Total cattle inventory. Number and value($) of: Cows, Heifers, Young heifers, Female calves, Young steer, Fattened steer, Bulls, Horses, Pigs, Male calves (obtained from INCORA, Cattlemen's Fund, Agricultural Credit Bank, Other)

9. Sources of financing other than INCORA: Agricultural Credit Bank, Other banks, Cattlemen's Fund, Other, Total (type of loan, date loaned and due, loan value, amount paid, due, overdue, interest rate, payment schedule)

10. Education and health. 10.1. How many members of the family go to school? 10.1.1. Men (boys) 10.1.2. Women (girls) 10.2. Distance from the house to the school in: 10.2.1. Time 10.2.2. Kms. 10.3. Have you or any family member attended courses in practical education? 10.3.1. Yes 10.3.2. No 10.3.3. What kind of courses? 10.3.4. How long did each course last? 10.3.5. Which agency gave each course? 10.3.6. What dates did you attend the courses? 10.3.7. What courses would you like to attend in the future? 10.3.8. Which months of the year is it easiest for you to attend courses? 10.3.9. How long (hours/days) would you be able to attend? 10.4. What hospital, health center or health clinic is closest to your house? 10.4.1. Distance in time 10.4.2. Kms. 10.4.3. Have you used these facilities? 10.4.3.1. Yes 10.4.3.2. No 10.4.3.3. Why 10.4.4. Date of your last visit

11. Income. 11.1. From cattle in the last six months: Fattened steer, Cows, Newborns, Others, Income from cattle "al partir", Milk, Cheese, Subtotal (unit, quantity, value, observations) 11.2. Do you earn income from the sale of hunting animals? 11.2.1. Yes 11.2.2. No 11.2.3. How much 11.3. Do you earn income from the sale of fish? 11.3.1. Yes 11.3.2. No 11.3.3. How much 11.4. Sale of agricultural products in the last six months: Corn, Rice, Plantain, Yuca, Other, Subtotal (unit, quantity, value, observations) 11.5. Sale of wood products in the last six months: Trees, Planks, Other, Subtotal (unit, quantity, value, observations) 11.6. Other income: Wages (head of family), Wages(other family members), Other income, Subtotal (unit, quantity, value, observations) 11.7. Total income

12. Observations.

Monitoring Interview Form for Credit Recipients, Annex 1

General Information

1. Did you have relatives or friends already settled in Caquetá when you arrived? Yes, No, In what ways did they help you?

2. What articles/money did you bring with you initially to your farm? Tools, Furniture, Money, Other

Health

1. Your family suffers from which illnesses most frequently?
2. Do you believe that your family is well fed? Yes, No, Why
3. Has the woman of the house received information on childcare? Prenatal: Yes, No, Postnatal: Yes, No, Do you believe this information is important?
4. Do you use contraceptive methods to plan your family? Yes, No, Method

Education

1. What is your opinion of the education your children receive at the local school?
2. Do you (the parents) give assistance to the teacher? Yes, No

INCORA
1. Do you feel satisfied with the credit services you have received from INCORA? Yes, No, Why
2. Do you feel satisfied with the social services - health clinics, schools, roads? Yes, No, Why
3. Do you feel satisfied with the technical services - veterinary, field trips, practical courses? Yes, No, Why
4. Do you feel satisfied with the land titling services? Yes, No, Why
5. What other services would you like to receive from INCORA?

Personal Aspects
1. Do you belong to a farmer's association? Yes, No, Communal Action Group, Borrowers Association, Cooperative, Other, What activities are these groups involved in?
2. What activities take up your time outside of work? Market, Church, Entertainment, Trips, Other
3. In general, are you and your family happy here in Caquetá? Yes, No, Why

Interview Form for Credit Applicants, Annex 2

Same as Annex 1 for the sections on general information, health, and education.

Credit
1. You have applied for credit from INCORA. Why did you apply to INCORA and not some other agency?
2. Why do you need credit? How will you invest it?
3. In addition to the credit program, INCORA has constructed schools, health clinics, and roads. It also offers veterinary services and courses on agriculture. Have you and your family benefited from any of these services? Yes, No, Which services
4. Do you believe that the credit-in-kind loaned to you would increase productivity on your farm? Yes, No, Why
5. Do you think that you would be able to comply with credit obligations? Yes, No, Why

Same as Annex 1 for the section on personal aspects.

Bibliography

Public Documents

Caja de Crédito Agrario, Industrial, y Minero

1977, 1978 Annual Financial Reports. Florencia.

Comité Interamericano de Desarrolo Agrícola (CIDA)

1966 *Tenencia de la tierra y desarrollo socioeconómico del sector agrícola: Colombia*. Washington, D.C.: Unión Panamericana, Secretaría General de la Organización de los Estados Americanos.

Departamento Administrativo Nacional de Estadística (DANE)

1977 *Boletin Mensual de Estadística* (314). Bogotá: División de Edición del DANE.

Instituto Colombiano de la Reforma Agraria (INCORA)

1967 *Cinco años de reforma agraria*. Bogotá: INCORA.

1972 *Proyecto Caquetá 1*. Bogotá: INCORA, Oficina de Divulgación.

1975 *Caminos Vecinales-INCORA Convenio, fase 2*. Florencia: INCORA.

1975 *INDERENA-INCORA Convenio, fase 2*. Florencia: INCORA.

1977 *Estudio sobre puestos de salud contruidos fase 1*. Florencia: INCORA.

1978 *Evaluación social de la via Albania-Curillo*. Florencia: INCORA.

1978 *Informe de actividades 1962-marzo 1978: Proyecto de Colonización del Caquetá*. Florencia: INCORA.

International Bank for Reconstruction and Development (World Bank)

1975 *Caquetá Rural Settlement Project Appraisal Report No. 501A—CO*. Washington, D.C.: World Bank.

1978 *Project Performance Audit Report: Colombia, Caquetá Land Colonization Project (Loan 739-CO)*. Washington, D.C.: World Bank, Office of Director-General Operations Evaluation.

1978 *Caquetá Land Colonization Project Completion Report*. Washington, D.C.: World Bank, Office of Director-General Operations Evaluation.

1981 *Supervision Report*. Washington, D.C.: World Bank, Latin American and the Caribbean Regional Office.

Ministerio de Agricultura and Instituto Colombiano de la Reforma Agraria

1975 *Reforma Social Agraria: Leyes y decretos reglamentarios*. Bogotá.

Ministerio de Agricultura and Caja de Crédito Agrario, Industrial, y Minero

1976 *Qué es el DRI*? Bogotá: Departamento de Comunicaciones.

United Nations, Department of Economic Affairs

1951 *Land Reform: Defects in Agrarian Structure as Obstacles to Economic Development*. New York: United Nations Publications, no. 1951. 11. B. 3.

1966 *Progresos en materia de reforma agraria*, cuarto informe. New York: United Nations, Food and Agricultural Organization and International Labor Organization.

United Nations, Industrial Development Organization (UNIDO)

1972 *Guidelines for Project Evaluation*. New York: Project Formulation and Evaluation Series, no. 2.

United Nations, International Labour Organization (ILO)

1977 *The Basic Needs Approach to Development*. Geneva: International Labor Organization Publications.

Books

Brucher, Wolfgang

1974 *La colonización de la selva pluvial en el piedemonte amazónico de Colombia*. Bogotá: Instituto Geográfico "Agustín Codazzi."

Bruyn, Severyn T.

1966 *The Human Perspective in Sociology: The Methodology of Participant Observation*. Englewood Cliffs, N.J.: Prentice-Hall.

Chenery, Hollis, et al.

1974 *Redistribution with Growth*. London: published for the World Bank and the Institute of Development Studies, University of Sussex, Oxford University Press.

Duff, Ernest A.

1968 *Agrarian Reform in Colombia*. New York: F. A. Praeger.

Goulet, Denis

1975 *The Cruel Choice*. New York: Atheneum.

Hirschman, Albert O.

1963 *Journeys toward Progress*. New York: Twentieth Century Fund.

1967 *Development Projects Observed*. Washington, D.C.: The Brookings Institute.

Kalmanovitz, Salamón

1978 *Desarrollo de la agricultura en Colombia*. Bogotá: Editorial la Carreta.

Lleras Camargo, Alberto

1961 *Sus mejores páginas*. Seleccionadas por Alberto Zalamea. Bogotá: Segundo Festival del Libro Colombiano, Companía Grancolombiana de Ediciones S.A.

Lleras Restrepo, Carlos, et al.

1962 *Tierra: 10 ensayos sobre la reforma agraria en Colombia*. Bogotá: Ediciones Tercer Mundo.

McHale, John and Magda Cornell

1978 *Basic Human Needs: A Framework for Action*. New Jersey: Rutgers State University, Transaction Books.

Mellor, John W.

1966 *The Economics of Agricultural Development*. Ithaca, N.Y.: Cornell University Press.

Nelson, Michael

1973 *The Development of Tropical Lands: Policy Issues in Latin America*. Baltimore and London: Johns Hopkins University Press.

PiDelta Ltda. Consultants

1973 *Plan de desarrollo del Proyecto de Colonización del Caquetá: etapa 1*, vol. 3. Bogotá: PiDelta Ltda.

Sánchez, Gonzalo G.
1977 *Las ligas campesinas en Colombia*. Bogotá: Ediciones Alcaraván.
Suchman, Edward A.
1967 *Evaluative Research: Principles and Practices in Public Service and Social Action Programs*. New York: Russel Sage Foundation.
Serrano, Luis F., ed.
1967 *La Reforma Social Agraria: la Ley 135 de 1961 y los otros estatutos legales que la complementan y desarrollan*. Bogotá.
Tobon, Alonso
1972 *La tierra y la reforma agraria en Colombia*. 2nd ed. Bogotá: Ediciones Cancer.
Tovar, Hermes
1975 *El movimiento campesino en Colombia durante los siglos XIX y XX*. 2nd ed. Bogotá: Ediciones Libres.
Uribe Uribe, R.
1955 *Por la América del Sur*. Vols. 1 and 2. Bogotá: Text of 1908.

Articles and Periodicals

Bonilla, Victor Daniel
1966 "Tolima 1: primer proyecto de la reforma agraria." *Revista de Economía Agraria*, julio-septiembre. Bogota: Ediciones Tercer Mundo.
Haney, Emil
1973 "El dilema del minifundio en Colombia." *Land Tenure Center*, reprint no. 85-S. University of Wisconsin, Madison. Reprinted from *Dualismo*, 1(1). Universidad Veracruzana, Veracruz, Mexico.
Tinnermeir, Ronald L.
1964 "New Land Settlement in the Eastern Lowlands of Colombia." Ph.D. dissertation, University of Wisconsin; abbreviated reprint ed. in *Land Tenure Center*, no. 13. University of Wisconsin, Madison.
World Bank Department of Information and Public Affairs
1977 "Rural Development: The Start is Promising, but the Problems are Formidable." *Report: News of the World Bank*, September October. Washington, D.C.

Reports

Cámera de Comercio de Florencia
1978 *Report: Regional Seminar on Cattle Production*. Florencia, Caquetá: Cámera de Comercio, INCORA, and ICA.
Tendler, Judith
1976 *Inter-Country Evaluation of Small Farmer Organizations. AID and Small Farmer Organizations: Lessons of the Honduran Experience*. Washington, D.C.: Office of Development Programs of the Latin American Bureau of the Agency for International Development (AID).
1978 *Piauí: Renters and Sharecroppers*. Washington, D.C.: a report for the World Bank.
Thirsk, Wayne R.
1978 "Some Facets of Rural Poverty in Colombia." *A Report Submitted to the U.S. Department of Agriculture*, General Working Document No. 2 (Colombia). University of Waterloo, Ontario, Canada.

Unpublished Material

Friedman, John
1978 "Basic Needs, Agropolitan Development, and Planning from Below." Paper presented at the United Nations Centre for Regional Development, Nagoya, Japan. (mimeographed)
Gómez, M. L., J. F González, N. I. Laverde, and Z. Torres
1977 "Incidencia socioeconómica del Proyecto de Colonización del Caquetá, etapa 1." Graduate thesis, Universidad Santo Tomás de Aquino, Bogotá.
Roberts, Ralph Leon
1975 "Migration and Colonization in Colombian Amazonia: Agrarian Reform or Neo-Latifundismo." Ph.D. dissertation, University of New York, Syracuse.

Primary Sources

INCORA
1978 Planning, Credit, and Rural Training Departments; Legal, Engineering, and Farm Settlement Sections. Interviews and unpublished data. Florencia, Caquetá.
Rural Families (85)
1978 Interviews with 85 rural families held between July 1978 and January 1979. Caquetá, Colombia.
Servicio Nacional de Erradicación de la Malaria (SEM)
1978 Interviews with the Regional Director of SEM and unpublished data. Florencia, Caquetá.

Index